ADVANCED
PRANIC HEALING

Books by Choa Kok Sui

PRANIC HEALING

ADVANCED PRANIC HEALING

PRANIC PSYCHOTHERAPY

ADVANCED PRANIC HEALING

CHOA KOK SUI

A PRACTICAL MANUAL
FOR COLOR PRANIC HEALING

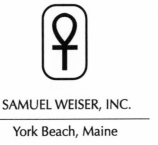

SAMUEL WEISER, INC.

York Beach, Maine

If an ailment is severe, or if symptoms persist, please consult a medical doctor immediately. Pranic healing is not intended to replace orthodox medicine, but rather to complement it. The author and the publisher are not responsible for any condition caused by interpreting information provided in the book.

First published in 1995 by
Samuel Weiser, Inc.
Box 612
York Beach, ME 03910-0612

Library of Congress Cataloging-in-Publication Data

Choa Kok Sui.
    Advanced pranic healing / Choa Kok Sui.
       p.   cm.
    Includes index.
    1. Healing.   2. Vital force.   3. Yoga, Hatha.   I. Title.
    RZ401.S836   1995
    615.5´3—dc20   95–13509
                                                   CIP

ISBN 0–87728–842–9
EB

Illustrations in the text by Benny Gantioque

Typeset in 10 point Galliard

Printed in the United States of America

04 03 02 01 00 99 98 97 96 95
10 9 8 7 6 5 4 3 2 1

The paper used in this publication meets the minimum requirements of the American National Standard for Permanence of Paper for printed Library Materials Z39.48-1984.

*To Divine Providence, Whose
blessings make everything possible.*

*To my Respected Teacher Mei
Ling and others for their patience,
instructions, and nurturing.*

*To Mike Nator for his tireless investigations;
and to others for their help and contributions.*

Table of Contents

Part II: ADVANCED PRANIC TREATMENTS

Part III: SUPPLEMENTARY HEALING

Affirmation for Receptivity • Touching the Heart Chakra • Forehead-Hand Chakras Technique • Invocation, Point of Entry • Descent of the Divine Light • Mass Healing • Distant Mass Healing • Combination of Instructive Healing and Divine Healing • Eucharistic Healing

Part IV: THE FUTURE OF PRANIC HEALING

Nutrition and Prana • Ginseng • Classifying Drugs by Using the Properties of Color Pranas • Etheric Beings, Currents, Planets • More Research Needed in the Field of Pranic Healing • Pranic Psychotherapy • Geometric Pranic Generator • Pranic Laser Therapy

List of Illustrations

To the people of the world:
May this book soothe your pain,
restore and maintain your health,
and initiate you
to higher spiritual teachings.

Globalizing Pranic Healing

Pranic Healing has been published in many different languages. To date the book is published (or in the process of being published) in English, German, Portuguese, Philippine, Indonesian Bahasa, Chinese, French, Spanish, Italian, Dutch, and Polish. Readers who are interested in taking the Master Choa Pranic Healing Course can contact the Institute as follows:

Vice President
Institute for Inner Studies, Inc.
Evekal Building
855 Passay Road
1200 Makati, Metro Manila
Philippines.
Telephone: (632) 819-1874; (632) 810-2808; (632) 818-2562
Fax: (632) 731-3828

In many developing countries, pranic healing is urgently needed. To help disseminate the science and art of pranic healing, interested readers may contact the World Pranic Healing Foundation as follows:

Executive Vice President
World Pranic Healing Foundation
P.O. Box 9101 MCS Mailing Center
Makati, Metro Manila
Philippines
Telephone: (632) 812-5001; (632) 812-4283
Fax: (632) 893-6144

Some readers may want to found a local Pranic Healers Association in their state or country. The objectives of such an association would be: 1) To regulate and standardize the practice of pranic healing; 2) To provide information on the latest findings and techniques in pranic healing; and 3) To promote the practice of pranic healing. This might event involve educating medical practitioners to consider pranic healing as one of the alternative treatments in many diseases. Interested readers can contact the Institute for Inner Studies at the address mentioned above.

Master Choa Kok Sui teaches courses in the following subjects:

Pranic Healing
Advanced Pranic Healing
Pranic Psychotherapy
Crystal Healing
Arhatic Yoga
Financial Healing
Psychic Self-Defense
Simplified Chi Kung and other Martial Arts

For more information, please contact the Institute for Inner Studies at the following address:

Institute for Inner Studies
Evekal Building
855 Passay Road
1200 Makati, Metro Manila
Philippines
Telephone: (632) 819-1874; (632) 812-2326; (632)813-2562
Fax: (632) 731-3828

For more information on workshops and healing sessions in your area, please contact

THE AMERICAN INSTITUTE OF ASIAN STUDIES
Mr. Stephen Co, United States Certified Pranic Healing Instructor
P.O. Box 1605
Chino, CA 91708-1605
Telelphone: (909) 465-0967

PART I: CONCEPTS, PRINCIPLES, AND TECHNIQUES

A professor visited a Roshi (Zen master) to learn about Zen. The professor was more interested in talking and trying to impress the Zen master than in learning. The Roshi poured tea into the professor's cup and continued pouring until it was overflowing. The professor alarmingly said, "The cup is full and cannot receive more!" The Zen master calmly replied, "You are full of preconceived ideas and opinions. To learn, you must empty your cup!" The professor respectfully bowed to the Roshi and remained silent.

—A Popular Zen Story

Miracles are fantastic events which utilize hidden laws of nature that most people are not aware of. Miracles do not break the laws of nature, they are actually based on them!

—C.K.S.

Color Pranas

INTRODUCTION

This book is predominantly based on the instructions given to the author by my teacher, Mei Ling. Other teachers also provided useful information. Teacher Mei Ling is one of the mentors of the author in his esoteric studies. Many clairvoyant investigations and experiments were done. It is also based on the author's and his students' experiments and experiences. Some of the concepts and techniques are "new" and different from other books on color healing. Instructions on the art of instantaneous healing of fresh wounds are given in a later chapter.

Many of the advanced techniques should be practiced by experienced pranic healers, and not by beginners. Improper understanding of the principles and instructions, and improper application of the advanced healing techniques may result in adverse effects on the patients. *Read through this book twice before applying any of the advanced techniques.*

Advanced pranic healing uses color pranas and chakral techniques to produce very rapid healing and to cure difficult ailments.

Air prana, solar prana, and ground prana are made of "white" or general prana. Air and ground pranas are called vitality globules in esoteric parlance because, when they are seen clairvoyantly or by a person with slightly more sensitive eyes, they appear as small spheres or globules of light. Vitality globules come in different sizes. Some contain more units of "white" prana and some contain less.

Ground vitality globules interpenetrate the ground and extend several inches away from it. They are more dense or more closely-packed and usually bigger than air vitality globules. *Some of the bigger air vitality globules can be easily seen by just staring at the sky for a few minutes especially just before sunset.* You do not need to be a clairvoyant to be able to see them. Many people are able to see them in a few sessions. With more practice, you will also be able to see ground vitality globules just a few inches away from the ground.

COLOR PRANAS

Vitality globules (conglomerations of units of white prana) are absorbed by the chakras where they are digested and broken down into their components. When white prana is digested, it produces six types of color pranas corresponding to the colors of the rainbow. A substantial amount of air prana is absorbed directly by the front and back spleen chakra. Air prana is broken down to different color pranas and distributed to the other chakras. Ground prana is absorbed through the sole chakras then goes to the basic chakra. A portion of the ground prana is directed upward to the spine and other chakras while a larger portion is directed to the perineum minor chakra, to the navel chakra, then to the spleen chakra where it is broken down and distributed to the other chakras. All these take place automatically, or at the subconscious level.

"White" prana is composed of red, orange, yellow, green, blue, and violet pranas.

HOW TO USE COLOR PRANA

Color prana is more specialized and more potent than white prana. Using color prana instead of white prana is just like approaching a specialist instead of a general practitioner. When using color prana, avoid projecting dark color prana since it may have adverse effects. In some cases, it may have a reverse reaction. For example, light red prana has a strengthening effect, but dark red prana has an overwhelming effect and will weaken the treated part. *When projecting color prana, it is safer and more effective to use a light or pastel color.*

The potency of a light color prana can be further diluted by combining it with white prana. For example, one can visualize the projected prana as luminous white at the core with light red at the periphery to strengthen an organ. *It is better and safer to combine a color prana of lighter shade with white prana. White prana is the harmonizing prana.* It is harmonizing in the sense that it provides the other color pranas required in healing and it redistributes excess color pranas from the treated area to other parts of the body. In general, better, faster, and safer results are obtained by combining white prana (about 70%) with light color prana (about 30%) than just light color prana since white prana provides the other color pranas required in healing. On rare occasions, if necessary, I use light color prana for more potent effects.

You may visualize the projected prana as: (1) luminous white at the core with the color prana at the periphery; (2) color prana at the core and the white prana at the periphery; or (3) light color prana thoroughly mixed with white prana. Visualize luminous white light (white prana) being projected. Then add a light tinge of the color prana, which results in a very light pastel color. Method 1 and method 2 are the same because it has been clairvoyantly observed that these two patterns change alternately, continuously, and rapidly from one pattern to the other. Method 3 produces more subtle pranic energy and is quite safe in general.

When energizing with color pranas, it is safer to flick the hand a few times before energizing with another color prana.

PROPERTIES OF COLOR PRANAS AND APPLICATIONS

Red Prana

Properties:

1. Strengthening
2. Warm
3. Expansive
4. Dilating
5. Distributive(improves circulation)
6. Constructive—rapid tissue or cellular repair
7. Sustains the visible physical body
8. Vitalizes the blood, tissues, and the skeletal system of the body
9. Stimulating and activating

Applications:

1. Strengthening sluggish and weakened organs or parts
2. Dilating blood vessels and air tubes

3. Improving circulation
4. Allergy relief
5. Healing internal and external wounds
6. Treating general tiredness or weakening
7. Treating paralysis
8. Reviving unconscious patients
9. Reviving or prolonging the life of dying patients

Use light whitish-red or light red prana. Do not use dark red prana because this has a reverse reaction; instead of strengthening, it will have a weakening effect on the part to be treated.

Light whitish red or light red prana has dilating effects on the blood vessels and air tubes. This is useful for treating heart and asthmatic patients. *Dark red prana should not be used because it can cause inflammation and constriction. It should also not be used on venereal ailments since it stimulates the rapid growth of venereal germs.*

Orange Prana

Properties:

1. Expelling
2. Eliminative
3. Decongesting
4. Cleansing
5. Loosening—loosens diseased energy
6. Melting
7. Extracting or abstracting
8. Splitting, exploding, and destructive

Applications:

1. Waste, toxins, germs, and diseased energy elimination
2. Allergies
3. Kidney and bladder ailments
4. Constipation
5. Menstrual problems
6. Blood clots
7. Arthritis
8. Cysts
9. Cold, cough, and lung problems

When using orange prana, only light whitish-orange or light orange prana is usually used. *Orange prana has a very potent effect; therefore, it should be avoided in treating delicate organs like the eyes. brain, and heart.* For safety reasons, avoid using orange prana on the following:

1. Head
2. Eyes
3. Brain
4. Areas very near the head
5. Jaw minor chakras
6. Heart
7. Front and back heart chakra
8. Spleen
9. Front and back spleen chakra

Energizing with orange prana on delicate organs may cause serious damage, like a detached retina or hemorrhage of the brain. *When energizing the lungs with orange prana directly through the back of the lungs, the hand(s) should be pointed away from the head.* It is not advisable to energize the jaw minor chakras with orange prana since these chakras also energize the brain. Do not also apply orange prana on the spleen or the spleen chakra because the spleen chakra is directly connected to all the major chakras including those on the head. Orange prana should be used with caution on the solar plexus chakra and on the navel chakra since it may cause loose bowel movements. Orange prana is used for treating constipation since it stimulates bowel movement. Orange prana should not be used on patients suffering from appendicitis because it may accelerate the rupture of the inflamed appendix. Orange prana is also used to facilitate the abstraction of consciousness in a dying patient.

Light whitish-orange has a strong cleansing effect, etherically and physically. Etherically, it expels used up and diseased energy. Physically, it is essential in the elimination of waste matter. Light whitish-orange and light whitish-red are used for treating allergies. Other color pranas can also be used in treating an allergy. But for more lasting and faster results, especially for a severe allergy, light whitish-orange and light whitish-red have to be used.

Green Prana

Properties:

1. Breaking down
2. Digestive
3. Decongesting

4. Cleansing
5. Detoxifying
6. Disinfecting
7. Dissolving
8. Loosening of diseased bioplasmic matter
9. Destruction or breaking down of dead and diseased cells

Applications:

1. Breaking down blood clots
2. Disinfecting
3. Treating colds
4. Treating fevers
5. Localized sweeping for decongesting and loosening stubborn diseased energy

Green or orange prana is usually used in decongesting and cleansing a diseased part by loosening the diseased bioplasmic matter. After being loosened, the diseased bioplasmic matter is removed by localized sweeping and the affected part is then energized. The loosening and expelling of the diseased bioplasmic matter by green or orange prana will enable fresh prana to enter the affected part, thereby restoring health to the treated part.

Green prana is milder and safer compared to orange prana. When internal organs are to be energized with orange prana, *it is advisable to use green prana as a safety precaution before projecting orange prana.*

Before energizing with more potent pranas, like orange, red, and violet, it is advisable to use light green prana first as a precautionary measure to avoid possible radical reaction or harm. *Energizing first with light green prana and then with light orange prana is very effective in decongesting, expelling, and cleansing physically and bioplasmically the part being treated.* Please note the sequence. Light green prana is used first to break down the diseased energy, then light orange prana to expel the loosened diseased energy—not orange prana first nor both simultaneously. When light orange-green prana (more of green prana and less of orange prana) is projected or when both orange prana and green prana are projected simultaneously, the effects of these pranas are multiplied several times; therefore, the effect is destructive to a certain degree and is used in dissolving deposits. When the darker shades of green prana and orange prana are used, the effect is quite destructive, hence they are used in treating certain types of cancers. *Blue prana is used first to localize the disintegrating effect of the projected pranic energy on the affected part.*

Yellow Prana

Properties:

1. Cohesion or cementing
2. Assimilating, multiplying, and growing
3. Stimulating nerves
4. Initiating or starting
5. Necessary for strong and healthy tissue, organs, and bones

Applications:

1. Broken bones
2. Skin problems
3. Cellular repair
4. Developing strong healthy tissues, organs, and bones
5. Improving assimilation

Yellow prana alone should not be used in treating wounds, burns, or broken bones because scar tissue or overgrowth will be formed. The proper treatments for these cases are given in a later chapter.

Blue Prana

Properties:

1. Disinfecting and disinflaming
2. Inhibiting
3. Localizing and contracting
4. Soothing and mild anesthetic
5. Cooling
6. Pliability or flexibility
7. Blood clotting

Applications:

1. Treating ailments due to infection
2. Removing pain
3. Reducing inflammation
4. Inhibiting chakras, organs, and motor action
5. Inducing rest and sleep
6. Stopping bleeding
7. Reducing fevers

I performed an experiment on a paralytic. Treatment was first given on the brain, then to the right arm. Light blue prana was directed to the affected right arm for several minutes. As a result, the patient had greater difficulty in raising his right arm. When light red prana was directed to the affected area, the patient was able to move his right arm with greater ease. The next day, there was an even greater improvement. This shows that blue prana has an inhibiting effect, while red prana has strengthening and stimulating effects.

Violet Prana

Violet prana has the properties of all the other five pranas combined and is potent. It is used for severe types of ailments. Light violet, light bluish-violet, and light greenish-violet pranas have regenerating effects and can be used to heal damaged organs and nerves. Light bluish-violet or light greenish-violet pranas are also used for rapid healing of fresh wounds. Violet prana is used to treat severe infections like syphilis. Do not use dark violet prana on respiratory ailments, since it will have a reverse reaction and will stimulate the growth of pulmonary virus. It is much safer to use light whitish-violet prana.

Violet prana has a high amplifying or multiplier effect on the properties of the other color pranas when it is projected simultaneously with another color prana. Never project violet and red pranas simultaneously since the effect is quite destructive. It will cause some of the energized cells to become very hot, to expand and burst. Do not project violet and orange pranas simultaneously since the effect is very destructive and will cause some of the energized cells to explode. Also do not project violet and yellow pranas simultaneously since it will cause rapid chaotic cell growth.

Violet prana has an amplifying or a multiplier effect before or after another color prana has been projected. Therefore, avoid using dark color prana when violet prana has been used or will be used, since it may produce adverse effects. To strengthen a weakened part, light whitish-red may be used. Or a more powerful technique is to project light whitish-red, then light whitish-violet on an affected part in order to rapidly strengthen it. The effect is quite powerful and fast. Do not use dark red since the effect is destructive.

Both white prana and violet prana have the properties of all the color pranas. The difference is that violet prana has a greater penetrating effect and is easier to assimilate than white prana. Therefore, violet prana has a faster effect than white prana.

Through clairvoyant observation, the indigo prana is normally not seen in any of the chakras and in any part of the bioplasmic body. That is why only six types of ordinary color pranas are discussed in this chapter.

The effect of the color prana is qualified and enhanced by the intention of the healer. For instance, blue prana can be used to inhibit a chakra or an organ by forming a firm intention to inhibit when projecting it.

Some students or practitioners of color healing may find the properties or qualities of green, yellow, and orange pranas strange or doubtful. This was also my initial reaction, but further study and experiments proved these are correct. By experimenting on color pranas and studying the pranas contained in the chakras and the organs controlled and energized by the corresponding chakras, it is possible to deduce and verify the correctness of the properties or qualities of the different types of color pranas discussed in this book.

Electric-Violet Pranic Energy

There are two types of violet pranic energy: ordinary violet pranic energy and electric-violet pranic energy. The former appears as luminous violet which is derived from the surrounding prana such as air, ground, and solar pranas. Electric-violet pranic energy appears as brilliant white with light violet at the periphery. This is derived from the higher self or higher soul where its entry point is the crown chakra, and hence is called *divine energy* or *soul energy*.

Electric-violet pranic energy has the properties of all the other color pranas and is many times more powerful than ordinary violet pranic energy. It has a rapid regenerating effect on damaged organs and nerves, and also a very strong disinfecting effect. *Electric-violet pranic energy has a consciousness of its own and is very effective for the rapid healing of severe ailments.*

Dark electric-violet pranic energy has a destructive effect on most people and can be used in treating tumors or cancers. In order to localize the effect, the part to be treated has to be energized first with dark blue pranic energy before using the dark electric-violet pranic energy or any other destructive pranic energy.

Electric-violet pranic energy has a greater amplifying or multiplier effect on the properties of the other color pranas than ordinary violet prana. Electric-violet pranic energy should not be simultaneously projected with red, orange, green or yellow because the effect will be very destructive. Therefore, it is not used with these in healing. There is also the possibility that the destructive energy may bounce back to the healer if the patient or subject is not receptive. Please take note of this.

Also, do not use dark color prana before or after electric-violet pranic energy has been projected. The effect is also quite destructive.

In certain instances, it is all right to use light whitish-color prana before or after electric-violet pranic energy has been projected. This technique is very potent, but there is also a greater risk. Improper application of the technique may result in a permanent adverse effect on the patient. There-fore, this technique should be used only by a master pranic healer or an ex-perienced, proficient, advanced pranic healer. *As a general guideline, avoid using other color pranas except blue prana if electric-violet pranic energy has been used or will be used.*

Electric-violet pranic energy is referred to in some esoteric literature as the "white light," but there is a slight difference between the two. Electric-violet light has been programmed by the higher soul; therefore, it has a con-sciousness of its own and knows exactly what is to be done. The brilliant white light has the same property as electric-violet light but has not been programmed by the higher soul. Therefore, the electric-violet light is more effective than just the "white light."

When projecting electric-violet prana, visualize the core as brilliant white with light violet at the periphery. Ordinary violet prana is visualized as luminous white at the core with light violet at the periphery. *Whether it is electric-violet prana or ordinary violet prana that will be projected depends upon the intention or the will of the healer, and the degree of development of the healer.*

The effectiveness of using electric-violet pranic energy depends upon the healer's ability to bring down this energy. The extent to which a healer can bring down the electric-violet prana depends on the degree of the develop-ment of his or her crown chakra and the size of the spiritual cord. The thick-ness of the spiritual cords of most people ranges from as thin as a spider web to the width of a single strand of hair—hardly noticeable when clairvoyantly seen. If the clairvoyant is not aware of its existence, he or she may not even notice it. Healers whose crown chakras are undeveloped and whose spiritual cords are quite thin will not be able to bring down sufficient divine energy or electric-violet pranic energy. One type of meditation that will rapidly activate the crown chakra and increase the size of the spiritual cord is through the reg-ular practice of Meditation on Twin Hearts mentioned in *Pranic Healing*.

The spiritual cords of some religious persons and advanced yogis, peo-ple who meditate or pray regularly, or who occupy responsible and impor-tant positions in life, are usually much thicker than those of ordinary people. They may have a diameter of half an inch or more. There are also ex-ceptional people whose spiritual cords are so big that they may be as big or even bigger than their heads. But these people are quite rare at the present level of human evolution.

Golden Pranic Energy

When electric-violet pranic energy comes in contact with the etheric or bio-plasmic body, it gradually turns into golden prana. The golden prana, when absorbed by the physical body, becomes light red. Golden prana has properties similar to those of electric-violet prana. Golden prana is milder and less fluidic than electric-violet prana. Golden prana has a less cleansing effect than electric-violet prana. *In general, it is better to use electric-violet prana for general energizing, and golden prana for localized energizing.* Electric-violet also has very potent psychological effects and is used for treating psychological ailments. The guidelines for golden prana are the same as those for electric-violet pranic energy.

Electric-violet pranic energy or the golden pranic energy is felt as a cooling and pleasant sensation by healthy persons. But in persons who are depleted or are not so healthy, the feeling is warm.

Saints of different religions are sometimes depicted with brilliant electric white light descending on their heads and a golden halo surrounding it. This golden halo is produced by the activated crown chakra and the radiation of the assimilated electric-violet pranic energy which has turned golden.

In Taoist Yoga, this energy is called "heaven ki" or "heaven energy." In Kaballah, it is called "pillar of light," referring to what clairvoyants literally see as a pillar of light. The Indian yogis call this pillar of light the spiritual bridge of light or "antakharana." Christians call this the "descent of the Holy Spirit" which is symbolized by a pillar of light with a descending dove. In Christian arts, this is shown in pictures of saints or of Jesus as a golden halo and a pillar of brilliant white light on top of the head with a descending white dove. This is to symbolize the descent of divine energy or holy spirit.

When spiritual practitioners have achieved a relatively high level of development, their etheric bodies are transformed into gold. They have developed, to a certain degree, the GOLDEN BODY. The gold first manifests externally, then it gradually manifests inwardly into the physical body. This is why some saints of different religions are sometimes depicted with a golden garment or a golden body. If the clairvoyant is not well trained, he or she will see the electric-violet light as brilliant white light and may not notice the golden aura behind the brilliant white light.

WHAT TO DO WHEN IN DOUBT

When in doubt as to what color prana to use, just use white prana for minor ailments, and light whitish-ordinary-violet prana for severe ailments. In general, it is better to use white prana, especially on infants, on very young children, and on old patients. On certain occasions, when white prana is not sufficiently effective, light color prana combined with white prana can be used.

DEGREE OF REFINEMENT OF PRANIC ENERGY

There are different degrees of refinement of pranic energy. If the energy body of the healer is gross, then the projected pranic energy is gross. If the healer has a more refined or subtle energy body, then the projected pranic energy is more refined or subtle. The effect of grosser pranic energy is that the patient tends to get congested and tends to experience radical reactions. For example, even if a small quantity of gross pranic energy is projected on the head area, the patient may experience dizziness. Or if the gross pranic energy is projected on the solar plexus chakra, the patient may experience difficulty in breathing.

The degree of refinement of the healer's energy body is dependent on several factors. One factor is the length and frequency of healing. Student healers or new healers tend to have more gross energy bodies initially, but will gradually develop more subtle or refined energy bodies with constant practice. This is why patients of apprentices or new healers tend to experience pranic congestion or radical reactions. The development of a more refined energy body can be hastened by a vegetarian diet, and by doing regular meditation, especially the Meditation on Twin Hearts.

Gross pranic energy is much bigger than refined or subtle pranic energy. Refined pranic energy has a more penetrating effect, the rate of assimilation is faster, and a greater quantity of pranic energy can be projected to patients without causing radical reactions. It is able to quickly penetrate the energy body and physical body of the patient with less resistance since it is so subtle. With gross pranic energy, it takes more time for the vital energy to seep into the energy and physical bodies of the patient. When very refined pranic energy is projected on the affected part, the rate of assimilation is very fast. This is clairvoyantly seen as rapid minute bubbling on the affected part. This is not seen when the projected pranic energy is not so refined. In other words, healers with more refined energy bodies produce faster rates of relief and cure than healers with gross energy bodies.

Ordinary healers have an inner aura that ranges from one to three feet, and the energy body is usually not so refined. More advanced pranic healers have an inner aura of six feet or more, and the energy body is more refined. Very advanced pranic healers may have an inner aura of more than fifty yards and the energy body is extremely refined.

If the healer has a very refined energy body, then more pranic energy can be projected to the patient without causing pranic congestion. For example, a very advanced pranic healer can increase the inner aura of the patient from three inches to about three feet without causing discomfort or pranic congestion on the patient. With an ordinary pranic healer whose energy body is relatively gross, increasing the patient's inner aura of an affected part from three to twelve inches may already cause discomfort or pranic congestion. A very advanced pranic healer can project a tremendous amount of very refined pranic energy which is assimilable within a very short period of time, thereby resulting in rapid healing.

To summarize, the energy body can be refined by:

a) A vegetarian diet
b) Meditating regularly
c) Healing regularly
d) Abstaining from smoking
e) Minimizing or avoiding consumption of alcoholic drinks
f) Abstaining from addictive and hallucinogenic drugs

Smoking, consuming drinks with high alcohol content, and taking addictive or hallucinogenic drugs must definitely be avoided because of the dirtying and clogging effect on the energy body.

MORE ABOUT KARMA

When a person does something with intention, whether good or bad, the karmic effect can reach tenfold. This is the principle behind tithing. When you plant a grain of rice, you harvest not only a grain of rice, but you harvest many times what you have planted. When you plant a mango seed, you get a mango tree that will produce many mangos.

When spiritual aspirants like pranic healers do something with intention, whether good or bad, the karmic effect can reach a hundredfold. This is no exaggeration and is to be taken literally. To deliberately misuse power or what has been taught in this book will bring severe karmic repercussions. "God cannot be mocked. A man reaps what he sows" (Galatians 6:7). Therefore, it is better to do good rather than evil deeds.

You do not have to blindly accept my words. You can experiment by doing something not too negative, and observe what happens. You can also try doing something positive, like tithing, and observe what happens. Very often, the karmic effect does not occur on a lump sum basis but on a piecemeal or staggered basis. But still the negative karmic effects are severe.

The law of karma is not fatalistic. It is self-determining or self-directing. It simply means that you are responsible and accountable for your deeds, words, feelings and thoughts. You cannot blame other people, your parents, your environment, or unseen forces for the problems or troubles you are experiencing. If you get yourself into trouble, then you should get yourself out of it with or without outside help. If you are experiencing "bad luck," or your condition is quite restrictive, or you are experiencing injustice, then you should meditate and learn whatever lessons are to be learned from them. You should do good deeds to generate good karma. Definitely, you should work hard and intelligently to improve your condition. *It is by learning your lessons, by doing good deeds, and by working hard and intelligently that you can reverse an adverse condition.* It is by working out or overcoming negative karma that one is purified and gains inner strength and wisdom.

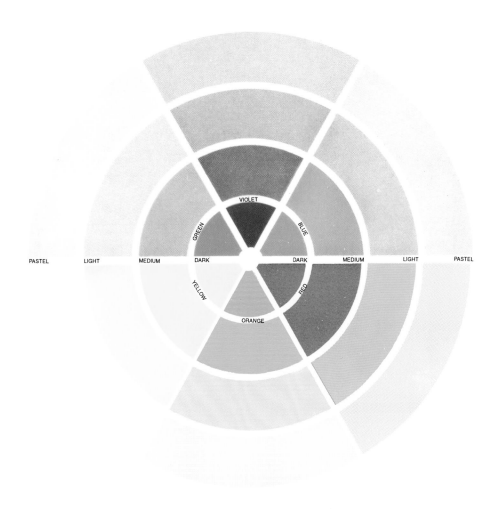

PASTEL LIGHT MEDIUM DARK DARK MEDIUM LIGHT PASTEL

VIOLET
GREEN BLUE
YELLOW RED
ORANGE

Color Pranas

light whitish red

light whitish green

light whitish orange

light whitish blue

light whitish yellow

light whitish violet

Light Whitish Color Pranas

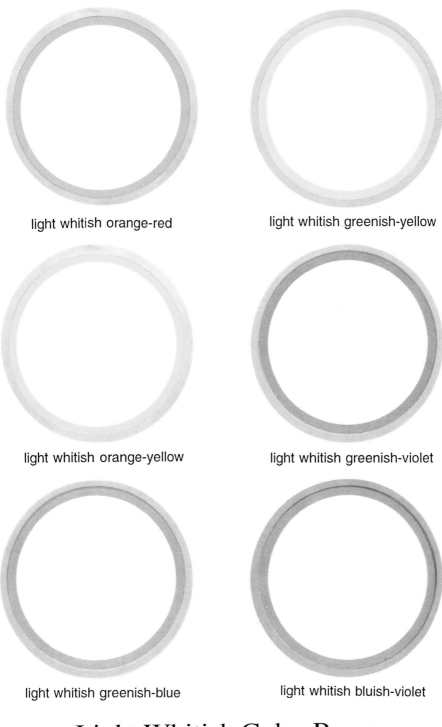

light whitish orange-red

light whitish greenish-yellow

light whitish orange-yellow

light whitish greenish-violet

light whitish greenish-blue

light whitish bluish-violet

Light Whitish Color Pranas

Golden Body of a Great Yogi

Eleven Major Chakras

THE CHAKRAS

The major chakras not only control and energize the vital organs of the body but also control and affect a person's psychological and spiritual conditions.

1. **Basic Chakra**. This chakra is located at the base of the spine or the coccyx area. It has four petals and contains red and orange pranas. It also contains a very minute amount of unnoticeable yellow prana. The red prana from the basic chakra is used for energizing and strengthening the entire visible physical body. The basic chakra controls and energizes the following:

   a) The muscular and skeletal systems
   b) The spine
   c) Production and quality of the blood
   d) The adrenal glands
   e) The tissues of the body and the internal organs
   f) Growth rate of cells
   g) Growth rate of children
   h) General vitality
   i) Body heat
   j) The heart and the sex organs

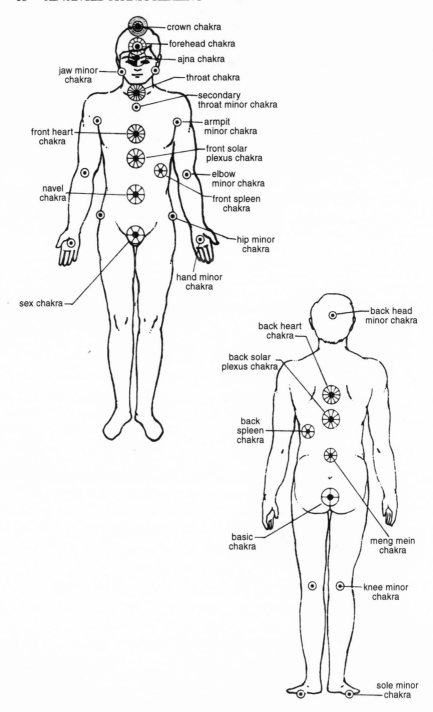

Figure 2-1. The eleven major chakras and other minor chakras.

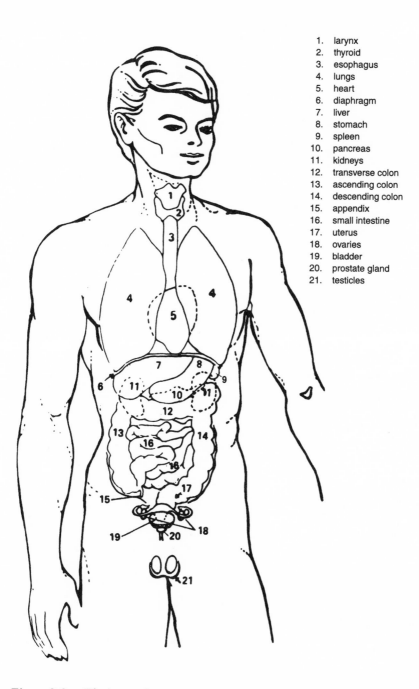

1. larynx
2. thyroid
3. esophagus
4. lungs
5. heart
6. diaphragm
7. liver
8. stomach
9. spleen
10. pancreas
11. kidneys
12. transverse colon
13. ascending colon
14. descending colon
15. appendix
16. small intestine
17. uterus
18. ovaries
19. bladder
20. prostate gland
21. testicles

Figure 2-2.   The internal organs.

Malfunctioning of this chakra may manifest as:

a) Arthritis and rheumatism
b) Spinal problems
c) Blood ailments and allergies
d) Slow healing of wounds and broken bones
e) Growth problems
f) Cancer and leukemia
g) Low vitality
h) Heart ailments
i) Brain ailments
j) Sexual ailments

The basic chakra controls and energizes the muscular system; therefore, the heart is also affected. Patients with severe heart ailments also have malfunctioning basic chakras. With some heart patients, the basic chakras instead of being predominantly red and orange are predominantly orange and yellow, which is an abnormal condition.

Part of the pranic energy of the basic chakra also goes to the brain; therefore, malfunctioning of the basic chakra may also seriously affect the brain. *Part of the transmuted basic energy is required for the proper functioning of the head chakras.*

Elderly people usually have depleted or very depleted basic chakras. This is why their bodies are weak and become smaller, their spines tend to curve, the healing of their wounds and broken bones tends to be slow, and they tend to develop arthritis. *A healthy basic chakra is a critical factor in one's youthfulness and health.*

The basic chakra is the center of self-survival or self-preservation. Persons with strong and active basic chakras tend to be more dynamic. But if the basic chakra is too overactivated, then the condition may manifest as hyperactiveness, restlessness or insomnia. Some people whose basic chakras are underactive tend to be sluggish, impractical, and unrealistic. In some severe cases, they tend to be completely out of touch with reality. Persons with suicidal inclination have weak and underactive basic chakras.

The minor chakras in the soles of the feet and the basic chakra are the major entry points for ground pranic energy.

2. **Sex Chakra**. This chakra is located at the pubic area. It has six petals and contains red and orange pranas. This chakra contains red prana of two different shades. It is clairvoyantly observed that when a person is urinating, the sex chakra and meng mein chakra produce more orange prana that is used in expelling and eliminating waste matter from the body. The sex chakra controls and energizes the following:

a) The sex organs
b) The bladder and urethra
c) The legs
d) The throat and head area

The ajna chakra, throat chakra and basic chakra have strong influences on the sex chakra. Malfunctioning of any of these chakras may adversely affect the sex chakra.

Malfunctioning of the sex chakra may manifest as:

a) Urinary problems
b) Impotency
c) Sterility
d) Enlarged prostate gland
e) Other sexual ailments

The sex chakra is the lower or physical creative center. The throat chakra is the higher correspondence of the sex chakra. Part of sex pranic energy is transmuted by the body to a higher form of pranic energy to be used by the throat and head chakras. *The transmuted sex energy is required for the proper functioning of the throat chakra, and the chakras in the head area.* Mentally retarded patients have depleted sex chakras. With older people, not only the basic chakra but also the sex chakra is depleted. This is one of the factors causing older people to become senile. The science and art of transmuting sex energy to creative energy and to a higher form of pranic energy to activate the brain cells is taught in Arhatic Yoga, the yoga of synthesis.

3. **Meng Mein Chakra**. This chakra is located approximately at the back of the navel. It has eight petals and contains predominantly orange prana and less red. It also contains smaller amounts of yellow prana and blue prana. It acts as a "pumping station" for the pranic energy from the basic chakra and is responsible for the *upward flow of pranic energy in the spine*. The meng mein chakra controls and energizes:

a) The kidneys
b) The adrenal glands
c) Other internal organs to a certain extent
d) Blood pressure regulation

Malfunctioning of the meng mein chakra may manifest as:

a) Kidney problems
b) Low vitality

    c) Blood pressure ailments
    d) Back problems

The normal size of the meng mein chakra is about 1/2 to 2/3 the average size of the other major chakras. At its normal size, the blood pressure is normal. If the meng mein chakra is overactivated or if the ratio is higher, then the blood pressure will be higher than the normal level. If the meng mein chakra is underactivated or the ratio is lower, then the blood pressure will be lower than the normal level. The meng mein chakra is closely related to the spleen chakra. If the spleen chakra is highly energized, the meng mein chakra will also be substantially energized. If the spleen chakra is activated, the meng mein chakra will also be partially activated. *This is why it is not advisable to energize the spleen chakra of a patient with hypertension*.

The malfunctioning of the solar plexus, meng mein, and basic chakras together with the malfunctioning of the ajna and heart chakras may manifest as abnormal growth rate of cells.

The meng mein chakra of infants, children, pregnant women, and elderly people should not be energized because of possible adverse effects. In the case of infants, children and elderly people, it may cause the blood pressure to go up. With pregnant women, it may cause the child to be stillborn. This chakra should be treated only by advanced pranic healers.

4. **Navel Chakra**. This chakra is located on the navel. It has eight petals and contains predominantly yellow, green, blue, red, and violet pranas. It also contains a little of orange prana. The navel chakra produces "synthetic ki" which facilitates or helps in the circulation of prana within the meridians. "Synthetic ki" facilitates the drawing in of prana by the etheric body. Persons with more "synthetic ki" can draw in more prana than those with less "synthetic ki." Persons with less "synthetic ki" feel low during poor weather. The navel chakra controls and energizes:

    a) The small intestine
    b) The large intestine
    c) The appendix
    d) The speed of giving birth
    e) The general vitality

Malfunctioning of the navel chakra may manifest as:

    a) Constipation
    b) Loose bowel movements
    c) Inability to assimilate food nutrients
    d) Appendicitis

   e) Intestinal ailments
   f) Difficulty in giving birth
   g) Low vitality

5. **Spleen Chakra**. The front spleen chakra is located at the middle part of the left bottom rib. The back spleen chakra is located behind the front spleen chakra. Both of them have the same functions. The spleen chakra has six petals. It is the major entry point of air prana or air vitality globules; therefore, it plays a vital part in our general well-being. The spleen chakra draws in air prana or "white" prana; and it breaks down the white prana into red, orange, yellow, green, blue, and violet pranas which are then distributed to the other major chakras. In other words, the spleen chakra energizes the other major chakras and thereby energizes the entire bioplasmic body and visible physical body. This means that the other major chakras and vital organs are substantially dependent on the spleen chakra for pranic energy. The normal size of the spleen chakra is about 1/2 to 2/3 the average size of the other major chakras. The spleen chakra:

   a) Controls and energizes the physical spleen
   b) Affects the pranic energy level or the general vitality of the body
   c) Affects the quality of the blood
   d) Affects the immune system of the body

Based on clairvoyant observation, the spleen chakra is usually, if not always, affected among patients suffering from severe infection. From the medical viewpoint, the physical spleen removes abnormal particles, especially germs from the blood, and it also produces antibodies.

Malfunctioning of the spleen chakra may manifest as:

   a) Ailments of the spleen
   b) Low vitality
   c) Lower immunity level
   d) Dirty blood or blood ailments
   e) Arthritis and rheumatism

Rheumatoid arthritis patients have dirty spleen chakras.

   The spleen chakra is closely related to the navel chakra. When the navel chakra is highly energized and activated, the spleen chakra also becomes substantially energized and partially activated, thereby drawing in more air prana. Thus, this increases the pranic energy level of the entire body.

   A person can be energized by just concentrating on the navel chakra. By concentrating on the navel chakra, it becomes activated and energized. This in turn substantially activates and energizes the spleen chakra which energizes the other chakras, thereby energizing the entire body. The navel chakra is also closely related to the meng mein chakra. *Therefore, it is not advisable for a patient with hypertension to meditate on the navel chakra since it may aggravate the condition.*

6. **Solar Plexus Chakra**. The front solar plexus chakra is located at the hollow area between the ribs; the back solar plexus chakra is located at the back of the solar plexus area. The solar plexus chakra has ten petals and contains red, yellow, green, and blue pranas. It also contains a little of orange and violet pranas.

More green prana is produced when a person is eating. When a person moves his or her bowel, the solar plexus and navel chakras produce a lot of orange prana and some yellow prana. When yellow prana comes in contact with orange prana, a triggering effect on the large intestine is produced. This is the reason why orange prana or yellow prana or both are used in treating constipation. The solar plexus chakra controls and energizes the following:

a) Diaphragm
b) Liver
c) Pancreas
d) Stomach
e) The large and small intestines to a substantial degree
f) The adrenal glands, heart, lungs and other parts of the body are also affected

The quality of the blood is also affected by the solar plexus chakra, since it controls and energizes the liver which detoxifies the blood. Patients suffering from rheumatoid arthritis, autoimmune ailments and lupus erythematosus have malfunctioning solar plexus chakras and livers. It is easier to energize the pancreas through the back solar plexus chakra.

An exhausted person can be revitalized rapidly by energizing the solar plexus chakra. The solar plexus chakra is one of the most important chakras because it controls, energizes, and affects so many vital organs, and because it is so easily disturbed or imbalanced by negative emotions.

Malfunctioning of the solar plexus chakra may manifest as:

a) Difficulty in breathing due to malfunctioning of the diaphragm
b) Diabetes
c) Ailments of the pancreas
d) Digestive ailments
e) Hepatitis
f) Ailments of the gall bladder
g) High cholesterol level

h) Heart ailments
i) Dirty blood or blood ailments

The solar plexus chakra is the center of positive and negative lower emotions, such as ambition, courage, perseverance, aggressiveness, anger, hatred, envy, greed, destructiveness, violence, cruelty, and so forth. When a person is very angry, the solar plexus chakra pulsates erratically. This causes the diaphragm to move erratically, resulting in irregular shallow breathing.

7. **Heart Chakra**. The heart chakra has twelve petals. The front heart chakra contains a lot of golden prana with some light red prana. The front heart chakra is located at the center of the chest. It controls and energizes the heart and the thymus gland.

The back heart chakra contains golden, red, orange, and yellow pranas. It controls and energizes the lungs, the heart, and the thymus gland.

The heart chakra also affects the ability of the body to fight infection. From a medical viewpoint, the thymus gland is an important factor in the defense system of the body.

Energizing the heart is done through the back heart chakra, which allows prana to easily flow into the heart, lungs, and other parts of the body without causing the physical heart to be congested.

The heart chakra is the center of higher or refined emotions. It is very closely related to the solar plexus chakra since both are emotional centers. To agitate the solar plexus chakra is also to agitate the heart chakra. *This is why negative emotions have detrimental effects on the physical heart in the long run.*

8. **Throat Chakra**. This chakra is located at the center of the throat. It has sixteen petals and contains predominantly blue prana with some green prana and violet prana. A lot of green prana is produced when a person is eating. The throat chakra controls and energizes the following:

a) Throat
b) Voice box or larynx
c) Air tube or trachea
d) Thyroid gland
e) Parathyroid glands
f) Lymphatic system
g) The sex chakra is also affected

Malfunctioning of this chakra may manifest as sterility and throat-related ailments like goiter, sore throat, loss of voice, and asthma.

The throat chakra is the center of the lower or concrete mind or lower mental faculty and is also the center for higher creativity.

9. **Ajna Chakra**. This chakra is located between the eyebrows. It has 96 petals and is divided into two divisions. Each division has 48 petals. With some persons, one of the divisions is predominantly light yellow and the other division is predominantly light violet. Others have whitish-green in one of the divisions and light violet in the other division. The predominating color pranas in the ajna differ from person to person. Its colors change according to the psychological state.

It controls and energizes the pituitary gland and the entire body. It is called the master chakra because it controls all the major chakras and the endocrine system, and affects the vital organs. Malfunctioning of the ajna chakra may manifest as diseases of the endocrine glands, eye ailments, cancer, and others.

The ajna chakra is the center of the higher or abstract mind and is also the center of the will or directive function.

10. **Forehead Chakra**. This chakra is located at the center of the forehead. It has 144 petals divided into twelve divisions. Each division contains twelve petals. The forehead chakra contains light violet, blue, red, orange, yellow, and green pranas.

The forehead chakra controls and energizes the pineal gland and the nervous system. Malfunctioning of the forehead chakra may manifest as ailments of the nervous system. The forehead chakra is the center of the lower Buddhic or cosmic consciousness.

11. **Crown Chakra**. This chakra is located at the crown of the head. It has 960 outer petals and twelve inner petals. The crown chakra has two sets of petals. The twelve inner petals contain predominantly golden prana and the 960 outer petals contain light violet, blue, yellow, green, orange, and red pranas. The front heart chakra looks like the inner petals of the crown chakra. *The crown chakra is the entry point of the divine energy or the electric-violet pranic energy.*

The crown chakra controls and energizes the brain and the pineal gland. Malfunctioning of this chakra may manifest as diseases of the pineal gland and the brain, which may manifest as physical or psychological illnesses.

The crown chakra is the center of the higher Buddhic or cosmic consciousness. The mental faculty can be compared to a blind man, while the Buddhic consciousness, to a person who can see. For a blind man to have an idea of the shape of an elephant, he has to spend a considerable amount of time touching the elephant and trying to deduce and synthesize the data gathered, while a person who can see will be able to know immediately the shape of an elephant. Buddhic consciousness is understanding a subject matter not through a long period of study nor through inductive or deductive reasoning but through *direct comprehension or perception*. Another term for Buddhic consciousness is *Christ consciousness*. Through Buddhic consciousness, a person feels oneness with all, loving kindness for all. It is through Christ consciousness that one feels oneness with God.

ENTRY POINTS OF PRANIC ENERGY

The entry points for earth pranic energy are the basic chakra and the sole chakras. For air prana, use the spleen chakra and the lungs. For divine energy or soul energy, the entry point is the crown chakra and the terminating point is the heart chakra. This is why the crown and heart chakras are predominantly gold.

NETWORK OF CHAKRAS

Each major chakra has a subchakra or several subchakras. This subchakra is called a minor chakra. Each subchakra may have a subsubchakra, called a minichakra. For example, the basic major chakra has many subchakras or minor chakras in the arms and legs. The hand minor chakra, which is a subchakra of the basic chakra, has subsubchakras which are the minichakras found on the fingertips and on the joints of the fingers. Those found in the fingertips are called finger minichakras. The human energy body is filled with big and small chakras or vortices of energy. These vortices of energy also correspond to acupuncture points. Knowing the location of the major chakras and their functions are usually sufficient for healing purposes. The locations of the other minor chakras will be discussed later in this book.

CHAKRAS AND AILMENTS

In elementary and intermediate pranic healing, students are concerned with whether or not the affected chakras are congested or depleted. In advanced pranic healing, the healers are concerned about the three following conditions of the chakras:

1. Congestion or depletion;
2. Overactivated or underactivated;
3. Improper type or amount of pranic energy in the chakras.

Whether a major chakra is overactivated or underactivated is relative to the sizes of the other major chakras. For example, if the solar plexus chakra is about six inches while the other chakras are about four inches, then the solar plexus chakra is overactivated. But if the solar plexus chakra is about three inches and the other major chakras are about five inches, then the solar plexus chakra is underactivated. Hypertension or high blood pressure and cancer are two common ailments that have something to do with the over-activation of certain chakras. In many instances, just cleansing the overacti-vated chakra will cause it to partially normalize. To get a more lasting result, treatment has to be done repeatedly.

Underactivated chakras can also cause ailments. If the solar plexus, meng mein and basic chakras are underactivated, then the person will be sluggish. If they are very underactivated, then the patient will be quite weak and sleepy most of the time.

Ailments could also be caused by improper type or amount of pranic energy contained in the chakra(s). For example, the following conditions are present in hyperthyroidism:

1. There is too much red prana in the solar plexus chakra.
2. There is a substantial amount of red prana in the ajna and throat chakras. Red prana is not supposed to be in the ajna and throat chakras.
3. The two conditions stated above are longstanding.

SIZES OF THE MAJOR CHAKRAS

The average size of the major chakras varies depending upon the evolution-ary development of the person. Table 1 provides general information.

Table 1. Size of the chakras.

Evolutionary Development	Sizes in Diameter
Mentally Retarded	two inches or less
Below Average	about two-and-half-inches
Average or Masses	about three to four inches
Intelligentsia	about four to five inches
Superior	about six or more inches
Advanced Yogis or Saints	about eighteen inches or more
Superpersons	two yards or more

Being a clairvoyant or psychic does not necessarily mean that the person is quite developed or has big chakras. As a matter of fact, some ordinary clairvoyants are quite emotional, and the average sizes of the major chakras are about four to five inches only.

Being a yogi or being on the spiritual path for more than ten or twenty years does not necessarily mean that the person is quite developed. As a matter of fact, I have encountered some so-called "yogis" or "spiritual practitioners" in which the average size of the major chakras is only about four to five inches in diameter. Many of these people have too much pride and suffer from delusions of spiritual superiority. They behave as though they know so much and are quite spiritually developed. They are just fooling themselves. Their esoteric knowledge is often superficial and contaminated with superstitious nonsense. Their spiritual cord or antakharana may be only hair-like, not even one inch in diameter. Based on spiritual or yogic standards, they are only in the nursery.

There are several spiritual or yogic systems of activating the chakras and awakening the kundalini. Arhatic Yoga is one of the systems that safely and rapidly activates the chakras and awakens the kundalini.

Preventive Healing

INTRODUCTION

In preventive healing, there are nine factors to be considered:

1. Diet
2. Breathing
3. Sufficient exercise
4. Etheric hygiene
5. Emotions and thoughts (emotional and mental hygiene)
6. Human relationships
7. Livelihood
8. Lifestyle
9. Preventive pranic treatment

DIET

Proper diet simply refers to clean nutritious food. Clean means the food must be physically and etherically clean. Physically, the food must be substantially free of dirt, germs, and chemical toxins. Etherically, the energy of the food must be clean and luminous. In general, meat contains a lot of dirty grayish energy. Pork is etherically quite sticky and very dirty; therefore it is better to abstain from it. In general, fish is cleaner than meat but is still slightly dirty. The energy content of vegetables and fruits is quite clean and luminous. Nutritious means that the "food mix" contains sufficient physical nutrients and much pranic energy or life force. Fresh food contains more life force than preserved ones. A person who is partially depleted can usually be revitalized within a short period by just eating two raw eggs. Taking one to two grams of bee pollen daily will be most healthful. Bee pollen is physically nutritious and contains life force.

Some healers are predominantly vegetarians. But under certain situations, like social gatherings, they also eat fish and meat to a limited degree. Extremist attitudes or fanaticism should be avoided.

For patients suffering from severe ailments, the energy body is quite dirty, and its ability to expel diseased energy is affected. Since vegetables and fruits are etherically quite clean, they will not unnecessarily burden the already overburdened energy body with the additional task of expelling more dirty energy. Fresh vegetables and fruits contain a lot of pranic energy or life force which is needed by the patient's body. *Therefore, it is advisable for a patient with severe ailments to become a vegetarian temporarily or permanently*. In the long run, the effect is usually quite substantial, if not quite dramatic.

Besides clean wholesome food, clean air and clean water are of course essential.

BREATHING

Basically, there are two ways of breathing: the correct way and the incorrect way. The correct way is abdominal breathing and the incorrect way is chest breathing. It is the diaphragm which enables the lungs to expand and to contract. The lungs by themselves do not have the capacity to expand in order to draw in air, or to contract in order to expel used air. With abdominal breathing, the abdomen is slightly pushed out during inhalation, causing the diaphragm to be pulled down which enables the lungs to draw in more air. During exhalation, the abdomen is slightly pulled in, causing the diaphragm to be pushed up which enables the lungs to exhale more used air. Also, more pranic energy is drawn in during inhalation and more used energy is expelled during exhalation.

With chest breathing, the abdomen is pulled in during inhalation, causing the diaphragm to be pushed up resulting in less air being drawn in.

During exhalation, the abdomen is pushed out, causing the diaphragm to be pulled down resulting in less air being expelled. Prolonged chest breathing also tends to congest the front heart chakra, resulting in chest pain and difficulty in breathing.

Abdominal breathing is natural. Infants and small children do it instinctively, without being taught by anybody. Observe for a few minutes how an infant breathes especially when asleep. The abdomen is expanded when inhaling and is contracted when exhaling. But as children grow up, they learn the wrong way to breathe, which is chest breathing.

EXERCISE

Exercising has a cleansing effect—physically and etherically. Physically, waste matter and toxins are eliminated through sweating. When a person is exercising, the auras of the energy body pulsate; whitish-gray light or used energy is expelled and fresh pranic energy is drawn in. The chakras, the meridians, and the organs are cleansed of used and diseased energy. *Blood and pranic circulations are greatly improved by regular exercise.* The body feels better and lighter after exercising. Regular physical exercise is a must to maintain a clean, highly vitalized, healthy body.

Based on clairvoyant observation, when a part of the physical body is being stretched and contracted or being rotated (in other words, when it is being exercised), the corresponding chakra pulsates, expelling used or diseased energy and drawing in fresh prana. The corresponding chakra becomes cleaner, brighter, and thicker. This is called the "principle of correspondence."

You can do an experiment to verify the validity of what has been stated.

1. Scan the throat chakra of the subject before the subject exercises.
2. Instruct the subject to bend the neck to the front then to the back repeatedly about thirty-six times.
3. Scan the throat chakra when the subject is doing the exercise and after the exercise.
4. If your hands are sensitive enough, you will notice that the throat chakra is becoming bigger and stronger as the subject continues to exercise the neck.

This is why, in Chinese chi kung, the patient is sometimes instructed to exercise an affected part for a period of time to facilitate the healing process. Another recommended experiment:

1. Scan the inner and outer auras of the subject before the subject exercises.
2. Instruct the subject to do Tai Chi or some other form of exercise for several minutes.
3. Scan the subject while he or she is doing the exercise.
4. You will notice that the auras of the subject are pulsating and expanding.

Tai Chi, chi kung exercises, hatha yoga, dancing, martial arts, sports, jogging, hiking or brisk walking, if done regularly, have very good effects on the body. The left and right parts of the body should be exercised equally. Otherwise, the part of the body which is not sufficiently exercised will become weaker and partially congested, which may manifest as pain or discomfort. Fifteen to thirty minutes of exercise daily or regularly will be sufficient. Exercising should be done with moderation, especially certain types of chi kung exercises which are quite powerful.

If people do regular physical exercise, health will greatly improve. We could reduce our huge national health bills. Also, elderly citizens will be more productive and will have fuller lives.

ETHERIC HYGIENE

Proper hygiene consists of physical hygiene, etheric hygiene, emotional hygiene, and mental hygiene. The emphasis of this section will be on etheric hygiene.

Smoking is a very unhygienic habit. Both the physical body and the etheric body are dirtied. In the case of chain smokers, the etheric body is polluted with dirty brown energy. Many of the meridians are partially blocked, thereby weakening the physical body in general. When the back meridian in the spine is partially blocked, the back solar plexus chakra, the meng mein chakra, and the basic chakra tend to become congested and overactivated, thereby making the smoker susceptible to hypertension. The etheric lungs and the back heart chakra are extremely dirty and are adversely affected. The front heart chakra is partially affected, making the habitually heavy smoker susceptible to heart problems, since the front heart chakra is closely connected to the dirty back heart chakra.

Habitually drinking liquor with a high alcohol content is etherically unhygienic. It makes the etheric body dirty and gross. Drug addiction dirties the etheric body. It damages the etheric body, making the addict susceptible to undesirable external psychic influences which manifest as severe psychological ailments.

In certain places, the land itself has a dirty etheric energy. This is clairvoyantly seen as light-grayish energy coming out of the ground. If the reclaimed land has been dumped with garbage, then the area is etherically dirty or polluted. These areas, in the long run, tend to adversely affect the physical and psychological health of their residents. It is just like living in a highly polluted city.

Certain places are likewise etherically quite dirty—hospitals, funeral parlors, cemeteries and others. For persons who are relatively weak, it is advisable to take a shower using water and salt to remove etheric dirt or the etheric contamination after visiting such places. For persons who are quite healthy, their energy bodies are usually quite capable of expelling the dirty energy, but it is still better to take a shower using water and salt just to be on the safe side.

If a room has been used for a long period of time by a very sickly person, then the room is filled with diseased energy, and it must be cleansed. If a room or a house has been occupied by a negative or psychologically disturbed person, then the room is not physically and psychologically conducive to anyone's well being. For some of you who are relatively sensitive, you may have experienced going to certain places which you do not feel good about for no apparent reason. This is because the place has been negatively impregnated. Etherically dirty rooms can be cleansed by:

1. Using water and salt;
2. Burning sandalwood incense;
3. Praying;
4. Exposing the room to sunlight.

Objects can also be etherically contaminated. As a general guideline, it is better to avoid lending your personal things to others to avoid etheric contamination. Likewise, it is advisable to avoid using the personal things belonging to other people. One of my students related an experience when he was feeling pain in one of the areas of his kidneys. He later found out that his driver had had a kidney ailment for quite some time. Since he also drives the car when the driver is absent, he was obviously contaminated with the driver's diseased energy when he repeatedly sat in the driver's seat. Contaminated objects can also be cleansed by using the same techniques as cleansing a room.

When buying or accepting secondhand things, especially pieces of jewelry, it is advisable to know the condition of the previous owner(s) since the characteristics of the previous owner are impregnated in personal belongings. If the previous owner was sickly or negative, then possessing a secondhand item from him or her would be unhealthy and unlucky.

You can also be contaminated when interacting with others. When interacting with a sick person, you may feel depleted since the sick person may subconsciously absorb some of your healthy pranic energy, and you may also accidentally absorb some of the diseased energy. When regularly embracing a loved one who is sick, you may tend to become sick, too. This is just like a very sick person embracing a big tree to absorb the tree's life force, and in the process transferring the diseased energy to the tree. In the long run, the tree may simply die. In deciding whether to allow yourself to be frequently embraced by a loved one who is quite sick, there are two main factors to be considered: first, the possible detrimental effect on your health; second, the emotional hurt that may be inflicted on the loved one if you do not embrace or allow yourself to be embraced by the loved one. You have to decide for yourself. Out of kindness and affection, you may lovingly embrace and be embraced. To correct the effects of being partially contaminated and depleted, take 3000 mg. of garlic oil since it contains a lot of orange prana and therefore has a strong cleansing effect. Since garlic contains a lot of orange prana, an overdose may cause diarrhea. To energize the body, take 2000 mg. of bee pollen, 2000 mg. Chinese or Korean red ginseng, and 400 to 800 iu of vitamin E.

It is a healthy practice to go to the beach regularly about once a month or once every two months. Sea water has a cleansing effect on the energy body. The body is highly energized with prana from the fresh air, sunlight, and ground.

EMOTIONS AND THOUGHTS (EMOTIONAL AND MENTAL HYGIENE)

Proper emotional and mental hygiene consists of internal and external hygiene. Internal emotional and mental hygiene simply means proper emotions and proper thoughts. Positive emotions and thoughts, such as happiness, kindness, joy, and enthusiasm tend to have beneficial effects psychologically, etherically, and physically.

In the next chapter, an experiment will be discussed to show that being happy, relaxed, or just smiling is beneficial and is enough to increase the energy level of the body.

In many instances, negative emotion is one of the critical factors, if not the most critical factor, in severe ailments. The solar plexus chakra is the center of lower emotions. Since most people are quite emotional, the solar plexus chakra tends to become quite dirty and malfunctions. The problem caused by unregulated emotions is compounded by living in a very stressful world. The solar plexus chakra is located at the center of the trunk; therefore, it is located very near to most of the vital organs. Malfunctioning of the solar plexus chakra tends to adversely affect the proximate organ or organs. The solar plexus chakra is either depleted or quite congested. Sometimes, the front solar plexus chakra seems to be normal, but the back solar plexus chakra is quite congested. Patients with this type of ailment tend to be tactful and usually do not express their negative feelings.

Harboring or explosively expressing negative feelings for a prolonged period may manifest as:

1. Glaucoma;
2. Migraine headaches;
3. Acute sinusitis;
4. Hyperthyroidism;
5. Respiratory ailments like asthma;
6. Heart ailments;
7. Diabetes;
8. Gastric or intestinal ulcers;
9. High cholesterol;
10. Infected liver (negative emotion weakens the body and the liver, thereby making it susceptible to infection);
11. Constipation;
12. Twisted intestines;
13. Damaged kidneys;
14. Hypertension;
15. Rheumatoid arthritis;
16. Cancer and other illnesses.

When negative emotions are accompanied by negative thoughts, the upper chakras—like the throat, ajna, forehead or crown chakras—will also be affected. This may manifest as hyperthyroidism, acute sinusitis, migraine headache, glaucoma, epilepsy, and other illnesses.

When negative emotions are accompanied by expressed or inhibited physical aggression, the lower chakras, like the meng mein chakra, and the basic chakra, will also be affected. This may manifest as hypertension, damaged kidneys, a herniated disk, skin ailments, rheumatoid arthritis, blood ailments, and other problems.

At the present level of human evolution, people are still quite centered in the emotions. They are focused or polarized in the solar plexus chakra;

therefore, *the solar plexus chakra should be thoroughly treated in most cases involving severe ailments.*

Although pranic healing can affect the emotional state of the patient, the rate of healing would be faster if the patient makes a conscious and persistent effort at regulating and improving his or her emotions. The cooperation of the patient is very important.

External emotional and mental hygiene means proper company, since emotions and thoughts are transmissible. Negative emotions and thoughts are infectious. This is why, after talking with persons with psychological problems, you may feel depressed and physically exhausted. Prolonged interaction with them may manifest as physical ailment(s). This is why many priests, nuns, social workers, psychologists, and psychiatrists, after closely interacting for many years with psychologically disturbed persons, tend to become psychologically affected and physically sick.

It is preferable to be sexually selective, since it is very easy to be etherically and psychologically contaminated through indiscriminate sexual interactions. After such an interaction, it is advisable to clean yourself physically, etherically, emotionally, and mentally.

Food should preferably be handled and prepared by persons in good health and with happy dispositions, since good energy and bad energy can easily be transmitted to food and objects.

Interacting with people who are optimistic, enthusiastic, radiant and very healthy is very psychologically and etherically beneficial. In the presence of an advanced spiritual teacher, you can easily be emotionally, mentally and spiritually uplifted if you are sufficiently receptive and have the proper reverence. Students can actually bathe in the powerful aura of a spiritual teacher.

FORGIVENESS & LOVING-KINDNESS

Some severe ailments are emotional in origin. Some patients carry deep-seated hurts or resentments toward another person or other people. Although pranic healing does greatly improve the condition of the patient, *the rate of healing would be much faster if the patient consciously exerts an effort to forgive those who may have actually or imaginarily hurt him or her.* Even though the solar plexus chakra and the other chakras are quite clean after pranic treatment, if the patient recalls the person(s) or the disturbing event, the solar plexus chakra will again become congested and dirty, which will in turn adversely affect some of the chakras and organs. Unless the patient learns to forgive, the healing will be slow or there will be a relapse. THE ACT OF

FORGIVING IS THERAPEUTIC AND IS NECESSARY FOR GOOD HEALTH. It helps normalize the solar plexus chakra and the other affected chakras.

Being habitually critical, irritable, or angry is also very unhygienic and bad for health in the long run. The remedy is, of course, to learn to appreciate the good qualities of others, to practice kindness and to learn to be calm. *It is easier to wear a pair of shoes than to try to flatten all the rough ground. It is easier to be kind, tolerant, and detached than to try to change and improve everybody.*

RELATIONSHIPS

Cruelty to fellow beings and to animals is one of the major causes of severe painful ailments. What you sow is what you reap (Galatians 6:7). This is the law. If one repeatedly causes pain to others, then one will also harvest intense pain in the form of a severe ailment. If someone repeatedly deprives others of physical sustenance (income, money, or food), then that person will also be deprived of physical sustenance. This may manifest as severe lung ailments wherein the person keeps gasping for life (sustenance). The affected body will gradually wilt. This will also have adverse financial effects.

Even prophets are not exempted from the law of karma. When Jesus asked "Who was John the Baptist?" the disciples understood that John the Baptist was Prophet Elijah (Matt. 17:12-13). Prophet Elijah was a very powerful prophet. After winning the contest against the pagan priests, he unfortunately got carried away and ordered the execution of the pagan priests (1 Kings 18:20-40). Likewise, King Herod ordered the head of John the Baptist chopped off (Matt. 14:8-11). We are all quite human and we make many mistakes. I have no intention of criticizing John the Baptist, but rather use this case to show the working of the law of karma.

Negative karma can be neutralized by:

1. Learning the lesson that has to be learned.
2. Using the Law of Forgiveness. It is in pardoning that we are pardoned (Matt. 6:12, Matt. 6:14-15).
3. Using the Law of Mercy. By showing mercy (being kind, helpful, charitable, and gentle) to others, mercy will also be shown to us (Matt. 5:7).

Avoid cruelty and show kindness to others; this is a major key to good health, to happiness, and to avoiding severe painful ailments.

LIVELIHOOD

The nature of your work, the psychological condition of co-workers, and the overall working environment of a person affect the health of the worker. In this so-called modern developed world, there is too much stress and tension. In other words, there is a lot of:

1. Work pressure;
2. Hurriedness;
3. Worry and anxiety;
4. Irritation, anger, and hurt feelings;
5. Excessive aggressiveness;
6. Bullying;
7. Harassment.

Severe stress or tension, in the long run, causes the solar plexus chakra and the other chakras to malfunction. This may manifest as a gastric ulcer, heart ailments, hyperthyroidism, severe sinusitis, a migraine headache, malfunctioning liver, damaged kidneys, general weakness, depression, and other maladies.

Meditation would definitely help in coping with stressful conditions. But then, there is a certain degree of limitation to what meditation can do for a specific person. In certain cases, the condition is so stressful that it may be wiser to look for a better job or a livelihood that is less demanding and has saner working conditions.

The psychological state of co-workers is also important since stress is psychically very infectious. People under great stress radiate stress energy to the surrounding people through their chakras and auras. Consciously or subconsciously, they transfer a great bulk of their stress energy by being nasty and rude to others. This type of behavior is unacceptable and quite uncivilized. In the future, such behavior will be considered coarse and barbaric. *It is very impolite and improper to dump one's psychic feces on others.* The proper way to dispose of stress energy is to meditate, to do self-pranic healing or to have pranic treatment. *Work productivity can be improved substantially by letting executives and workers have regular pranic treatment.*

Prolonged stress is a psychological ailment which will adversely affect the physical body. In more developed countries, stress is a national epidemic. It is the right of each worker to have not only a physically safe working environment but also a psychologically healthy environment to work in. It is just a matter of time that this basic human right will be recognized and respected.

SELF-PRANIC HEALING FOR STRESS

With people who are undergoing a lot of stress, the solar plexus chakra is very congested and overactivated. The solar plexus chakra is filled with dirty red energy. The other chakras are also affected. Here are methods for self-pranic healing for stress.

1. Apply self-localized sweeping on the front solar plexus chakra thirty times or more. The sweeping should be done slowly and in a counterclockwise motion. Throw the dirty energy to the basin with water and salt. This will substantially reduce the stress.
2. Do deep pranic breathing for twelve cycles or more in order to further normalize the solar plexus chakra, to achieve inner calmness, and to recharge oneself. Or do the Meditation on Twin Hearts.
3. Repeat the procedure several times a day if necessary. (Meditation on Twin Hearts is preferably done not more than once or twice a day since it may cause pranic congestion.)
4. If stress is severe, contact an advanced pranic healer for regular preventive pranic psychotherapy treatment.

LIFE-STYLE

The life style of a person is an important health factor. Avoid undesirable habits and excessiveness such as:

1. Smoking cigarettes or tobacco;
2. Alcoholism;
3. Drug abuse;
4. Excessive work—hard work or industriousness is indeed a virtue but working fourteen to sixteen hours a day for several months or years is definitely excessive and *definitely bad for the health and bad for family life*;
5. Excessive fun—having fun is great, but too much fun or too much night life for a prolonged period is quite exhausting and will definitely have adverse effects on the health.

Some of the questions that should be asked are: Is the money and excessive luxury worth the inner emotional problem, the failing physical health, and deterioration of family life? What about the quality of life? What about the psychological and spiritual well-being of the children and of the spouse? What about one's inner peace and happiness? What about one's spiritual well-being and one's spiritual development? Are these not as important or even more important than excessive material possession and excessive luxury? Being rich and prosperous is indeed a blessing. But wealth should be acquired intelligently and not at such a heavy price.

PREVENTIVE PRANIC TREATMENT

As a person grows older, the chakras gradually atrophy and become depleted. These correspondingly cause the physical body and its organs to gradually deteriorate. To improve one's health, to reduce tension, and to slow down the rate of aging, it is advisable to undergo regular preventive pranic treatment. For older people, preventive pranic treatment can be applied once or twice a week depending upon the need. For younger people, the treatment can be done at further intervals.

Procedure:

1. Scan the patient, then rescan during pranic treatment.
2. Apply general sweeping twice.
3. Apply localized sweeping thoroughly on the front and back solar plexus chakra, on the liver (front, side, and back), on the stomach, and the pancreas.
4. Energize the solar plexus chakra with white prana.
5. Apply localized sweeping thoroughly on the crown chakra, forehead chakra, ajna chakra, back head chakra, on the left and right sides of the brain, the eyes, and the ears.
6. Energize the crown, forehead, ajna, and back head chakras with white prana.
7. Apply sweeping thoroughly on the jaw minor chakras, the throat chakra, the secondary throat minor chakras and on the back of the neck.
8. Energize the left and right jaw minor chakras, the throat chakra and the secondary throat minor chakras with white prana.
9. Apply localized sweeping on the front and back heart chakra and on the lungs (front, side, and back).
10. Energize the back heart chakra with white prana.
11. Apply sweeping thoroughly on the front and back spleen chakra.
12. Apply sweeping thoroughly on the left and right kidneys and on the meng mein chakra.
13. Apply localized sweeping thoroughly on the spine.
14. Apply localized sweeping on the navel and on the lower abdominal area thoroughly.

15. Energize the navel chakra with white prana.
16. Apply localized sweeping on the sex chakra and energize it with white prana.
17. Apply localized sweeping thoroughly on the basic chakra and energize it with white prana.
18. Apply localized sweeping on the left and right legs, with emphasis on the hip, knee and sole minor chakras.
19. Energize the hip, knee, and sole minor chakras with white prana.
20. Apply localized sweeping thoroughly on the left and right arms, especially on the armpit, elbow, and hand minor chakras.
21. Energize the armpit, elbow, and hand minor chakras with white prana.
22. Stabilize, then release the projected pranic energy. Avoid overenergizing the patient.
23. Repeat treatment once or twice a week.

By following the guidelines in this chapter and by undergoing regular preventive pranic treatment, a person can have a happier and healthier life.

Advanced Pranic Healing Techniques

BASICS OF PRANIC HEALING

No matter how advanced a pranic healer is, he or she will have to go back to the basics of pranic healing. For example, even if a healer is quite powerful, the patient still has to be receptive or be made receptive for healing to take place. The healer should remember the following basic concepts and techniques in pranic healing:

1. The two basic principles in pranic healing: cleansing and energizing.
2. The external and internal causes of diseases.
3. The seven basic techniques in pranic healing:
    a) sensitizing;
    b) scanning;
    c) cleansing;
    d) increasing receptivity;
    e) energizing;
    f) stabilizing;
    g) releasing or cutting the etheric link.
4. The proper disposal of diseased energy.
5. Washing the hands to avoid contamination.

6. When a healer should not heal.
7. Five things to avoid in pranic healing.
8. Critical factors in healing.
9. Invocative healing and the assigning of healing angels.
10. The karmic aspect of ailments.
11. Integrated approach in healing.

Scanning and repeated rescanning are necessary for proper diagnosis and proper feedback. Scan and rescan the patient thoroughly. Both cleansing and energizing should be done thoroughly. It is very important to stabilize with light whitish-blue prana after energizing. Be detached and release the projected pranic energy after the pranic treatment by cutting the etheric link. The patient should be instructed not to wash the treated part for twelve to twenty-four hours after pranic treatment. Patients with severe ailments should be instructed not to take a shower or bath within twenty-four hours after pranic treatment. To minimize or avoid being contaminated with diseased energy, flick your hand repeatedly even when energizing. Also, always wash your hands with water or with water and salt after healing. Advanced pranic healing students are sometimes so engrossed with sophisticated healing techniques that they forget the basics of pranic healing, thereby committing fundamental mistakes.

When energizing, (especially powerful healers) please also remember these important points: *If the projected pranic energy is impregnated with compassion and loving-kindness, the rate of assimilation is faster, resulting in a faster rate of healing.* If the projected pranic energy is impregnated with too much will, the rate of assimilation is very much slower, and it has a "stunning effect" on the cells, resulting in a slower rate of healing or, in some cases, a destructive effect. If the projected pranic energy is impregnated with anger or irritation, the effect will be destructive. The patient will get worse instead of getting better.

PRINCIPLES OF PRANIC HEALING

Certain basic concepts are easier to understand and remember if they are labeled.

1. **Principle of Life Force.** For physical life to exist, it must have life force or vital energy. Life force is essential to physical life. It is also necessary for the existence of more subtle life forms. This life force has been called by various names: prana, ruah, chi, manna, and many other names. Rapid healing is brought about by increasing the life force or pranic energy level of the affected part or the whole body.

2. **Principle of Pervasiveness.** Life force or vital energy is all around us. It is pervasive; we are actually in an ocean of life force. Based on this principle, a healer can draw in pranic energy or life force from the surroundings, and give it to the patient without exhausting himself or herself.

3. **Principle of Diseased Energy.** Disease not only exists in physical form but also in energy form. Disease in energy form is called diseased energy or diseased bioplasmic matter. Clairvoyantly, diseased energy is seen as greyish or dark.

4. **Principle of Transmittability.** Life force or vital energy can be transmitted from one person to another person or object, or from one object to another object or a person.

5. **Principle of Contamination.** Diseased energy is transmissible. It could be transmitted from a patient to another person or to a healer. The diseased energy of a subject could contaminate a person, an object, an animal, or a plant. Therefore, to avoid contamination, it is extremely important for healers to flick their hands when sweeping and after energizing, and to wash their hands and arms after cleansing and energizing.

6. **Principle of Controllability.** Life force and diseased energy can be controlled and directed through the will or through "mind intent."

7. **Principle of Cleansing and Energizing.** In healing, giving life force is not enough; it is also necessary to remove the diseased energy. Removing the diseased energy is called cleansing. Giving life force to a patient or an object is called energizing. The rate of healing can be accelerated by applying the principle of cleansing and energizing.

8. **Principle of Radical Reaction.** When energizing is done without removing the diseased energy, a crisis may take place in the form of temporary worsening of the condition. This is called radical reaction. This could be avoided or minimized by thorough cleansing.

9. **Principle of Receptivity.** A patient has to be receptive or at least neutral in order to receive the projected pranic energy. Being relaxed also helps increase the degree of receptivity. Without receptivity, the projected pranic energy will not be absorbed, or only a minimal amount of it will be absorbed. Patients may not be receptive because: they are biased toward this type of healing, they do not like the healer personally, they do not want to get well, or they are in general not receptive about anything.

10. **Principle of Stabilizing.** Projected pranic energy tends to leak out if it is not stabilized. Stabilization is done by energizing the treated part with

light whitish-blue prana, or covering the treated part with pastel blue prana with a "wiping" motion of the hand. Symptoms tend to recur if stabilization is not done.

11. **Principle of Releasing.** For healing to take place, it is necessary for the projected pranic energy to be released. Otherwise, a substantial portion of it will return to the healer. Releasing is done by being detached and by cutting the etheric link. The healer can be warm and caring but at the same time detached. Here, being detached does not mean being cold.

12. **Principle of Correspondence.** What affects the energy body or the etheric body will tend to affect the physical body. And what affects the physical body will tend to affect the energy body. When the energy body is healed, the physical body will also be healed.

13. **Principle of Interconnectedness.** The body of the patient and the body of the healer are interconnected with each other since they are part of the Earth's energy body. On a more subtle level, it means that we are part of the solar system. We are interconnected with the whole cosmos. This principle of interconnectedness is also called the **Principle of Oneness.**

14. **Principle of Directability.** Life force can be directed. It follows where your attention is focused; it follows thought. Distant pranic healing is based on the principle of directability and the principle of interconnectedness.

SCANNING

Scanning is divided into two parts:

   a) Activating and sensitizing the chakra(s) used in scanning;
   b) Tuning in. This is done by just "looking" at the part to be scanned or by just forming an intention to scan a specific part or area.

Scanning, like hearing or seeing, is selective. This is why a good healer is able to scan properly even if there are several persons beside the patient. The healer is able to scan the skin tissue or the internal organs by just forming the intention, since scanning is selective or discriminating. Difficulty in scanning is often due to any of the following:

   a) The pranic student doubts or worries; therefore, he or she does not follow instructions.
   b) Instead of scanning, the pranic student is analyzing or anticipating. But he or she is definitely not scanning.

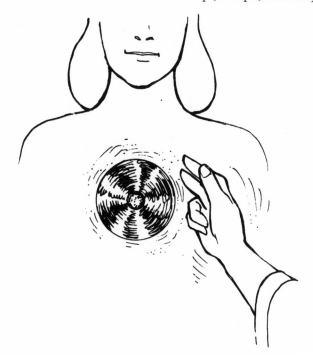

Figure 4-1.   Scanning sideways to determine the size of the chakra.

   c) In fewer instances, the student is simply too mental and too willful; therefore, he or she has very poor sensitivity. This problem can be overcome by months of persistent practice.

In advanced pranic healing, scanning is done to determine:

   a) Whether there is pranic congestion or depletion;
   b) And whether the chakras are overactivated, underactivated, or normal. This is done by scanning the chakras sideways with two fingers.

A chakra is normal, overactivated, or underactivated only in relation to the other chakras. Therefore, when scanning a chakra, it must be compared with the other chakras to determine its size relative to those of the other chakras. A chakra is overactivated when it is much bigger than the other chakras. For example, if the throat chakra and the solar plexus chakra are six inches in diameter, while those of the other chakras are only about four inches, then the throat and solar plexus chakras are overactivated. This means the patient has hyperthyroidism, or may suffer from it in the future if the condition is not corrected. Another example is, if the throat chakra is about two inches in diameter and the other chakras are about four inches, then the throat chakra is underactivated. This means the patient has hypothyroidism or may develop it in the future if the condition is not corrected.

The size of the chakra could be influenced by drugs or herbs. For example, the author was scanning a patient with hyperthyroidism and was surprised to discover that the throat chakra was quite small or underactivated while it was supposed to be big. He later found out that the patient had been taking medicine for quite some time. Scanning the affected chakra could be used to help determine whether the dosage of the medicine is enough or has to be reduced. Scanning can also be used to determine the effectiveness of a prescribed medicine. For example, patients suffering from hypertension have overactivated meng mein chakras. The normal size of the meng mein chakra is about one-and-one-half to two inches in diameter for adults whose major chakras have an average size of about three inches. With a patient whose average chakral size is about three inches and who is suffering from hypertension, the meng mein chakra may have a diameter of three to five inches or more. If after an hour or two, the meng mein chakra is still about four inches in diameter, it may mean the medicine is not sufficiently effective or the dosage is not enough.

ENERGIZING WITH COLOR PRANAS

There are three methods of energizing with color pranas:

1. Visualizing;
2. Using the chakral technique;
3. Combining visualization and chakral techniques.

In the visualization approach, you simply do pranic breathing, or the hand chakras technique, and visualize the specific color prana coming out of your hand. Do not visualize the specific color prana being drawn in; just visualize the specific color prana projecting out of your hand chakra. For example, if you want to energize with green prana, you simply visualize green light projecting out of your hand chakra. Practice regularly so that you can be sure that the color prana projected is the intended one. It is quite possible that you may be visualizing green prana projecting out of your hand chakra but what is actually coming out is light blue prana. Or you may be trying to project light red prana but what is coming out is dark red. Practice is necessary to become proficient in projecting color pranas.

In the chakral technique, you simply choose a source chakra that provides the specific color prana or pranas required. For example, if you want to treat an infection with blue or greenish-blue prana, you can draw in prana from the surroundings through your throat chakra and project the blue or greenish-blue prana through your hand chakra. This can simply be done by doing pranic breathing and, simultaneously, concentrating on your throat chakra and your hand chakra. You should form an intention to draw in prana through your throat chakra and project it out through the hand chakra. This is the same as the energizing technique taught in elementary pranic healing. Instead of concentrating on the left and right hand chakras, you simply concentrate on your throat chakra and your hand chakra. *The chakral technique can be used for both cleansing and energizing.*

In many instances, just using the chakral technique is not enough. It is necessary to combine the visualization technique with the chakral technique in order to project the right type and the right shade of prana. If the healer is not proficient in visualization, he or she should at least have the intent to project the specific type of prana required and the right shade of prana.

BASIC-HAND CHAKRAS TECHNIQUE

In the basic-hand chakras technique, the basic chakra is used as the source chakra, and the hand chakra as the projecting chakra. Earth and air pranas are drawn by the basic chakra and projected out through the hand chakra. Instead of using the hand chakra, the finger can be used. This is called the basic-finger chakras technique.

Procedure:

1. Concentrate on the basic chakra and the hand chakra simultaneously. Concentration is done by just feeling the base of the spine and the center of the energizing palm.
2. Do not overconcentrate. Just relax and do deep pranic breathing.
3. Visualize the required pranic energy being projected out from the hand chakra. You do not have to strain or overexert your willpower. You do not have to visualize the required pranic energy flowing up from the basic chakra to the hand chakra, for this is too strenuous. It will cause your concentration to become erratic. Just visualize the required pranic energy coming out of your hand. This is very important.

The following pranic energy can be projected by using the basic-hand chakras technique:

1. Red;
2. Orange;

Figure 4-2.   Basic-hand chakras technique.

3. Yellow;
4. Orange-red (more of orange, less of red);
5. Orange-yellow (less of orange, more of yellow).

Light whitish orange-red is used for the rapid healing of fresh wounds. Light whitish orange-yellow is used for rapid healing of broken bones and torn tendons.

Light whitish-red is visualized as luminous white (about 70%) at the core with light red (about 30%) at the periphery. Apply the same visualization procedure for light whitish-orange (white is about 80% or more and light orange is about 20% or less), and light whitish-yellow (white is about 80% and yellow is about 20%). Or visualize luminous white light (white prana) being projected, then add a tinge of light red prana. Apply the same procedure for light whitish-orange and light whitish-yellow.

Light whitish-orange-red is visualized as luminous white (about 70%) at the core with light red (about 15%) at the periphery and a little light orange (about 15%) at the periphery of light red. The proportion of orange and red is about 50-50, with red prana slightly greater than orange prana. Apply the same visualization procedure for light whitish-orange-

Figure 4-3. Basic-finger chakras technique.

yellow. With light whitish-orange-yellow, the white is about 70%, the yellow is about 15%, and the orange is about 15%. The proportion of orange and yellow is about 50-50, with light yellow slightly more than light orange.

THROAT-HAND CHAKRAS TECHNIQUE

With the throat-hand chakras technique, the throat chakra is used as the source chakra and the hand chakra as the projecting chakra. If the finger is used instead of the hand, it is called the throat-finger chakras technique.

Procedure:

1. Concentrate on the throat chakra and the hand chakra simultaneously. Concentration is done by just feeling the throat and the center of the energizing palm.
2. Do not overconcentrate. Just relax and do deep pranic breathing.

Figure 4-4.   Throat-hand chakras technique.

3. Visualize the required pranic energy being projected out of the hand chakra.

The following pranic energy can be projected by using the throat-hand chakras technique:

1. Blue;
2. Green;
3. Greenish-blue.

Light whitish-greenish-blue is used to treat fresh burns, infections, inflammations, food poisoning, and also to stop bleeding.

Light whitish-blue is visualized as white (about 70%) at the core and light blue (about 30%) at the periphery. Light whitish-green is visualized as white (about 70%) at the core and light green (about 30%) at the periphery. Or visualize luminous white light (white prana) being projected, then add a tinge of light blue. Apply the same procedure for light whitish-green.

Figure 4-5.   Throat-finger chakras technique. For a powerful healer the hand is placed on the heart to soften the projected pranic energy.

Light whitish-greenish-blue is visualized as white (70%) at the core, light blue (about 20%) at the periphery and light green (about 10%) at the periphery of light blue.

CROWN-HAND CHAKRAS TECHNIQUE

With the crown-hand chakras technique, the crown chakra is used as the receiving chakra and the hand chakra as the projecting chakra. If the finger is used instead of the hand, it is called the crown-finger chakras technique.

Procedure:

1. Concentrate on the crown chakra and the hand chakra simultaneously. Concentration is done by just feeling the top of your head and the center of your palm.
2. Do not overconcentrate. Just relax and do deep pranic breathing.

Figure 4-6.   Crown-hand chakras technique.

    3. Visualize the required pranic energy being projected out of the
    hand chakra.

It is not advisable to use the ajna as a source chakra because, for powerful
and willful healers, the use of the ajna-hand chakras technique will have destructive effects on the patient.

    Divine healing energy from your "higher self" or your higher soul and
air prana are drawn and absorbed by the crown chakra and projected out
through your hand chakra. The soul pranic energy is electric-violet, elec-
tric-white, or golden in color. How much soul pranic energy or divine
healing energy can be drawn depends upon the spiritual development of
the practitioner. The more developed the practitioner, the bigger is the
crown chakra and the thicker is the "spiritual cord" connecting the crown
chakra and the higher self. With an ordinary person, the spiritual cord is
hardly visible.

Figure 4-7. Crown-finger chakras technique.

The crown-hand chakras technique can be used to project the following types of pranic energy:

1. Electric white prana (divine healing energy);
2. Electric violet prana (divine healing energy);
3. Golden prana (divine healing energy);
4. Ordinary violet prana;
5. Ordinary bluish-violet prana (less of blue, more of violet);
6. Ordinary greenish-violet prana (less of green, more of violet);
7. Greenish-yellow prana.

Please note, there are two types of violet pranic energy: electric-violet pranic energy and ordinary violet pranic energy. Electric-violet pranic energy should not be projected simultaneously with green, yellow, orange, and red since the effect is quite destructive.

Electric-violet prana has the properties of the other color pranas. It has a consciousness of its own, and knows where to go and what to do. It has a regenerating effect and is much more powerful than ordinary violet prana. *Electric-violet prana is used mostly in severe ailments.*

Ordinary violet prana, ordinary bluish-violet prana, and ordinary greenish-violet prana can be used to regenerate damaged organs, nerves, and brain cells. They can also be used to rapidly heal fresh wounds. Greenish-yellow also has a regenerating effect.

The crown-hand chakras technique is simple and easy to learn. Ordinary healers can bring down only a minute amount of divine healing energy or electric-violet pranic energy, since their crown chakras are quite small and the spiritual cord is only as thin as a cobweb or a hair strand. It is advisable to do the Meditation on Twin Hearts regularly to accelerate the development of one's crown chakra and spiritual cord. Overmeditating should be avoided since the energy that will be generated is too strong and will weaken the physical body.

Electric-violet prana is visualized as "brilliant" white (about 70%) at the core with light violet (about 30%) at the periphery. Ordinary light whitish-violet prana is visualized as "luminous" white (about 70%) at the core with light violet (about 30%) at the periphery. Ordinary light whitish-violet can be visualized as luminous white light (white prana), then add a tinge of light violet.

Ordinary light whitish-bluish-violet is visualized as luminous white (about 70%) at the core, with light violet (about 20%) at the periphery and light blue (about 10%) at the periphery of light violet. Ordinary light greenish-violet is visualized as luminous white (about 70%) at the core with light violet (about 20%) at the periphery and light green (about 10%) at the periphery of light violet. Light whitish-greenish-yellow is visualized as white (about 70%) at the core with light yellow (about 15%) at the periphery and light green (about 15%) at the periphery of light yellow.

CLOCKWISE ENERGIZING TECHNIQUE

The patient's absorption of the projected prana can be hastened by moving the healer's hand in a clockwise motion. This will cause the treated chakra to move predominantly clockwise, thereby rapidly drawing in the projected pranic energy.

PRACTICE SCHEDULE

To become proficient in projecting the different color pranas, it is necessary to have a lot of practice.

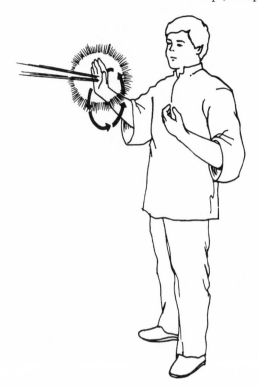

Figure 4-8. Clockwise energizing technique.

Procedure:

1. Do pranic breathing for about five cycles. This is to still the mind and to energize the body.
2. Practice the basic-hand chakras technique and project the following color pranas for about twenty seconds each:
   a) light whitish-red;
   b) light whitish-orange;
   c) light whitish-yellow;
   d) light whitish-orange-red;
   e) light whitish-yellow-orange.
3. Practice the throat-hand chakras technique and project the following color pranas for about twenty seconds each:
   a) light whitish-blue;
   b) light whitish-green;
   c) light whitish-greenish-blue.

4. Practice the crown-hand chakras technique and project the following color pranas for about twenty seconds each:
   a) ordinary light whitish-violet;
   b) ordinary light whitish-greenish-violet;
   c) ordinary light whitish-bluish-violet;
   d) light whitish-greenish-yellow.

Practice this every day for about one to two months. It will take only about five minutes per session.

SPIRITUAL CORD OR SPIRITUAL ROOTING

You can perform this experiment in order to prove to yourself the existence of the spiritual cord and the descent of the divine energy.

1. Look for a regular meditator, priest, monk, nun, or a person holding a high responsible position.
2. Request him or her to sit down.
3. Scan sideways the area one foot above the head. Move your hand slightly back and forth. Can you feel something?

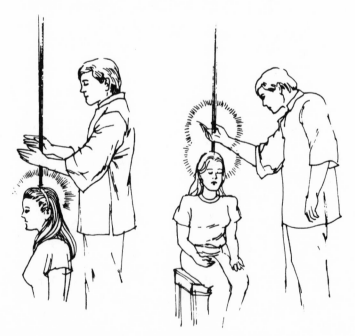

Figure 4-9. Scanning the spiritual cord.

4. Scan upward the area one foot above the head. Move your hand slightly up and down with the palm facing up. Your hand should be about one foot on top of the subject's head. Can you feel energy coming down?
5. Instruct the subject to meditate, to pray or to do the crown-hand chakras technique.
6. Repeat steps 3 and step 4.

If you are sensitive enough, you should be able to feel the spiritual cord and the descent of divine energy. You can perform this experiment with different types of people.

IMPROVING THE CONNECTION OF THE FRONT AND BACK MERIDIANS

The pranic energy level of a person or a healer can easily be increased by just putting the tip of the tongue on the palate. This has the effect of im-

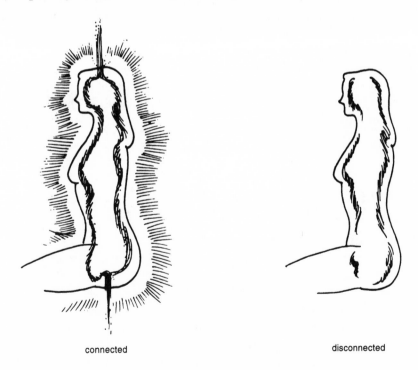

connected   disconnected

Figure 4-10. Increasing pranic energy level by connecting the tongue to the palate.

proving the connection between the back energy channel and the front energy channel, resulting in more divine pranic energy being drawn in by the crown chakra and more ground pranic energy being drawn in by the sole chakras and the basic chakra. Consequently, the inner aura of the person or the healer increases substantially. You can perform this experiment:

1. Scan the inner aura of the subject. Note the size and the "pressure" of the inner aura.
2. Request the subject to bring the tip of his or her tongue in contact with the palate.
3. Scan the inner aura of the subject again. Note the size and "pressure" of the inner aura before and after the "contact" was made. If you are sufficiently sensitive, you will notice a substantial increase in the size and "pressure" of the inner aura.
4. Request the subject to disconnect the tip of his or her tongue from the palate.
5. Scan the inner aura of the subject again. You will notice that there is a substantial decrease in size and "pressure" of the inner aura.

From this, we can conclude that the pranic energy level of a person can be temporarily increased by putting the tip of the tongue on the palate. And that a healer can increase his or her healing power when giving pranic treatment just by connecting the tip of the tongue with the palate. This is a common chi kung practice.

BEING RELAXED OR SMILING INCREASES THE FLOW OF PRANIC ENERGY

When a person is relaxed, happy, or smiling, there is a smooth and free flow of pranic energy. The circulation of pranic energy is improved, more pranic energy is drawn, and more used energy is expelled. It is advisable to be relaxed or to smile when energizing since this will make the healer more powerful; therefore, more pranic energy can be projected. You can perform a simple experiment by requesting somebody to scan your inner aura and the projected pranic energy when you are quite serious and when you are relaxed or smiling. You will find that your inner aura is stronger and more pranic energy is projected when you are relaxed or smiling.

AVOID ENERGIZING WITH THE EYES

Some healers use their eyes in energizing patients. This practice, when done frequently for even a short period, will damage the eyes. When you energize, an etheric or bioplasmic link is established between the projecting chakra and the diseased part. Diseased energy is absorbed by the projecting chakra through the etheric link. Although the projecting chakra is turning predominantly counterclockwise, it is also alternately turning clockwise. When turning clockwise, it partially absorbs some of the diseased energy. Consequently, the eyes will be damaged if used regularly in projecting prana to the diseased parts. This is also why healers sometimes experience diseased energy creeping up the arms when they are energizing with their hand chakras.

It is not advisable to energize directly from your major chakra to the diseased part of the patient for the same reason. It is better to energize with the hand chakra or finger chakra since the hands and fingers are easier to clean and are not very delicate compared to the eyes, brain, or heart.

Sometimes, even though the healer is using his or her hand chakra to energize the affected part, the healer also unintentionally energizes with his or her eyes, thereby damaging the eyes in the long run. This usually happens to healers who tend to stare intensely at the affected part when they are healing.

HOW LONG SHOULD ENERGIZING BE DONE?

There is no definite answer to the above question. This is left to the healer's discretion. Certain factors have to be considered, like the condition of the patient, the severity of the ailment, the rate of pranic energy consumption of the affected part and the proficiency of the healer. Some healers prefer to energize intensely and rapidly while others prefer to energize moderately and gradually. Advanced healers whose energy is quite subtle can energize a chakra in just a few seconds. Sometimes, color prana is projected only for three or four seconds. For mild ailments, the entire treatment may take less than a minute. It is very important to rescan and determine whether energizing is sufficient or not.

INVOCATION BEFORE HEALING

Since many of the healing techniques presented in this book are quite potent, it is advisable to invoke for Divine Blessing, the help of mighty angelic beings, and your spiritual guides to assist and protect the patient from possible errors when you are giving pranic treatment.

ADVANCED GENERAL SWEEPING

General sweeping can be done with light whitish-green prana in order to loosen the diseased energy and to facilitate its removal.

COUNTERCLOCKWISE SWEEPING TECHNIQUE

The cleansing process can be hastened by moving the hand in a counterclockwise motion once or twice, then flicking the hand. The process is repeated as many times as necessary until the affected part is thoroughly cleansed. This technique, when combined with advanced localized sweeping, will rapidly clean the affected part and will produce very fast relief.

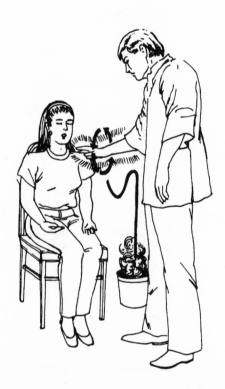

Figure 4-11.   Counterclockwise sweeping technique.

ADVANCED LOCALIZED SWEEPING FOR LOOSENING OR DECONGESTING

If the diseased energy is difficult to remove or is quite stubborn, it is advisable to apply localized sweeping alternately with light whitish-green prana and light whitish-orange prana to loosen the stubborn diseased energy. Please note the sequence: green prana first and then orange prana. This approach is much safer. If cleansing is done properly on the affected part, there will be rapid partial or complete relief. This technique is much faster than ordinary localized sweeping. In some instances, from the ordinary person's viewpoint, the effect is almost miraculous.

The sex chakra, basic chakra, and the minor chakras on the arms and legs can be cleansed rapidly and thoroughly by sweeping alternately with light whitish-green and light whitish-orange. Do not use orange prana on delicate organs or on prohibited areas.

CLEANSING DELICATE ORGANS

If the affected part is quite delicate or is near a delicate organ, apply localized sweeping with light whitish-green. Or apply localized sweeping alternately with light whitish-green prana and ordinary light whitish-violet prana. These techniques also produce fast relief and are quite safe.

The crown, forehead, ajna, back head, jaw, throat, secondary throat, heart, solar plexus, spleen, and navel chakras can be cleansed rapidly and thoroughly by sweeping alternately with light whitish-green prana and ordinary light whitish-violet prana, or just by sweeping with light whitish-green prana.

Sometimes an ailment such as nearsightedness or farsightedness can be caused by the partial clogging of very fine bioplasmic channels. Used-up prana and diseased energy in the eyes are loosened up and broken down into very fine particles by energizing with light whitish-green prana. Project a little of light whitish-yellow prana to group these fine particles together for easier removal, then apply localized sweeping. Yellow prana is preferable to blue prana because blue prana tends to remove not only the used-up prana but also the fresh prana.

Please remember that light green prana is used in loosening and cleansing delicate organs like the eyes and the brain. Orange prana is not used because it is too powerful, and may result in undesirable side effects. There is no point in taking unnecessary risks.

Advanced pranic healing techniques, when applied properly, will usually produce fast and incredible results.

General Applications

INTRODUCTION

Most of the advanced healing techniques or procedures taught in this book can easily be applied by students of advanced pranic healing. But a few of the more advanced healing techniques or procedures included here are to be used only by experienced, proficient, advanced pranic healers. A practitioner of advanced pranic healing is considered experienced and proficient if he or she has been regularly practicing advanced pranic healing for about a year; he or she must be skillful in projecting color pranas and, in general, must have been consistently able to heal severe ailments effectively and rapidly.

Students of pranic healing can become more powerful, effective healers by regularly practicing Arhatic Yoga. Arhatic Yoga causes the chakras to become bigger and to move a lot faster. It causes the energy body and the auras of the practitioner to become bigger, denser, and more refined, thereby enabling the practitioner to heal very fast and more effectively.

ACTIVATING THE CHAKRA

Activating the chakra is sometimes needed for more advanced and faster healing. How long the chakra will remain activated depends upon the need and the skill of the healer.

1. Scan the chakra to be activated frontally and sideways.
2. Apply localized sweeping thoroughly. This is very important. *An underactivated chakra can be gradually normalized by cleansing it regularly.*
3. From the solar plexus chakra up to the crown chakra, ordinary light whitish-violet or ordinary light violet prana is used for activating.
4. For chakras below the solar plexus chakra, light whitish-red prana or light red prana is used for activating.
5. When energizing, simultaneously will or visualize the chakra becoming bigger and brighter.
6. Rescan the chakra.
7. To make the chakra remain activated for a long time, stabilize it by projecting a little of light whitish-blue prana to prevent the projected red prana from leaking. If dark blue prana is used or too much light blue prana is projected, it will have an inhibiting effect. If stabilization is not done, then the chakra will remain activated for only a few minutes. Whether to stabilize or not to stabilize, and whether a chakra should remain activated for only a few minutes or for a few hours or even for a few days, depends upon the need and the condition of the patient.
8. Release the projected pranic energy.

INHIBITING THE CHAKRA

1. Scan the chakra to be inhibited frontally and sideways.
2. Apply localized sweeping thoroughly. This is very important. *An overactivated chakra can be gradually normalized by just cleansing it*

thoroughly. It is more difficult to inhibit an overactivated chakra unless it has been sufficiently cleansed.

3. Energize the chakra with light blue prana to inhibit it.
4. When energizing, simultaneously will or visualize the chakra becoming smaller.
5. Rescan the chakra.
6. Release the projected pranic energy.

STRENGTHENING

Light whitish-red prana is used in strengthening the organs or parts that have been weakened. Using light whitish-red prana is safer than using light red prana. Avoid using dark red prana since this has a weakening effect and may cause inflammation. From the throat up to the head, use ordinary light whitish-violet instead of red prana for strengthening.

1. Scan the patient, then rescan during pranic treatment.
2. Apply localized sweeping thoroughly on the affected part.
3. Energize the weakened part or organ with a little of light whitish-green prana, then with light whitish-red prana. To further strengthen the affected part, you may energize it with ordinary light whitish-violet. This has to be done with caution since the technique is quite powerful. *Never energize simultaneously with red and violet pranas since the effect is quite destructive*.
4. From the throat up to the head, use light whitish-green prana, then more of ordinary light whitish-violet prana.
5. Stabilize and release the projected pranic energy.

INHIBITING

Blue prana can be used to inhibit a chakra and its corresponding organ(s) if required. For example, a patient suffering from gastric ulcer has an overactivated solar plexus chakra and stomach. The solar plexus chakra and the stomach are filled with dirty red energy. The solar plexus chakra and the stomach can be inhibited by cleansing them thoroughly and energizing them with light whitish-blue prana. It is clairvoyantly observed that patients who are recovering from gastric ulcer have a lot of blue prana in the solar plexus chakra.

1. Scan the patient, then rescan during pranic treatment.
2. Blue prana can be used to inhibit an organ or part that is over-active.
3. Apply localized sweeping thoroughly on the overactive organ.
4. Energize the overactive organ with light whitish-green prana, then with more of light whitish-blue prana or light blue prana.
5. Do not use dark blue because the organ may be overinhibited, and this may cause constriction.
6. Release the projected pranic energy.

LOCALIZING

In certain cases, it is better to energize first the part to be treated with light whitish-blue prana or light blue prana in order to localize the pranic energies that will be projected. Localizing is used in the following situations:

1. To minimize wastage and to produce faster healing results by local-izing the projected pranic energies to the affected part. For example, when healing a fresh wound, light blue prana is used first to localize or to minimize the dispersal of the light whitish-orange-red prana that will be projected. If blue prana is not used first, then a large part of the projected light whitish-orange-red prana will be dispersed to other parts of the body instead of con-centrating on the affected part, thereby resulting in slower healing.

2. To localize the disintegrating effect of the destructive types of pranic energies only to the affected parts. The use of light blue prana or dark blue prana depends upon the degree of destructiveness of the pranic energy that will be used. It is very important that a sufficient amount of blue prana be projected, otherwise the destructive energies will spread to other parts. This may cause unnecessary problems. If dark green prana and dark orange prana will be used, then dark blue prana should be projected. If the de-structive energies will be projected for a long period, then blue prana should first be projected for a longer time. In other words, the blue prana should be slightly more than the destructive energies that will be projected.

TREATING INFANTS AND OLD PEOPLE

In treating infants, it is also advisable to avoid using dark green prana be-cause this may affect the future development of the organs being energized. Localized sweeping and energizing with white prana are usually sufficient. There is no point in taking unnecessary risks.

In treating infants and old people, it is advisable to avoid using dark blue prana especially on the solar plexus and heart chakras because of its strong inhibiting effects on the functioning of the organs.

RELIEVING PAIN: BLUE PRANA

Blue prana has a soothing effect and is used for relieving pain. Green prana is used to loosen the diseased energy. Just cleansing the affected part thoroughly will substantially reduce the pain. Cleansing the affected part is as important as energizing with blue prana.

1. Scan the patient, then rescan during pranic treatment.
2. Energize the affected part with light whitish-green prana to loosen the diseased energy.
3. Apply localized sweeping thoroughly on the affected part until there is partial relief.
4. Energize the affected part with light whitish-green prana, then with a lot of light whitish-blue prana.
5. Release the projected pranic energy.
6. Repeat treatment if necessary.

This treatment will relieve the affected part. For better and more lasting results, a more complete pranic treatment has to be applied.

Fire can be extinguished by pouring water on it or by exploding it. Pain can also be removed by cleansing the affected part alternately with light whitish-green prana and light whitish-orange prana. This has a dispersing effect or a mini-regulated exploding effect on the diseased energy, thereby cleansing and relieving the affected part. The affected part is energized with light whitish-green then with light whitish-blue to further soothe the affected part. Or the affected part is energized with light whitish-red prana to improve pranic and blood circulation, which further hastens the rate of relief and healing. This technique is quite fast and potent but has to be used with care. Do not use orange prana on the head, on delicate organs or areas near them.

HEADACHE

1. Scan the crown chakra, forehead chakra, ajna chakra, back head chakra, the entire head, and neck. Headaches could be caused by pranic depletion or congestion on these parts. The eyes, the temples, the spine, and the solar plexus chakra should also be scanned.

2. If the headache is due to eye strain, apply localized sweeping thoroughly on the eyes and the temple.

3. Apply localized sweeping thoroughly on the crown chakra, forehead chakra, ajna chakra, back head minor chakra, and on the affected head area. Energize them with light whitish-green, light whitish-blue, then ordinary light whitish-violet. If the cause is pranic congestion, localized sweeping is usually sufficient to remove the pain.

4. Or just ask the patient which part is aching and apply localized sweeping and energizing alternately on the affected part until the patient is relieved.

5. Release the projected pranic energy.

MIGRAINE HEADACHE

Migraine or persistent headaches, in general, are due to emotional problems or stress. The solar plexus chakra is very congested and filled with pent-up emotion. This pent-up emotion is clairvoyantly seen as dirty red energy. Part of this congested red energy goes to the spine then to the head area causing some of the blood vessels in the head area to dilate. This manifests as persistent headache.

1. Scan the patient, then rescan during pranic treatment.

2. Apply localized sweeping thoroughly on the front and back solar plexus chakra and on the liver. The back solar plexus chakra is usually quite congested. If the sweeping is done properly, the patient should experience substantial relief. Energize the solar plexus chakra with light whitish-green, light whitish-blue, then ordinary light whitish-violet. Thorough cleansing is important.

3. Apply localized sweeping on the spine and on the upper back to remove the dirty red energy.

4. Apply localized sweeping on the front and back heart chakra. Energize the back heart chakra with light whitish-green then with more of ordinary light whitish-violet. Visualize the heart chakra as becoming bigger. This is to give the patient a sense of peace.

5. Apply localized sweeping thoroughly on the affected head area, on the ajna, forehead, crown, and back head chakras.

6. Energize the ajna, forehead, crown, and back head chakras and the affected part with light whitish-green, light whitish-blue and ordinary light whitish-violet.

7. Stabilize and release the projected pranic energy.

TOOTHACHE

1. Scan the affected part, then rescan during treatment.
2. Apply localized sweeping thoroughly on the affected parts with light whitish-green prana.
3. Energize the affected part with light whitish-green prana, with light whitish-blue prana, then with ordinary light whitish-violet prana.
4. Release the projected pranic energy.
5. Repeat treatment if necessary. Instruct the patient to see a dentist. This treatment can be applied by dentists on their patients after tooth extraction or oral surgery to minimize infection.

PYORRHEA

1. Scan the patient, then rescan during pranic treatment.
2. Apply localized sweeping alternately on the affected parts with light whitish-green prana and ordinary light whitish-violet prana.
3. Energize the affected parts with light whitish-green prana, with light whitish-blue prana, then with ordinary light whitish-violet prana.
4. Apply localized sweeping thoroughly on the jaw minor chakras and on the throat chakra. Energize them with white prana.
5. Apply localized sweeping thoroughly on the basic, navel, and solar plexus chakras. Energize them with white prana.
6. Stabilize and release the projected pranic energy.
7. Repeat treatment two to three times a day for the next several days or for as long as necessary.

ENERGIZING THE BASIC CHAKRA AND THE PERINEUM CHAKRA

To facilitate the flow of pranic energy from the basic chakra to the legs in order to strengthen them, just energize the basic chakra and the perineum minor chakra. The act of energizing the perineum minor chakra is like turning on a water faucet. You do not have to ask your patient to assume an embarrassing position just to energize the perineum minor chakra. Just visualize his or her perineum in front of your hand chakra, then proceed to clean and energize it with light whitish-red prana.

HOW TO STRENGTHEN THE LEGS

1. Scan the patient, then rescan during pranic treatment.
2. Apply localized sweeping on the basic chakra and on the perineum minor chakra, and energize them with light whitish-red prana. This will cause an increase in the flow of pranic energy from the basic chakra to the legs.
3. Apply localized sweeping on the navel and sex chakras, and energize them with light whitish-red prana. A substantial portion of prana from the sex chakra automatically goes down to the legs.
4. Apply localized sweeping on the entire legs and on the hip, knee, and sole minor chakras alternately with light whitish-green prana and light whitish-orange prana.
5. Energize the hip, knee, and sole minor chakras on the legs with light whitish-red prana.
6. Stabilize and release the projected pranic energy.
7. Repeat treatment several times a week for as long as necessary.

This pranic treatment can be applied in cases of weak legs, leg fractures, arthritis, and paralysis of the legs.

HOW TO STRENGTHEN THE ARMS

1. Scan the patient, then rescan during pranic treatment.
2. Apply localized sweeping on both arms entirely and the arm minor chakras, alternating with light whitish-green prana and light whitish-orange prana.
3. Apply localized sweeping on the armpit minor chakra. Energize it with light whitish-red prana. Clean the armpit minor chakra by raising the arm of the patient and by applying localized sweeping on the armpit. This is very important. Difficulty in raising the arm or pain in the elbow or fingers could be caused by pranic congestion or depletion of the armpit minor chakra. Cleansing and energizing this minor chakra usually brings rapid relief.
4. Apply localized sweeping on the elbow and hand minor chakras. Energize them with light whitish-red prana.
5. Apply localized sweeping and energizing with white prana on the nipple chakra. A person with arm problems like old sprains may have a depleted nipple chakra. There is a meridian connecting the nipple chakra to the armpit, elbow, and hand minor chakras.

6. Apply localized sweeping on the basic and navel chakras, and energize them with light whitish-red prana.
7. Stabilize and release the projected pranic energy.
8. Repeat treatment several times a week for as long as necessary.

This treatment can be used on weak arms, arm fractures, arthritis, and paralysis of the arm.

BROKEN BONES: ORANGE-YELLOW PRANA

Light orange-yellow prana is used for the rapid healing of fractures. Use the basic-hand chakras technique for projecting orange-yellow prana.

1. Scan the affected part, then rescan during treatment.
2. Apply localized sweeping on the affected part and on the affected arm or leg alternately with light whitish-green and light whitish-orange.
3. Energize the affected part with light whitish-blue prana for soothing and localizing effects.
4. Energize the affected part with light whitish-orange-yellow prana for the rapid healing of the broken bone. Visualize the core as luminous white (about 70%) with light yellow (about 15%) at the periphery and light orange (about 15%) at the periphery of light yellow—slightly more yellow prana than orange prana.
5. Apply localized sweeping on the minor chakras of the affected arm or leg, and energize them with light whitish-red prana.
6. Apply localized sweeping on the basic and navel chakras. Energize them with light whitish-red prana.
7. Stabilize and release the projected pranic energy.
8. Repeat treatment several times a week for as long as necessary. Or for very rapid healing, you may repeat the treatment once a day or more for as long as necessary. The rate of recovery is very fast compared to that without pranic treatment.

CONCUSSION

1. Scan the affected part, then rescan during treatment.
2. Apply localized sweeping alternately with light whitish-green prana and ordinary light whitish-violet on the affected part. Energize the

affected part with light whitish-blue prana, with light whitish-green prana, then with ordinary light whitish-violet prana.
3. Release the projected pranic energy.
4. For fresh concussions, repeat treatment several times for the next few hours.
5. For old concussions, repeat the treatment once or twice a day for the next few days.

In general, the rate of healing will be very fast for fresh concussions.

CONTUSION

1. Scan the affected part, then rescan during treatment.
2. For fresh contusions, apply localized sweeping on the affected part alternately with light whitish-green prana and light whitish-orange prana.
3. Energize the affected part with light whitish-blue, light whitish-green, and light whitish-orange.
4. Repeat treatment several times for the next few hours.
5. For old contusions, apply localized sweeping on the affected part alternately with light whitish-green prana and light whitish-orange prana.
6. Energize the affected part with light whitish-green prana, light whitish-orange prana, then light whitish-red prana. Do not use orange prana on or near delicate organs.
7. Repeat treatment once or twice a day for the next several days.
8. Release the projected pranic energy.

For fresh contusions, the rate of healing will be quite fast.

BACK INJURY

1. Scan the patient, then rescan during pranic treatment.
2. Apply localized sweeping on the spine and the affected part thoroughly and alternately with light whitish-green and light whitish-orange. Do not apply orange prana on or near the head.
3. Energize the affected part with light whitish-blue prana, with light whitish-green, then with more of ordinary light whitish-violet.
4. Apply localized sweeping on the front and back solar plexus chakra, and energize it with white prana.

5. Apply localized sweeping on the basic and navel chakras, and energize them with light whitish-red prana.
6. Stabilize and release the projected pranic energy.
7. Repeat treatment three times a week

FRESH BURNS: GREEN AND BLUE PRANAS

Blue prana is used for treating burns because of its soothing and cooling effects. But blue prana also has a localizing effect which tends to prevent the red hot energy from coming out. This is why green prana is also used to facilitate the removal of red energy.

1. Scan the affected part, then rescan during treatment.
2. Apply localized sweeping on the affected part alternately with light whitish-green prana and light whitish-blue prana.
3. Energize thoroughly the affected part with light whitish-green prana then with more of light whitish-blue prana.
4. Apply sweeping and energizing alternately on the affected part until the patient is relieved.
5. Release the projected pranic energy.

Orange prana is not used in sweeping fresh burns since it tends to intensify the red hot energy. If the treatment is done properly, the result will be quite amazing.

OLD MINOR BURNS: GREEN AND RED PRANAS

1. Scan the affected part, then rescan during treatment.
2. Apply localized sweeping alternately on the affected part with light whitish-green and light whitish-orange. Do not use orange prana on the head area, or on or near a delicate organ. In delicate areas, sweeping with light whitish-green will be sufficient.
3. Energize the affected part with light whitish-blue prana for soothing effects, and light whitish-green prana, then with light whitish-red prana for rapid healing. The proportion of light whitish-green and light whitish-red should approximately be equal for better results. If the affected part is on the head area, use ordinary light whitish-violet instead of light whitish-red.
4. To further hasten the healing process, apply localized sweeping on the basic and navel chakras. Energize them with light whitish-red.

5. Stabilize and release the projected pranic energy.
6. Repeat treatment for the next several days.

OLD SEVERE BURNS: GREEN AND RED PRANAS

1. Scan the patient, then rescan during pranic treatment.
2. Apply sweeping on the affected part alternately with light whitish-green and light whitish-orange. Do not use orange prana on the head area, or on or near a delicate organ. In delicate areas, sweeping with light whitish-green will be sufficient.
3. Energize the affected part with light whitish-green prana, with light whitish-blue prana, then with ordinary whitish-light violet. This is to soothe the pain, to minimize infection and to hasten the healing process. Repeat steps 2 and 3 several times a day.
4. After several days when the pain has been substantially relieved, energize the affected part with light whitish-green prana, then with light whitish-red prana for rapid healing. If the affected part is on the head area, use ordinary light whitish-violet instead of light whitish-red.
5. Apply localized sweeping on the basic and navel chakras. Energize them with white prana in order to further accelerate the healing process.
6. Stabilize and release the projected pranic energy.
7. Repeat treatment once or twice a day for as long as necessary.

HOW TO STOP BLEEDING: BLUE PRANA

Light blue prana and light greenish-blue prana are used to stop bleeding. Use the throat-hand chakras technique.

1. Scan the patient, then rescan during pranic treatment.
2. Apply localized sweeping on the affected part.
3. Energize the affected part with a little light whitish-green prana for a cleansing effect. This is important.
4. Energize the affected part with light whitish-blue prana to stop bleeding.
5. Apply localized sweeping on the basic and navel chakras. Energize them with light whitish-red prana.
6. Stabilize and release the projected pranic energy.

For hemophilia, energize the affected part with light whitish-greenish-blue. The basic chakra has to be cleansed and energized with light whitish-red. Repeat treatment until the bleeding stops. Greenish-blue prana is not used in general sweeping because it may have adverse effects on some patients. This technique is based on the instruction given to me by my Respected Teacher Mei Ling.

OLD WOUNDS: GREEN AND RED PRANAS

Green prana is not used on fresh wounds because its effect is slower, and it tends to make the wound wet or "watery." It is used for the rapid healing of old wounds. A lot of green prana is required in breaking down dead cells. To heal old wounds, light whitish-green prana and light whitish-red prana (about 50% green and 50% red) are used on the affected parts.

1. Scan the patient, then rescan during pranic treatment.
2. Apply localized sweeping on the affected part alternately with light whitish-green prana and light whitish-orange prana. This is to clean the affected part thoroughly. Do not use orange prana on delicate organs or areas near them.
3. Energize the old wound with a little light whitish-blue prana for a localizing effect.
4. Energize the old wound with light whitish-green, then with light whitish-red for rapid healing.
5. To further hasten the healing process, apply localized sweeping on the basic and navel chakras and energize them with light whitish-red prana.
6. Stabilize and release the projected pranic energy.
7. Repeat treatment if necessary.

INSTANTANEOUS HEALING OF A FRESH WOUND: ORANGE-RED PRANA

Instantaneous healing of a wound is applicable only if the wound is fresh and the subject is healthy, relatively young, and receptive. The rate of instantaneous healing ranges from several minutes to about an hour or more. How long it will take depends on the age and the health of the subject, the proficiency of the healer and the size of the wound. The healer may take several short rests when energizing.

The basic chakra, which is the source of orange-red prana, is used for the in-stantaneous healing of a fresh wound. The red prana is about fifty percent and the orange prana is about fifty percent. The red prana is slightly more than the orange prana. The red and orange pranas are projected simultaneously, not one after the other. The effect is slower if orange prana is projected first, then red prana next, or vice versa, compared to the simultaneous projection of orange-red prana. Orange prana has a cleansing or expelling effect. If too much orange prana is used, it may increase the bleeding. Red prana has a strengthening effect and increases the growth rate of cells. Light whitish-orange-red prana accelerates the growth rate of cells, thereby causing rapid or instantaneous healing of the fresh wound.

Orange prana causes the rapid splitting of the cells. Red prana causes the cells to grow rapidly and mature. And white prana provides the other color pranas needed. White prana is as essential as orange-red prana. The fresh inner wound will close and heal very fast, but the outer skin which is composed of dead cells will not close. Therefore, after healing, there will be a thin cut line on the outer skin. This technique will produce a much faster result on young healthy subjects.

If the wound is gaping, it is necessary to have the wound sewn or taped together, or clipped by your fingers when healing.

This technique is used only on fresh wounds. It cannot be used on delicate internal organs because too much orange prana may cause damage to the internal organ being treated. Orange-red prana should not be used on the brain and the nervous system because of the possible bursting effect and the production of abnormal or "mongoloid" cells.

It is important that the patient's basic chakra be energized and activated. This is necessary in order to have enough pranic energy to produce instantaneous healing of the wound. For less powerful healers, using the basic chakra of the healer alone may not be enough, taking longer to fully or substantially heal. The instantaneous healing technique, the "master healing technique," and some advanced healing techniques were taught to me by my Respected Teacher Mei Ling.

1. Energize and activate the patient's basic chakra with light whitish-red prana. Visualize the basic chakra pulsating and becoming bigger.
2. Apply localized sweeping on the fresh wound. Energize it with a little light whitish-green, then with light whitish-blue prana to reduce the bleeding and for a localizing effect.
3. Energize the fresh wound with light whitish-orange-red prana by using the basic-hand chakras technique. Visualize the core as luminous white (about 70%), with light red (about 15%) at the periphery, and light orange (about 15%) at the periphery of the light red.

Orange-red prana also stops bleeding without causing the forma-
tion of scabs.

4. Simultaneously, apply "short circuiting" on the patient's basic
chakra. This is done by drawing pranic energy from the patient's
basic chakra with one of your hand chakras, then directing it to the
wound with your other hand chakra. This step can be omitted by
powerful healers.

5. Visualize the wound closed or healed. Your visualization does not
have to be clear. What is important is the intention. Continue with
the treatment until the wound is completely healed. You may take
several short rests when treating.

Do not apply this technique on areas near delicate organs.

Ordinary light whitish-greenish-violet or ordinary light whitish-bluish-
violet can also be used for the rapid healing of a fresh wound.

Does instantaneous healing of a wound require an exceptional person?
No, it does not require an exceptional person, but the healer should at least
be proficient in intermediate pranic healing. Please experiment first with
small cuts. In the first few sessions, it may take you longer to heal the wound
rapidly or instantaneously. If you want to become a good healer, merely
reading and speculating about pranic healing is not enough. The only way to
learn pranic healing is through lots and lots of practice and experiments.

REGENERATION: GREEN-YELLOW PRANA
AND GREEN-VIOLET PRANA OR LIGHT
WHITISH-GREEN, LIGHT WHITISH-ORANGE
AND LIGHT WHITISH-RED

Ordinary light whitish-greenish-violet prana (about 70% white, 20% ordinary violet, and 10% green) and light whitish-greenish-yellow prana (about
70% white, 15% yellow, and 15% green prana) are used in regenerating
brain cells, nerve cells, and internal organs.

Non-delicate organs can also be gradually regenerated by energizing with
light whitish-green, light whitish-orange, then light whitish-red. The interaction of these three color pranas will gradually regenerate the affected organ.
Energize the affected organ directly without passing through the corresponding chakra. *This technique is used to regenerate the lungs, kidneys, and liver.*

The rate of healing depends on the degree of damage, the physical and
psychological conditions of the patient, the karmic factor, and the healer's
degree of proficiency in healing. It may take several months up to an indef-
inite period of time.

1. Scan the patient, then rescan during pranic treatment.
2. Clean the affected chakra and organ with light whitish-green prana then with ordinary light whitish-violet.
3. Energize the affected part or organ with light whitish-blue for a localizing effect.
4. If the affected part or organ is delicate, energize it through the corresponding chakra with light whitish-greenish-violet prana then with light whitish-greenish-yellow prana.
5. If the affected organ is not delicate, energize it with light whitish-green, light whitish-orange, then light whitish-red.
6. Apply localized sweeping on the front and back solar plexus chakra and energize with light whitish-green, then with more of ordinary light whitish-violet.
7. Apply localized sweeping on the basic and navel chakras. Energize them with light whitish-red.
8. Stabilize and release the projected pranic energy.
9. Repeat treatment thrice a week for as long as necessary. The treatment may take from about six months to a year or more.

ORANGE-YELLOW PRANA

Orange-yellow prana is not used in healing fresh or old wounds because its use tends to form ugly scars or keloids. Orange-yellow prana is used on skin-grafting or bone-grafting. Light whitish-orange-yellow prana is projected on the area where the bone or skin was taken. Use the basic-hand chakras technique.

Orange-red prana is less effective in such a case because it does not have the ability to "fill" the hole or gap where the skin or bone was taken.

RAPID GROWTH: RED AND YELLOW PRANA

When red prana and yellow prana are used one after the other, rapid growth of cells is produced. This can be used to stimulate hair growth.

Never use dark red prana and dark yellow prana. Never energize simultaneously with yellow-red prana, or red prana and yellow prana, because this will cause rapid chaotic growth.

This can also be applied on plants to induce faster growth. You may perform an experiment on the rapid growth of plants for about one month with the use of red prana and yellow prana. Energize the root with light whitish-red prana first, followed by a little light whitish-yellow prana. Use about 95%

light whitish-red prana and about 5% light whitish-yellow prana. Too much yellow prana will have an adverse effect. Stabilize the projected pranic energy. Never energize with both pranas simultaneously. Yellow-red prana is destructive and will result in a very rapid chaotic multiplication of cells. When yellow-red prana is applied on a plant or tree, it will result in the destruction of the plant or tree being energized. Yellow-red prana is not used in healing.

REDUCING THE RISK OF
REJECTION OF TRANSPLANTED ORGANS

Red prana and yellow prana can also be used to facilitate the assimilation and acceptance by the body of a newly transplanted organ. This will reduce the risk of rejection. This is done by cleansing the transplanted organ and energizing it with light whitish-red prana, then with a little light whitish-yellow prana. Use about 95% light whitish-red prana and about 5% light whitish-yellow prana. It is safer not to energize the basic chakra of the patient in order to avoid stimulating the immune system.

PRANIC HEALING APPLIED IN SURGERY

Pranic healing is useful for treating patients before, during, and after surgery. Pranic healing can be used to reduce bleeding, to minimize the possibility of infection, to strengthen the body and the part or organ to be operated on, and to accelerate the rate of recovery.

Minor Surgery

1. Scan the patient, then rescan during pranic treatment.
2. Apply localized sweeping on the part to be operated on. Energize it with light whitish-green prana, light whitish-blue prana, then ordinary light whitish-violet prana. This is to minimize infection and to reduce bleeding.
3. Repeat Step 1 on the operated part after surgery. Or you may apply the technique for instantaneous healing of a fresh wound. (See page 79.)
4. Apply localized sweeping on the basic and navel chakras, and energize them with light whitish-red prana. This is to hasten the healing process.
5. Stabilize and release the projected pranic energy.
6. If necessary, repeat treatment for the next several days.

Major Surgery

1. Scan the patient, then rescan during pranic treatment.
2. Apply general sweeping twice.
3. Apply localized sweeping thoroughly on the basic, navel, and solar plexus chakras. Energize the basic and navel chakras with light whitish-red prana. Energize the solar plexus chakra with white prana.
4. Apply localized sweeping and energizing with ordinary white prana on the part to be operated on and its corresponding chakra.
5. Steps 2,3 and 4 are applied immediately before the operation as well as several days or weeks before the operation. This is to strengthen the body.
6. Before the operation, apply localized sweeping on the part to be operated on. Energize it with light whitish-green then with more of ordinary light whitish-violet.
7. During surgery, if required, the healer may apply pranic healing to strengthen the body and to reduce bleeding.
8. After surgery, general sweeping should be applied several times a day to clean the entire body. The energy body is grayish after an operation.
9. Apply localized sweeping on the area operated on, and energize it with light whitish-green then with more of light whitish-violet.
10. To further hasten recovery, apply localized sweeping thoroughly on the basic, navel, and solar plexus chakras. Energize the basic and navel chakras with light whitish-red prana. Energize the solar plexus chakra with white prana.
11. Apply localized sweeping on the depleted chakras. Energize them with light whitish-green, then with more of light whitish-violet.
12. Stabilize and release the projected pranic energy.
13. Repeat treatment for the next several days or weeks.

FOOD POISONING

1. Scan the patient, then rescan during pranic treatment.
2. Apply localized sweeping thoroughly on the abdominal area, the solar plexus, and navel chakras. The emphasis should be on the lower abdominal area.

3. Energize the solar plexus chakra and the navel chakra with light whitish-greenish-blue prana. The emphasis should be on the navel chakra. Apply more localized sweeping.
4. Stabilize and release the projected pranic energy.
5. If symptoms persist, instruct the patient to see a medical doctor immediately.

INSOMNIA

People with healthy and active basic chakras are dynamic. But people with overactivated basic chakras are hyperactive, restless, and have difficulty sleeping. Patients suffering from insomnia have overactivated basic chakras.

The overactivation of the basic chakra could be caused by emotional factors. The solar plexus chakra is usually overactivated and congested. The crown, forehead, ajna, and throat chakras are partially affected.

1. Scan the patient, then rescan during pranic treatment.
2. Apply general sweeping twice.
3. Apply localized sweeping thoroughly on the solar plexus chakra and the basic chakra. This will gradually normalize the basic and solar plexus chakras. In many cases, if this step is applied properly, the patient will tend to fall asleep.
4. If it is necessary, inhibit the basic chakra and the solar plexus chakra with light whitish-blue prana. Blue prana is soothing and sleep inducing.
5. Apply localized sweeping on the crown, forehead, ajna, and throat chakra.
6. Apply localized sweeping on the navel chakra and energize it with white prana to strengthen the body.
7. Stabilize and release the projected pranic energy.

DISINTEGRATING DEPOSITS

Green prana and orange prana are used for disintegrating.

1. Scan the patient, then rescan during pranic treatment.
2. Apply localized sweeping on the part to be treated.
3. Energize the part to be treated with medium blue prana for a localizing effect. It is important that sufficient blue prana is projected, otherwise the destructive energy will spread to other parts of the body.

4. Energize the part to be treated with medium green prana, then medium orange prana. It is safer to use medium green and orange than dark green and orange.
5. Stabilize and release the projected pranic energy. Repeat treatment for the next several days.

CYSTS

In many cases, the solar plexus chakra of people who have cysts is congested and filled with grayish-red prana. The affected part is also congested and filled with grayish-red prana. The congested dirty red pranic energy in the cyst is connected with and derived from the congested red pranic energy in the solar plexus chakra. *It has been observed that prolonged pranic congestion on certain parts of the body tends to cause cysts or even abnormal growth of cells.*

1. Scan the patient, then rescan during pranic treatment.
2. Apply localized sweeping thoroughly on the front and back solar plexus chakra and energize it with light whitish-green then with light whitish-blue prana. This is very important. For patients with cysts, the solar plexus chakra is usually, if not always, very congested.
3. Apply localized sweeping thoroughly on the cyst with light whitish-green and light whitish-orange prana. This is to remove the congested dirty red prana.
4. Energize the affected part with light blue prana for a localizing effect.
5. Energize the affected part with light green then with light orange. *Do not use orange prana near delicate organs.*
6. Release the projected pranic energy.
7. Repeat treatment three times a week for as long as necessary.
8. Instruct the patient not to eat spicy foods since these contain a lot of red prana. Also, instruct the patient to practice simple meditation to help regulate his or her emotions, since cysts are often caused or aggravated by negative emotions or by stress. This is why most patients with cysts have congested solar plexus chakras.

CLEANSING THE INTERNAL ORGANS TECHNIQUE

The solar plexus chakra is the clearing house for pranic energies from the lower and higher chakras. It is located at the center of the trunk where most of the internal organs are located. The internal organs can be cleansed by sweeping the solar plexus chakra and by energizing it with light whitish-blue, light whitish-green, and light whitish-orange. This is clairvoyantly seen as green and orange pranas gradually spreading to and cleansing the internal organs and the whole body. Blue prana is used to make the technique safer. *This healing technique can rapidly cleanse a congested solar plexus chakra which is a major cause of many severe ailments.* It is very important that the orange prana projected should be light whitish-orange prana, not medium or dark orange prana. *This healing technique should be used only by the more experienced advanced pranic healers.*

1. Scan the patient, then rescan during pranic treatment.
2. Apply general sweeping twice.
3. Apply localized sweeping thoroughly on the front and back solar plexus chakra.
4. Energize the front solar plexus chakra with a little light whitish-blue, then with more of light whitish-green, and light whitish-orange.
5. Or energize the front solar plexus chakra with light whitish-green, then light whitish-orange. This is more powerful and faster than Step 4, but this requires greater skill. Improper application may cause loose bowel movements, and other possible adverse effects, especially with patients whose hearts are weak.
6. If the patient experiences a radical reaction or pain in certain part(s) of the body, apply localized sweeping immediately until there is complete relief.
7. Release the projected pranic energy.

This healing technique is very useful for treating severe ailments especially severe infections. It is preferable not to apply this technique on intestinal infections since it may cause loose bowel movements or internal bleeding to become worse. Do not apply this technique on pregnant women.

CLEANSING THE SOLAR PLEXUS CHAKRA

Many severe ailments are emotional in origin, which indicates that the solar plexus chakra is affected. Applying ordinary sweeping on the front and back solar plexus chakra will take too much time. The amount of sweeping necessary on the front and back solar plexus chakra will be substantially reduced by applying the counterclockwise sweeping technique. The receptivity and the rate of healing can be increased by treating the solar plexus chakra thoroughly.

If the emotional problem is longstanding, there is a tendency for more dirty red energy to continue to spring out even after thorough cleansing of the solar plexus chakra. In such a case, energize the front and back solar plexus chakra with light whitish-blue, light whitish-green, and light whitish-orange. Green and orange pranas have cleansing and expelling effects, while blue prana is used to make this technique safer. After energizing, apply localized sweeping again on the front and back solar plexus chakra. Thorough sweeping is important. This technique is to be used only by the more experienced advanced pranic healer.

The more skillful advanced pranic healers may just energize the solar plexus chakra with light whitish-green prana and light whitish-orange prana. Then, apply thorough localized sweeping again on the front and back solar plexus chakra to facilitate the removal of congested pent-up emotions.

In the later chapters, the instruction *"Apply localized sweeping thoroughly on the solar plexus chakra"* will have the following meanings:

A) For ordinary advanced pranic healing students, it refers to the "counterclockwise sweeping technique" with light whitish-green applied on the front and back solar plexus chakra;

B) For the more experienced advanced pranic healers, it refers to the "counterclockwise sweeping technique," and the "cleansing the solar plexus technique" used in appropriate cases;

C) For the more skillful, experienced, proficient advanced pranic healers, it refers to the counterclockwise sweeping technique and the "cleansing the internal organs technique" but without using light whitish-blue prana in appropriate cases.

CLEANSING THE BLOOD

The blood can be cleansed by energizing the lungs with light whitish-green, then with light whitish-orange. The green prana and orange prana will be absorbed by the blood passing through the lungs, thereby cleansing the blood, the blood vessels, and the whole body. The light whitish-orange prana may cause the patient to perspire. *This technique is very useful for treating ailments of the blood and of the arteries, and for severe infections.* Do not apply this healing technique on pregnant women.

1. Scan the patient, then rescan during pranic treatment.
2. Apply general sweeping once or twice.

Figure 5-1. The fingers should be pointed away from the head when energizing the lungs with orange prana.

3. Apply localized sweeping on the front, side, and back of the lungs.

4. Energize the lungs directly through the back of the lungs with light whitish-green then with light whitish-orange. When energizing the lungs with orange prana, the fingers should be pointed away from the head.

5. If the patient is depleted, energize the lungs with light whitish-red for a strengthening effect.

6. Stabilize by covering or "coating" the back of the lungs with light whitish-blue.

7. The spleen, liver, and kidneys purify the blood. Apply localized sweeping on them and energize with white prana.

8. If the patient experiences a radical reaction or pain in certain part(s) of the body, apply localized sweeping immediately until there is complete relief.

9. Stabilize and release the projected pranic energy.

FEVER

In the case of fever, the body is depleted but the solar plexus chakra is congested and overactivated, and filled with dirty red energy. If the solar plexus chakra is energized without first cleansing it thoroughly, the fever may go up. The basic chakra is depleted but overactivated. It is preferable not to energize it directly because the fever may go up further.

The key factors are: a) to clean the entire body thoroughly and to remove the congested dirty red prana from the solar plexus chakra in order to cool the body down; b) to further cool the body down by energizing the solar plexus chakra with light whitish-green and light whitish-blue prana; c) to treat the affected part(s); and d) to enhance the body's defense system.

1. Scan the patient, then rescan during pranic treatment.
2. Apply general sweeping with light whitish-green prana then with light whitish-blue prana several times.
3. To soothe, disinfect, and rapidly cool the body down, apply localized sweeping thoroughly on the front and back solar plexus chakra and the liver. Energize the front solar plexus chakra with light whitish-green prana, then with a lot of light whitish-blue prana. The emphasis is on thorough cleansing of the solar plexus chakra.
4. To facilitate the expelling of diseased energy, energize the front solar plexus chakra with light whitish-orange prana. This step is to be used only by experienced advanced pranic healers. Do not apply this step if the patient is suffering from loose bowel movements or intestinal bleeding.
5. Apply localized sweeping on the front and back heart chakra. Energize the back heart chakra with light whitish-green, then with more of ordinary light whitish-violet. This is to stimulate the thymus gland which helps fight infection.
6. Apply sweeping thoroughly on the left and right lungs. Energize the lungs directly through the back of the lungs with light whitish-green, then light whitish-orange. Do not energize through the back heart chakra since orange prana is being used. When energizing the lungs with orange prana, the fingers should be pointed away from the head. This is good for cleansing the blood and for lung infections.
7. Apply localized sweeping on the front and back spleen chakra.
8. Cleanse the lower abdominal area and the navel chakra. Energize the navel chakra with light whitish-green prana, light whitish-blue prana, then ordinary light whitish-violet prana. This is good for

strengthening the body and for treating intestinal infections. It is preferable not to use green prana on the navel chakra if there is intestinal bleeding unless the healer is very skillful in controlling the shade of the projected pranic energy.

9. Apply localized sweeping thoroughly on the basic chakra.
10. Apply localized sweeping on the hand and sole chakras. Energize them with ordinary light whitish-violet prana. This is to stimulate the production of white blood cells. Do not repeat this step on the same day since it may cause a reverse reaction.
11. Apply localized sweeping on the crown chakra, forehead chakra, ajna chakra, back head minor chakra, jaw minor chakras, and throat chakra. Energize them with light whitish-green, light whitish-blue, then ordinary light whitish-violet.
12. With infants and small children, just use white prana for the entire treatment. General sweeping should be emphasized and energizing should be done gently and gradually.
13. Repeat treatment two to three times a day. If the fever is persistent, consult a medical doctor and an advanced pranic healer immediately.
14. If the fever is quite high or recurrent, clean thoroughly the basic chakra and energize with a little light whitish-blue prana. Simultaneously, will the basic chakra to become smaller. This has to be done with care since the temperature may drop temporarily to a little below the normal level.
15. Stabilize and release the projected pranic energy.

Sometimes fevers in children could be emotional in origin. When the parent or parents are quite angry or irritated, not necessarily at the child but with somebody else, the aura becomes dark red and radiates angry energy. The child may become contaminated by the dark red energy, thereby weakening the child's body and making it susceptible to inflammation and infection.

MASTER HEALING TECHNIQUE: BASIC-MENG MEIN CHAKRAS TECHNIQUE

The technique of energizing and activating the basic and meng mein chakras is an important technique in healing. The basic chakra energizes the entire physical body. Energizing and activating the basic chakra alone will increase the pranic energy level of the body to a limited degree. As stated earlier, the meng mein chakra acts as a pump to facilitate the distribution of pranic energy from the basic chakra to the other parts of the body. To be more accurate, it acts as an accelerator since it increases the rate of vibration of the prana coming from the basic chakra. This is why the rate of vibration of pranic energy from the basic chakra is higher when coming out of the meng mein chakra than when entering it. Without energizing and activating the meng mein chakra, the pranic energy from the basic chakra will have difficulty in spreading rapidly to other parts of the body. This is just like having a big factory in full production but with a very poor marketing department to distribute the products.

When these two chakras are energized and activated, pranic energy from the basic chakra will gush out with tremendous speed through the back meridian and spread to all parts of the body. The entire body and the internal organs are energized and strengthened, and they become much brighter and more reddish. Energizing and activating the basic and meng mein chakras is considered the "master healing technique." *This powerful healing technique can be used to treat many types of ailments but should be applied with caution.* This Master Healing Technique can be used for the following:

1. Energizing and strengthening the internal organs and the entire body. This technique is very useful for patients who are weak or very depleted and have ailments involving the internal organs. *With some depleted patients, the energizing and strengthening effects are almost instantaneous.* It can also be used to make strong young athletes even stronger. *Using this technique is just like taking steroids the natural way.*

2. Greatly increasing and strengthening the body's immunity and defense system. This technique is used on severe types of infection like pulmonary tuberculosis. *It is preferable not to use this healing technique on patients who have venereal disease or have had venereal disease, since this technique tends to produce a lot of red prana which may activate the venereal germs and thus worsen the condition of the patient.* Due to the pervasiveness of people with venereal disease, this technique should be used with caution.

3. Accelerating the healing process several times. This can also be used on some severe types of ailments.

4. For emergency cases to revive unconscious or very weak patients. When the basic and the meng mein chakras are energized, pranic energy from the basic chakra rushes up to energize the brain and the entire body. It should not be used on old dying patients or on those who are right at the point of death since it will further shorten life.

5. Accelerating tissue repair or the growth rate of cells. This can also be used on patients before and after surgery. Do not apply this technique on transplant cases since the body's defense system will be stimulated.

This Master Healing Technique is also used as a supplementary or supportive healing technique with the main pranic treatment. For example, if the patient has a lung ailment, the lungs should be treated (main pranic treatment), and the basic and meng mein chakras can be energized and activated to further increase the rate of healing. The main pranic treatment can be given before or after applying the Master Healing Technique.

One of the effects of using this powerful healing technique is that it tends to increase the sexual drive. Patients should be advised about this and should be told to avoid or minimize sexual activities during treatment to conserve pranic energy which is intended to accelerate the healing process.

This powerful healing technique is relatively safe if the following guidelines are observed:

1. Never use this powerful healing technique on pregnant women. The energy generated can overwhelm or destroy the delicate chakras of the unborn baby. There is the possibility of miscarriage or stillbirth.

2. Do not use this technique on patients with hypertension or high blood pressure since this will only make the patients worse.

3. Do not use this on patients suffering from pranic congestion throughout the body. This sometimes happens to esoteric students who overpractice or incorrectly practice the advanced type of chi kung or yoga.

4. Do not overenergize and activate the meng mein chakra since it may result in high blood pressure and possibly an allergy throughout the body. The patient may feel quite weak and uneasy for the next few days because of too much pranic energy. Also, the brain will be partially affected and the patient may find it difficult to concentrate.

5. Avoid energizing the spleen chakra if this technique will be used or has been used because it may cause the body to be overenergized. The side effects will be similar to overactivating and overenergizing the basic and meng mein chakras.

6. This technique should not be used on patients suffering from glaucoma.

7. It should not be used on patients suffering from leprosy because it will accelerate the rate of deterioration. The basic chakra of a leprous patient is

very dirty. The use of this technique will rapidly spread the diseased energy throughout the body.

8. It should not be used on patients suffering from cancer since it will cause the cancer to spread faster. Cancer patients have overactivated basic, meng mein, and solar plexus chakras. It is preferable not to use this on patients with tumors.

9. It is preferable not to apply this technique on patients suffering from inflammation of the liver because it may result in cirrhosis due to the rapid growth of cells.

10. Do not use this healing technique on leukemia patients since it will worsen their condition.

11. Do not use this healing technique on patients suffering from severe heart ailments. The heart has a strong tendency to draw or attract pranic energy. The use of this advanced healing technique on a patient with a serious heart ailment may result in pranic congestion manifesting as cardiac arrest.

12. This healing technique should only be used on patients whose ages range from 15 to 45. Infants and children may suffer brain damage due to too much pranic energy rushing upward. With children, their chakras are not quite developed, and subjecting them to intense pranic energy may cause a serious imbalance in their bioplasmic bodies. For older patients, this technique will have detrimental effects since their bodies, chakras and endocrine glands have partially atrophied and cannot withstand too much pranic energy. Infants, children, weak and aged patients should be gently and gradually energized.

Procedure:

1. To get better results, apply general sweeping two or three times to enable the pranic energy to flow freely to different parts of the body. Also instruct patients to connect the tip of their tongue to their palate.
2. Scan the basic and meng mein chakras frontally and sideways to determine the degree of activation. The normal size of the meng mein chakra is about 1/2 to 2/3 the average size of the other chakras. The ratio can be increased to 1/1. The blood pressure will increase slightly.
3. Apply localized sweeping on the basic chakra and energize it with light red prana. To reduce the potency of the technique, use light whitish-red prana. You may will or visualize the basic chakra to become bigger by one or two inches in diameter.

4. Apply localized sweeping on the meng mein chakra. Energize it with light red prana. To reduce the potency of the technique, use light whitish-red prana. It is safer not to visualize or will the meng mein chakra to become bigger, since, if it is highly overactivated, this will result in hypertension. When the meng mein chakra is energized with light red prana or light whitish-red prana, it will pulsate, rotate faster, and become slightly bigger without visualizing or willing it to become bigger.

5. How long should the basic and meng mein chakras be energized? There is no definite answer. For not-so-powerful healers, about three to seven breathing cycles. For very powerful healers, only a few seconds. The meng mein should not be energized for too long.

6. Rescan the basic and meng mein chakras frontally and sideways to determine the degree of activation. Get feedback from the patient immediately. If the patient feels dizzy or feels pain on the back of the head, apply localized sweeping thoroughly from the head to the tail of the spine. Apply sweeping thoroughly on the meng mein chakra and basic chakra until the patient is relieved.

For powerful healers, the willpower should not be used in full force. Otherwise, the patient may suffer undesirable side effects due to overactivation of the basic chakra and the meng mein chakra.

This Master Healing Technique can be toned down by just energizing the basic and meng mein chakras with white prana. Do not visualize or will the chakra to become bigger and brighter. This milder form of the Master Healing Technique is still quite potent and can easily energize and strengthen a depleted patient in a short time. It can be used on patients whose ages range from 12 to 60, but with caution. It should not be used on infants. The same master healing technique guidelines should be followed when using this milder form of the Master Healing Technique.

The potency of the basic and meng mein chakras technique can be graduated from the most potent to the mildest as follows:

Basic Chakra	Meng Mein Chakra
1. Light red prana	Light red prana
2. Light red prana	Light whitish-red prana
3. Light whitish-red prana	Light whitish-red prana
4. Light red prana	White prana
5. Light whitish-red prana	White prana
6. White prana	White prana

This basic and meng mein chakras technique should be used only by experienced and proficient advanced healers, not by beginners.

SUPER HEALING TECHNIQUE

The Master Healing Technique, combined with the cleansing the blood technique and cleansing the internal organs technique, can be used to rapidly treat a wide range of severe ailments. The two cleansing techniques purify the body thoroughly while the Master Healing Technique provides a tremendous amount of pranic energy. This combination of healing techniques is called the "super healing technique." This healing technique is also used as a supplementary or supportive healing technique together with the main pranic treatment. In general, the Super Healing Technique, when applied skillfully on the right patient and for the right ailment, will produce very rapid healing. In some instances, it seems almost "miraculous."

It is important to apply general sweeping. Also, apply localized sweeping on the major chakras, the important or affected minor chakras and the internal organs, especially the affected ones before or after the application of this healing technique. This is to avoid or minimize radical reactions. *The Super Healing Technique should be used only by experienced and proficient advanced healers, not by beginners.*

PRANIC HEALING PROCEDURE

There are two factors to be considered in studying the causes of ailments: the external factors and the internal factors. External factors are physical causes like germs, toxins, improper diet, side-effects of drugs, and others. In this book, the internal causal factors of ailments will be emphasized. There is a tendency among healers and holistic health practitioners to overemphasize the internal factors. This has to be avoided since the physical causes of ailments are as important as the non-physical causes. A more balanced and integrated perception is achieved by considering both types of factors. It is also advisable to instruct the patient to consult a reputable medical doctor if the ailment is severe or if symptoms persist.

Based on my observation, many of the severe ailments are partially or predominantly caused by stress or negative emotions. In order for the patients to get well fast, it is necessary to thoroughly treat the solar plexus chakra which is the seat of lower emotions, and to activate the heart chakra which produces a sense of inner peace. The patient has to cooperate by avoiding stress and by regulating the emotions. Doing simple meditation is also helpful.

The rate of recovery of a particular organ does not only depend on the affected chakras but also on the health of the other chakras and organs. Therefore, to produce better and quicker results, *it is advisable that the other chakras which are not affected or mentioned are also cleansed and energized.* The meng mein and spleen chakras can be cleansed, but energizing them will have to be determined on a case-by-case basis.

The treatment is divided into two parts: relieving the patient and correcting the conditions causing the ailments. For example, the healer may relieve a patient of headache by treating the head area and correct the condition by treating the eyes if the cause of the headache is eyestrain. As another example, the healer can relieve an asthmatic patient by treating the throat chakra, the secondary throat chakra, and the back heart chakra. This condition can be corrected by treating the ajna chakra, the basic chakra, and the bones.

In studying the advanced pranic treatments for different ailments, it is better to try to understand why certain chakras are being treated and why certain color pranas are being used, rather than trying to memorize the procedures. The healer can consult the book or notes before giving pranic treatment if it is needed. There are healers who sometimes consult the book or their notes and meticulously follow the instructions. They are very careful and thorough. In general, they usually get better and faster results than other healers. Thoroughness in treatment is essential to rapid effective healing. The following list explains the procedure.

1. Visually examine the patient.
2. Interview the patient and establish rapport.
3. Scan the major chakras, the relevant minor chakras, vital organs, the spine and the affected part thoroughly. Though an affected chakra may seem to have no relation to the ailment and may be quite a distance from the affected part, this chakra may be a major contributing factor to the ailment. *Thorough scanning is an important factor to proper treatment.*
4. Apply general sweeping several times.
5. To increase receptivity, instruct the patient to silently affirm several times: "I fully accept the healing energy with thanks."
6. If the affected part is congested, thorough cleansing should be emphasized.
7. If the affected part is depleted, energizing should be emphasized.
8. If the affected chakra is overactivated, then it should be thoroughly cleansed and inhibited by using blue prana.

9. If the affected chakra is underactivated, then it should be thoroughly cleansed and activated by energizing with light whitish-red prana for the lower chakras, or with ordinary light whitish-violet for the upper chakras.
10. Use the necessary color pranas to correct or remedy the ailment. In cases where you are not sure of what color pranas to use, then just use white prana for simple ailments or light whitish-green prana and ordinary light whitish-violet prana for severe ailments.
11. It is also advisable to clean and energize the other chakras that are not affected to further hasten the rate of recovery.
12. Stabilize the projected pranic energy.
13. Release the projected pranic energy by visually cutting the etheric cord between you and the patient.
14. Repeat treatment if necessary.
15. For minor ailments or disorders, instruct the patient not to wash the treated part for at least 12 hours. For severe ailments, instruct the patient not to take a bath or shower for at least 24 hours. Water absorbs some of the pranic energy that has been projected to the patient's body.
16. Healers, please wash your arms and hands after sweeping and after energizing to avoid contamination.

WHAT TO DO WHEN YOU ARE NOT SURE

1. Apply general sweeping several times.
2. Apply localized sweeping on all major chakras, on the more important minor chakras, and on all vital organs.
3. Energize with light whitish-green prana and with more of ordinary light whitish-violet on all major chakras and the important minor chakras except the meng mein chakra. Energize the spleen chakra with caution.
4. Stabilize and release the projected pranic energy.
5. Repeat the treatment regularly.

You can use this procedure for most ailments.

PART II:
ADVANCED PRANIC
TREATMENTS

Immunity and Defense System

IMMUNE SYSTEM

The immune (and defense) system is predominantly controlled by the skeletal system and the lymphatic system. The skeletal system is controlled and energized by the basic chakra. The lymphatic system is controlled and energized by the throat chakra.

The production of red and white blood cells is controlled by the basic chakra since it controls and energizes the bone marrow. It is also affected by the meng mein chakra which affects the flow of pranic energy from the basic chakra to the bones and to the other parts of the body.

The bone marrow in the arms and legs is controlled and energized by the basic chakra through the minor chakras in the arms and legs. The bone marrow in the spine is controlled and energized by the basic chakra. The bone marrow in the ribs, breastbone, and scapula is controlled and energized by the basic chakra through the heart chakra. The bone marrow in the skull is controlled and energized by the basic chakra through the back head minor chakra. Before adulthood, red and white blood cells are produced in the marrow in all bones. In adults, the production is done mainly in the marrow of the hipbones, spine, ribs, and breastbone.

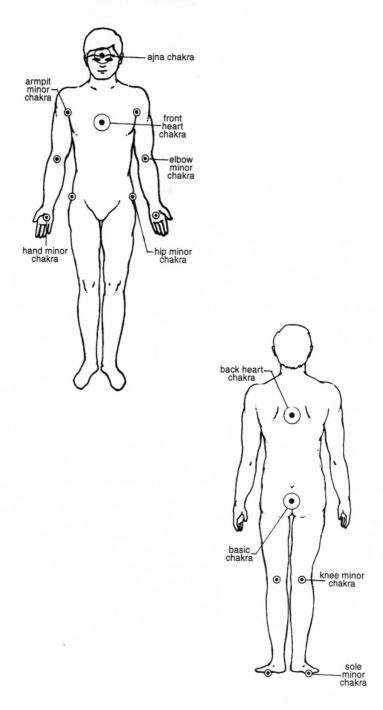

Figure 6-1. Chakras affecting the production of white blood cells.

When the basic chakra is cleansed and energized with white prana or light whitish-red prana, the bone marrow is stimulated to produce more red and white blood cells. Energizing the basic chakra strengthens the body and also enhances its immunity and defense system. The effects are hastened and magnified by energizing the meng mein chakra with white prana or light whitish-prana. This is why the Master Healing Technique is quite powerful.

The bone marrow can also be stimulated to produce more white blood cells by energizing it directly with light whitish-red prana or ordinary light whitish-violet prana. Ordinary light whitish-violet is more potent than light whitish-red. But light whitish-red is safer than ordinary light whitish-violet. If too much light whitish-violet prana is projected to the bone marrow, there will be a reverse reaction. It is not advisable to energize the bone marrow with ordinary light whitish-violet more than once a day.

For patients suffering from fever, it is not advisable to energize the basic chakra directly because if it is overenergized, it will cause the fever to rise. By energizing the minor chakras on the soles of the feet, the basic chakra is indirectly energized without being overenergized, thereby enhancing the defense system of the body without worsening the fever.

For patients suffering from venereal ailments, it is preferable not to energize the basic chakra directly unless the healer is an experienced, proficient, advanced pranic healer. If the basic chakra is overenergized, it will produce too much red pranic energy which will stimulate the growth of venereal germs.

The solar plexus chakra, which is the center for lower emotion, is a major factor affecting the immunity and defense system. Through emotional negative outbursts, the whole body including the basic chakra and the other chakras becomes depleted, causing the physical body to become susceptible to infection. Through prolonged harboring of negative emotions, the solar plexus chakra, the basic chakra, and the other major chakras malfunction, thereby adversely affecting the immunity and defense system. The immunity and defense system is also affected by the solar plexus chakra through the liver which purifies the blood.

The crown, forehead, and ajna chakras also affect the immunity and defense system of the body. The crown chakra is the entry point of electric-violet pranic energy which stimulates the immunity and defense system. Electric-violet pranic energy has a very strong disinfecting property. The forehead and ajna chakras facilitate the flow of electric-violet pranic energy to other parts of the body. The ajna chakra ensures that the other chakras work harmoniously with each other. The crown, forehead, and ajna chakras also produce a lot of green, blue, and ordinary violet pranic energies which have a strong disinfecting property.

LYMPHATIC SYSTEM

The throat chakra affects the immunity and defense system since it controls and energizes the lymphatic system which filters virulent microbes and destroys them. The lymphatic system produces antibodies and an important variety of white blood cells called lymphocytes. The lymphocytes have a "memory" of invading microbes and are responsible for the immunization of the body against infections. The throat chakra, through the jaw minor chakras, controls and energizes the tonsils. The thymus gland is controlled and energized by the throat chakra and the heart chakra. Thymus produces T-lymphocytes or T-cells, which fight off viruses, fungi, parasites, cancer cells, and transplanted foreign tissues and organs. The thymus is responsible for regulating the immune and defense system from attacking the body's own tissues or organs. The spleen is controlled and energized by the spleen chakra and the throat chakra. The spleen filters and destroys abnormal cells and disease causing germs. The throat chakra through the navel chakra controls and energizes the lymph nodes in the abdominal area. The throat chakra—through the armpit, elbow, hand, perineum, hip, knee, and sole minor chakras—controls and energizes the lymph nodes in the arms and legs.

INFECTION AND INFLAMMATION: GREEN, BLUE, AND VIOLET PRANAS

1. Scan, then rescan the affected part.
2. Apply localized sweeping on the affected part alternately with light whitish-green and light whitish-orange. Thorough cleansing is important. Do not apply this technique on or near the head, the heart, or the spleen chakra.
3. If the affected part is on or near the head, the heart, or the spleen chakra, apply localized sweeping on the affected part alternately with light whitish-green and ordinary light whitish-violet.
4. Energize the affected part with light whitish-green, with light whitish-blue, then with ordinary light whitish-violet.
5. If infection and inflammation are severe, repeat this treatment three to four times a day for the next several days or until the condition stabilizes since the rate of pranic consumption is quite fast.
6. If infection is severe, apply the treatment for enhancing the body's defense system once or twice a day for the next several days or until the patient's condition stabilizes.

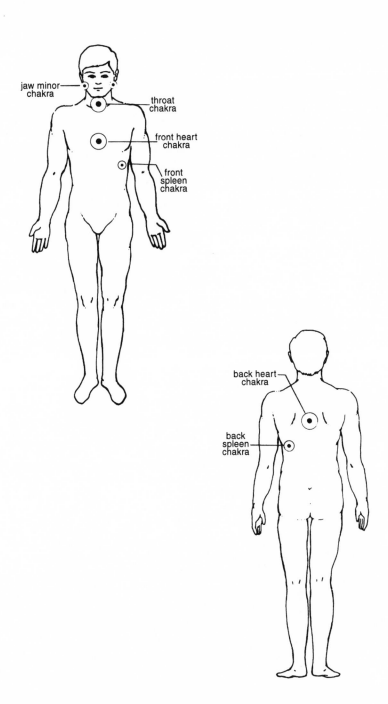

Figure 6-2.   Chakras controlling and energizing the lymphatic system.

7. The frequency of treatment can be reduced to three times a week when the patient's condition substantially improves.
8. Stabilize and release the projected pranic energy.

Green prana breaks down diseased energy. It has loosening, decongesting, cleansing, and disinfecting effects. Blue prana has disinfecting, inhibiting, containing, localizing, cooling, and soothing effects. For severe types of infection, use violet prana because it has the strongest disinfecting effect. Other pranas also have a disinfecting property but with less effectiveness.

Blue prana disinfects by its inhibiting action and by its localizing and containing effects. Green prana disinfects by its disintegrating effect. When greenish-blue (about 30% green and 70% blue prana) is used, the potency is increased several times. Preferably, greenish-blue should not be used in general sweeping because some patients cannot withstand it and because of its possible detrimental effects.

Greenish-blue prana is used for severe infection or inflammation, and it should be used with caution on delicate organs. It is preferably not used on patients younger than 20 years old or patients older than 45 years old because it has a constrictive effect on delicate organs. When used regularly for a certain period of time, it may produce adverse effects. Greenish-blue prana is also used to treat food poisoning and insect bites.

STIMULATING AND STRENGTHENING THE BONE MARROW

The immunity and defense system can be enhanced by stimulating and strengthening the bone marrow which produces the white blood cells. This is done by strengthening the basic chakra. The basic chakra is strengthened just by cleansing and energizing it with white prana or light whitish-red prana.

1. Scan the patient, then rescan during pranic treatment.
2. Apply general sweeping twice. Always remember that cleansing the body is as important as energizing it.
3. Apply localized sweeping on the basic chakra. Energize it with white prana or with light whitish-red prana.
4. To further strengthen the body, apply localized sweeping on the navel chakra and energize it with white prana or with light whitish-red prana.
5. Or, instead of Step 4, apply localized sweeping on the meng mein chakra and energize it with white prana or light whitish-red prana.

The meng mein chakra has to be scanned before energizing, and rescanned after energizing. This step is to be used only by experienced, proficient, advanced pranic healers.

6. Apply localized sweeping thoroughly on the front and back solar plexus chakra. Energize it with white prana. This is important since most patients have a malfunctioning solar plexus chakra which is the major contributing factor in the weakening of the immunity and defense system of the body.

7. Stabilize and release the projected pranic energy.

STIMULATING AND STRENGTHENING THE SPLEEN

The spleen purifies the blood flowing through it by filtering and destroying abnormal cells and disease causing germs. By stimulating and strengthening the spleen, the immunity and defense system will be enhanced. Patients suffering from severe infection have dirty and sluggish spleen chakras. The physical spleen is also adversely affected. Therefore, in severe infection cases, it is a must to treat the spleen chakra.

The pranic energy level of the entire body can be greatly increased by cleansing and energizing the spleen chakra. This has a strengthening effect on the whole body.

The treatment of the spleen chakra has to be done with caution. With infants and small children, overenergizing the spleen chakra may cause them to faint because of pranic congestion. This also happens sometimes with adults. With a hypertensive patient, energizing the spleen chakra may cause the blood pressure to rise further. The spleen chakra is closely connected with the meng mein chakra. Energizing the spleen chakra will cause the meng mein chakra to become partially more energized. Activating the spleen chakra will cause the meng mein chakra to become partially more activated. It is advisable to scan the spleen chakra and the meng mein chakra frontally and sideways before energizing the spleen chakra, then to rescan them after energizing.

1. Scan the patient, then rescan during pranic treatment.
2. Apply general sweeping twice.
3. Apply localized sweeping thoroughly on the front and back spleen chakra with light whitish-green.
4. Apply localized sweeping on the navel chakra.
5. Energize the navel chakra with white prana or light whitish-red prana. This will energize the spleen chakra without overenergizing

it. This procedure is effective in stimulating and strengthening the spleen, and at the same time is very safe to use.

6. The more experienced and skillful pranic healer may energize the spleen chakra directly with white prana, light whitish-red prana or ordinary light whitish-violet prana.

7. Stabilize and release the projected pranic energy.

STIMULATING AND STRENGTHENING THE THYMUS

The thymus produces T-lymphocytes which fight off viruses, fungi, and parasites. By stimulating and strengthening the thymus, the immunity and defense system is enhanced. The solar plexus chakra must also be treated since it is closely connected to the heart chakra.

1. Scan the patient, then rescan during pranic treatment.
2. Apply general sweeping twice.
3. Apply localized sweeping thoroughly on the front and back solar plexus chakra and on the liver.
4. Energize the solar plexus chakra with light whitish-green, light whitish-blue, then with ordinary light whitish-violet.
5. Apply localized sweeping thoroughly on the front and back heart chakra. Energize the back heart chakra with a little light whitish-green then with more ordinary light whitish-violet. Visualize pranic energy going into the thymus. Do not stabilize the projected pranic energy to the heart chakra to avoid pranic congestion.
6. Release the projected pranic energy.

By cleansing and energizing the heart chakra, the spine, ribs, and breastbone are stimulated to produce more blood including white blood cells.

PURIFYING THE BLOOD

The blood is purified by energizing the lungs through the back with light whitish-green, light whitish-orange, and ordinary light whitish-violet. Therefore, it hastens the rate of recovery especially in severe infections.

ENHANCING THE IMMUNITY AND DEFENSE SYSTEM

The immunity and defense system can be enhanced by stimulating and strengthening the skeletal system and the lymphatic system.

1. Scan the patient, then rescan during pranic treatment.
2. Apply general sweeping twice.
3. Apply localized sweeping thoroughly on the affected part(s). Energize the affected part(s) with light whitish-green, light whitish-blue, and ordinary light whitish-violet pranas.
4. Apply localized sweeping on the lungs. Energize the lungs through the back of the lungs with light whitish-green prana, light whitish-orange prana, and ordinary light whitish-violet prana. The healer's fingers should be pointed away from the head. By purifying the blood, the whole body, including the affected part, will be substantially purified.
5. Apply localized sweeping on the basic chakra and energize it with white prana or light whitish-red. If the patient has a fever or venereal disease, do not energize the basic chakra. Just apply localized sweeping thoroughly on it.
6. Apply localized sweeping on the minor chakras of the arms and legs. Energize them with light whitish-red or ordinary light whitish-violet. If the patient has a fever or venereal disease, just use ordinary light whitish-violet. Do not use light whitish-red. Steps 4 and 5 are used to stimulate the production of white blood cells in the bone marrow. If ordinary light whitish-violet prana is used, do not repeat this step on the same day.
7. Apply localized sweeping thoroughly on the front and back spleen chakra and on the navel chakra. Energize the navel chakra with ordinary light whitish-violet. This is to further increase the pranic energy level of the body and to indirectly energize the spleen chakra.
8. If the spleen is painful, energize directly the spleen chakra with light whitish-green then ordinary light whitish-violet. Apply more localized sweeping on the front and back spleen chakra. Avoid overenergizing the patient.
9. Apply localized sweeping thoroughly on the front and back solar plexus chakra and the liver. Energize the solar plexus chakra with light whitish-green prana, light whitish-blue prana, then ordinary light whitish-violet prana. This is to normalize the solar plexus chakra (which is usually malfunctioning in patients) and to strengthen the liver which has a cleansing effect on the blood.

10. Apply localized sweeping thoroughly on the throat chakra. Energize it with light whitish-green, light whitish-blue, then ordinary light whitish-violet. This is to stimulate the lymphatic system.

11. Apply localized sweeping thoroughly on the front and back heart chakra. Energize the back heart chakra with light whitish-violet. This is to strengthen and stimulate the thymus gland. This will also stimulate and strengthen the bone marrow in the spine, ribs, and breastbone.

12. Apply localized sweeping on the crown, forehead, ajna, and back head chakras. Energize them with a little light whitish-green then with more ordinary light whitish-violet prana.

This procedure is very thorough and could be used to treat severe infectious ailments like hepatitis, AIDS, and others.

MINOR AND SEVERE INFECTIONS

For minor infections, the affected part(s) has to be cleansed thoroughly and alternately with light whitish-green prana and light whitish-orange prana. If the affected part(s) is delicate, apply localized sweeping with light whitish-green prana only or light whitish-green prana and ordinary light whitish-violet prana. Energize the affected part(s) with light whitish-green, light blue, and ordinary light whitish-violet.

For severe infections, the affected part(s) has to be cleansed thoroughly before energizing. Energize the affected part(s) with light whitish-green, light blue, and gold prana. Energizing has to be done fully. The pranic treatment on the affected part(s) has to be repeated about three to four times a day until the condition has stabilized or substantially improved. The procedure for enhancing the immunity and defense system has to be applied on the patient.

SKIN INFECTIONS

Apply localized sweeping on the affected part alternately with light whitish-green and light whitish-orange. Do not apply orange prana on or near the head, the heart, or the spleen chakra. Just apply localized sweeping alternately with light whitish-green and ordinary light whitish-violet on these areas. Energize the affected part with light whitish-green, with light whitish-blue, then with ordinary light whitish-violet.

EYE INFECTIONS

Apply localized sweeping thoroughly on the eye(s) with light whitish-green. Apply localized sweeping on the ajna chakra and on the back head minor chakra. Energize them with light whitish-green, light whitish-blue, then with ordinary light whitish-violet. Visualize pranic energies going to the eyes. Apply more localized sweeping on the eyes.

EAR INFECTIONS

Apply localized sweeping on the affected ear with light whitish-green. Energize the affected ear with light whitish-green, light whitish-blue, then with ordinary light whitish-violet. Apply localized sweeping on the jaw minor chakra below the affected ear. Energize the jaw minor chakra with light whitish-green then with more ordinary light whitish-violet.

TONSILLITIS AND MUMPS

Apply localized sweeping on the jaw minor chakras, throat chakra, and secondary throat minor chakra alternately with light whitish-green and ordinary light whitish-violet. Cleansing must be done thoroughly. Energize the jaw minor chakras, throat chakra, and the secondary throat chakra with light whitish-green, light whitish-blue, and ordinary light whitish-violet.

RESPIRATORY INFECTIONS

For a nasal infection, apply localized sweeping on the ajna chakra alternately with light whitish-green and ordinary light whitish-violet. Energize it with light whitish-green, light whitish-blue, then with ordinary light whitish-violet.

For a throat infection, apply localized sweeping on the jaw minor chakras, throat chakra, and secondary throat minor chakra alternately with light whitish-green and ordinary light whitish-violet. Then energize them with light whitish-green, light whitish-blue, and ordinary light whitish-violet.

For bronchial and lung infections, apply localized sweeping on the lungs alternately with light whitish-green and light whitish-orange. Energize the lungs through the back of the lungs with light whitish-green, light whitish-orange, and ordinary light whitish-violet. When energizing the back of the lungs with orange prana, the healer's fingers should be pointed away from the head. Light whitish-blue prana, which has a disinfecting effect, is preferably not used on lung infections since it tends to slow down the expelling effect of orange prana.

GASTROINTESTINAL INFECTIONS

Apply localized sweeping on the front and back solar plexus chakra, navel chakra, and the abdominal area alternately with light whitish-green prana and ordinary light whitish-violet prana. Energize the front solar plexus chakra and the navel chakra with light whitish-green, light whitish-blue, and ordinary light whitish-violet. The emphasis of the treatment is on cleansing. Orange prana should not be used because it will cause diarrhea to become worse. For the more severe case, the front and back spleen chakra has to be cleansed thoroughly with light whitish-green prana then energized with light whitish-green prana and ordinary light whitish-violet prana. With more severe infections like amebiasis, typhoid fever, and others, the procedure for enhancing the immunity and defense system has to be applied.

LIVER INFECTIONS

Apply localized sweeping thoroughly on the front and back solar plexus chakra with light whitish-green prana. Apply localized sweeping on the liver (front, side, and back) alternately with light whitish-green and light whitish-orange. This has to be done thoroughly. Energize the front solar plexus chakra with light whitish-green, light whitish-blue, and ordinary light whitish-violet. Visualize the pranic energy going to the liver. The liver has to be treated several times a day until the condition has substantially improved. The spleen is also affected. Apply localized sweeping on the spleen with light whitish-green prana. Energize it with light whitish-green, then with ordinary light whitish-violet. This is to be done with caution. The procedure for enhancing the immunity and defense system must be applied.

This entire procedure can be used as pranic treatment for malaria. It is important to apply the purifying the blood technique. The front, side, and back of the lungs have to be cleansed thoroughly. Energize the lungs through the back with light whitish-green prana and light whitish-orange prana. Do not use medium or dark green prana and orange prana since it will aggravate the rupturing of the red blood cells. For healers who are not sufficiently experienced and skillful, it is safer just to use white prana or ordinary light whitish-violet.

URINARY INFECTIONS

For an infection of the urethra and bladder, apply localized sweeping on the sex chakra alternately with light whitish-green and light whitish-orange. Thorough cleansing is very important. Energize the sex chakra with light whitish-green, light whitish-blue, and ordinary light whitish-violet.

For a kidney infection, apply localized sweeping on the kidneys alternately with light whitish-green and light whitish-orange. Apply localized sweeping on the meng mein chakra. Energize the kidneys directly with light whitish-green, light whitish-blue, and ordinary light whitish-violet. Apply more sweeping on the meng mein chakra. If it is overactivated, inhibit it with light blue prana.

VENEREAL DISEASE

Energize the sex chakra with light blue prana. Then apply localized sweeping on it thoroughly and alternately with light whitish-green and light whitish-orange. Thorough cleansing is very important. Energize the sex chakra with light whitish-green, light whitish-blue, and ordinary light whitish-violet.

Disorders of the Eyes, Ears, and Throat

EYES AND EARS

The eyes and ears are controlled and energized by the crown, forehead, and ajna chakras. The eyes have corresponding eye minor chakras. The ears have corresponding ear minor chakras. The left eye and ear are influenced and energized more by the ajna chakra. The right eye and ear are influenced and energized more by the forehead chakra and crown chakra. The back head minor chakra energizes the whole head. It affects and energizes the eyes and ears. The temple minor chakras also affect the eyes. The jaw minor chakras energize the head including the eyes and ears. The condition of the eyes and ears also depends on the healthiness of the whole body. With middle-aged and elderly patients, the other major chakras have to be treated also.

NEARSIGHTEDNESS, FARSIGHTEDNESS, ASTIGMATISM, CROSS-EYES, WALLEYES

1. Scan the patient, then rescan during pranic treatment.
2. Apply localized sweeping thoroughly on the ajna chakra. Energize the eyes through the ajna chakra with light whitish-green prana.

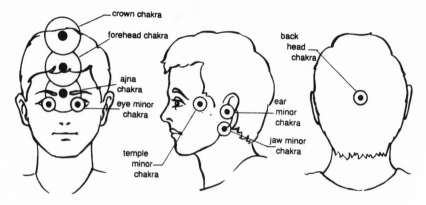

Figure 7-1. *Chakras affecting the eyes and ears.*

This is to clean and to loosen the diseased and used-up pranas in the minute nadis of the eyes. Energize the eyes with a little light whitish-yellow prana.* This is to facilitate the removal of the diseased and used-up energies.

3. Apply localized sweeping thoroughly on the eyes. Energize the eyes through the ajna chakra with light whitish-green, light whitish-yellow,* ordinary light whitish-violet, and less light whitish-blue prana. Visualize pranic energies going inside the eyes. The interaction of light whitish-green, light whitish-yellow,* and ordinary light whitish-violet has regenerating and strengthening effects on the eyes. Light whitish-blue prana gives pliability to eyes and stabilizes the projected pranic energy.

4. Apply localized sweeping on the temple minor chakras, forehead chakra, crown chakra, brain, back head minor chakra, and jaw minor chakras alternately with light whitish-green prana and ordinary light whitish-violet prana.

5. Energize the back head chakra with less light whitish-green and more ordinary light whitish-violet prana. Visualize the pranic energies going into the eyes.

6. Energize the forehead chakra, crown chakra, temple minor chakras, and the jaw minor chakras with light whitish-green prana, then with more ordinary light whitish-violet prana.

7. If the patient is middle-aged or elderly, it is advisable to clean the throat, heart, solar plexus, navel, and basic chakras; then energize

---

*Use the crown-hand chakras technique for projecting light whitish-yellow to regenerate delicate organs. The effect of yellow prana from the crown chakra is different from that of the basic chakra.

them with white prana. The heart chakra is energized through the back heart chakra.

8. Stabilize and release the projected pranic energy.
9. Repeat the treatment two to three times a week. The patient should avoid or minimize wearing eyeglasses for the duration of the treatment as this tends to neutralize the effects of the treatments. If the preceding steps are followed, it is likely that some patients will be completely healed within three months. The rate of healing will depend on the patient's age, the condition of the patient's eyes, and the proficiency of the healer.

Once the patient has been healed, he or she should not overuse the eyes and should go back for periodic treatments, especially if the eyes are weakening. This is just like visiting the dentist once or twice a year.

EYE INFECTIONS

It is clairvoyantly observed that some patients suffering from eye infections have holes in their outer auras. A portion of the health aura droops and the health rays are entangled. In many cases, the other parts of the body are also substantially affected. Very often, the application of general sweeping makes the difference between a rapid rate of healing and a slower rate of healing.

1. Scan the patient, then rescan during pranic treatment.
2. Apply general sweeping twice.
3. Apply localized sweeping on the eyes thoroughly and alternately with light whitish-green prana and ordinary light whitish-violet prana.
4. Apply localized sweeping on the ajna chakra. Energize the eyes through the ajna chakra with light whitish-green, with light whitish-blue, then ordinary light whitish-violet prana. Visualize pranic energies going inside the eyes. The eyes can be cleansed and energized several times a day to further accelerate the healing process.
5. Apply localized sweeping on the back head chakra. Energize it with less light whitish-green prana, then with more ordinary light whitish-violet prana. Visualize the eyes being energized and becoming brighter.
6. Apply localized sweeping thoroughly on the jaw minor chakras and the throat chakra. Energize them with white prana.

7. Apply localized sweeping on the front and back heart chakra. Energize the back heart chakra with light whitish-green prana, then with more ordinary light whitish-violet prana.

8. Apply localized sweeping on the lungs—front, side, and back. Energize the lungs directly through the back of the lungs with light whitish-green, then light whitish-orange prana. When energizing the lungs directly with orange prana, the healer's fingers should be pointed away from the patient's head.

9. Apply localized sweeping on the front and back spleen chakra and on the basic chakra.

10. Apply localized sweeping on the solar plexus chakra, liver, and navel chakra. Energize the solar plexus chakra and navel chakra with white prana.

11. Stabilize and release the projected pranic energy.

12. Repeat the entire treatment once a day for the next several days.

CHRONIC RED EYES

The solar plexus chakra is usually congested and filled with too much red pranic energy. Part of this excess red pranic energy goes to the ajna chakra and the eyes.

1. Scan the patient, then rescan during pranic treatment.

2. Apply localized sweeping thoroughly on the front and back solar plexus chakra and the liver. Energize the solar plexus chakra with light whitish-green, light whitish-blue, and ordinary light whitish-violet prana.

3. Apply localized sweeping on the front and back heart chakra. Energize the back heart chakra with less light whitish-green prana, then with more ordinary light whitish-violet prana.

4. Apply localized sweeping on the eyes thoroughly and alternately with light whitish-green prana and ordinary light whitish-violet prana.

5. Apply sweeping thoroughly on the ajna chakra, then energize the eyes through the ajna chakra with light whitish-green, then with more light whitish-blue prana.

6. Apply localized sweeping on the back head minor chakra, forehead chakra, and crown chakra. Energize them with white prana.

7. Stabilize and release the projected pranic energy.

8. Repeat treatment three times a week for as long as necessary.

FLOATER

A floater is one or more spots that appear to drift in front of the eye. This is caused by a shadow cast on the retina by vitreous debris or from the separation of the vitreous humor from the retina.

1. Scan the patient, then rescan during pranic treatment.
2. Apply localized sweeping on the ajna chakra. Energize the eyes through the ajna chakra with light whitish-green prana. This is to clean and to loosen the diseased and used-up pranas in the minute nadis of the eyes. Energize the eyes with a little light whitish-yellow prana. This is to facilitate the removal of the diseased and used-up energies.
3. Apply localized sweeping thoroughly on the eyes. Energize the eyes through the ajna chakra with less light whitish-green, and with more light whitish-yellow, then with more ordinary light whitish-violet prana. Visualize pranic energies going inside the eyes.
4. Apply localized sweeping on the temple minor chakras, forehead chakra, crown chakra, brain, back head minor chakra, and jaw minor chakras alternately with light whitish-green prana and ordinary light whitish-violet prana.
5. Energize the back head minor chakra, crown chakra, forehead chakra, temple minor chakras, and the jaw minor chakras with light whitish-green prana, then with more ordinary light whitish-violet prana.
6. If the patient is middle-aged or elderly, it is advisable to clean and energize the throat, heart, solar plexus, navel, and basic chakras with white prana. The heart chakra is energized through the back heart chakra.
7. Stabilize and release the projected pranic energy.
8. Repeat the treatment two to three times a week.

GLAUCOMA

In many cases, glaucoma is caused by irritation, frustration, and tension. The eye minor chakras, solar plexus chakra, ajna chakra, and back head minor chakra are substantially affected.

1. Scan the patient, then rescan during pranic treatment.
2. Apply localized sweeping thoroughly on the front and back solar plexus chakra and the liver. Energize the solar plexus chakra with light whitish-green, with light whitish-blue prana, then with ordinary light whitish-violet. For experienced, proficient, advanced pranic healers, you may use the "cleansing the solar plexus chakra technique."

3. Apply localized sweeping on the front and back heart chakra. Energize the back heart chakra with light whitish-green prana then with more ordinary light whitish-violet prana. Visualize the front heart chakra becoming bigger and brighter.

4. Apply localized sweeping thoroughly on the throat chakra and energize it with light whitish-green, then with ordinary light whitish-violet prana.

5. Apply localized sweeping thoroughly on the eyes, the temples, and the ajna chakra. Energize the eyes through the ajna chakra and the temples with whitish-green prana, with light whitish-blue prana, then with more ordinary light whitish-violet. Apply localized sweeping and energizing alternately until there is substantial or complete relief.

6. Apply localized sweeping on the forehead chakra, crown chakra, and back head minor chakra alternately with light whitish-green prana and ordinary light whitish-violet prana. Energize them with light whitish-green prana, then with ordinary light whitish-violet prana.

7. If the eye(s) has been damaged, energize the eyes through the back head minor chakra with light whitish-greenish-yellow, then with ordinary light whitish-greenish-violet prana. Visualize the eyes becoming brighter. Regeneration of the eye(s) may take six months to one year or more. The cooperation of the patient is very important.

8. Apply localized sweeping on the basic and navel chakras. Energize them with white prana. This is to strengthen the body.

9. Stabilize and release the projected pranic energy.

10. Repeat treatment three times a week for about two to three months.

CATARACT

Cataracts are usually connected with the aging process, and sometimes with pancreatic diabetes. Therefore, treating the eyes alone is not enough. It is necessary to treat the major chakras, especially the lower ones.

1. Scan the patient, then rescan during pranic treatment.

2. Apply localized sweeping thoroughly on the ajna chakra. Energize the eyes through the ajna chakra with light whitish-green prana. This is to clean and to loosen the diseased and used-up pranas in

the minute nadis of the eyes. Energize the eyes with a little light whitish-yellow prana. This is to facilitate the removal of the diseased and used-up energies.

3. Apply localized sweeping thoroughly on the eyes. Energize the eyes through the ajna chakra with light whitish-green prana, then with ordinary light whitish-violet prana. Visualize the pranic energies going into the eyes.

4. Apply localized sweeping on the forehead chakra, crown chakra, brain, temple minor chakras, and back head minor chakra. Energize the eyes through the back head chakra with light whitish-green prana, then ordinary light whitish-violet prana. Visualize the pranic energies going into the eyes.

5. Energize the crown chakra, the forehead chakra, and the temple minor chakras with light whitish-green prana, then ordinary light whitish-violet prana.

6. Apply localized sweeping on the jaw minor chakras, on the throat chakra, and on the secondary throat minor chakra. Energize them with white prana.

7. Apply localized sweeping on the front and back heart chakra. Energize the heart through the back heart chakra with some light whitish-green prana then with more ordinary light whitish-violet prana.

8. Apply localized sweeping on the front and back solar plexus chakra, navel chakra, sex chakra, and basic chakra. Energize them with white prana.

9. Apply localized sweeping on the front and back spleen chakra and on the meng mein chakra. Do not energize them.

10. Stabilize and release the projected pranic energy.

11. Repeat the treatment three times a week The result varies with patients. Some are cured while others notice a certain degree of improvement only after several months of treatments.

OUTER EAR INFECTIONS

1. Scan the patient, then rescan during pranic treatment.

2. Apply general sweeping twice.

3. Apply localized sweeping on the affected part and on the affected ear chakra thoroughly and alternately with light whitish-green prana and ordinary light whitish-violet prana. This is very important.

4. Energize the affected part and the affected ear minor chakra with light whitish-green, light whitish-blue, and ordinary light whitish-

violet prana. The affected ear can be cleansed and energized several times a day to further accelerate the healing process.

5. Apply localized sweeping on the back head minor chakra and on the jaw minor chakra below the affected ear. Energize them with white prana.

6. Apply localized sweeping on the throat chakra, then on the secondary throat minor chakra. Energize them with light whitish-green prana, then with ordinary light whitish-violet prana.

7. Apply localized sweeping on the front and back heart chakra. Energize the back heart chakra with less light whitish-green prana, then with more ordinary light whitish-violet prana.

8. Apply localized sweeping on the lungs—front, side, and back. Energize the lungs directly through the back of the lungs with light whitish-green prana, then with light whitish-orange prana. When energizing the lungs with orange prana, the healer's fingers should be pointed away from the patient's head.

9. Apply localized sweeping on the front and back spleen chakra and on the basic chakra.

10. Apply localized sweeping on the solar plexus chakra, liver, and navel chakra. Energize the solar plexus chakra and navel chakra with white prana.

11. Stabilize and release the projected pranic energy.

12. Repeat treatment once a day for the next several days.

MIDDLE AND INNER EAR INFECTIONS

In some cases, middle and inner ear infections could be caused by a stuffy nose. Therefore, the ajna chakra may have to be treated.

1. Scan the patient, then rescan during pranic treatment.

2. Apply general sweeping twice.

3. Apply localized sweeping on the affected ear thoroughly and alternately with light whitish-green prana and ordinary light whitish-violet prana. This is very important.

4. Energize the affected ear with light whitish-green, light whitish-blue, and ordinary light whitish-violet prana. The affected ear can be cleansed and energized several times a day to further accelerate the healing process.

5. Apply localized sweeping on the ajna chakra. Energize it with light whitish-green, light whitish-blue, and ordinary light whitish-violet prana.

6. Apply localized sweeping on the back head minor chakra and on the jaw minor chakra below the affected ear. Energize them with white prana.

7. Apply localized sweeping on the throat chakra, then on the secondary throat minor chakra. Energize them with light whitish-green prana, then with ordinary light whitish-violet prana.

8. Apply localized sweeping on the front and back heart chakra. Energize the back heart chakra with less light whitish-green prana and with more ordinary light whitish-violet prana.

9. Apply localized sweeping on the lungs—front, side, and back. Energize the lungs directly through the back of the lungs with light whitish-green prana, then with light whitish-orange prana. When energizing the lungs with orange prana, the healer's fingers should be pointed away from the patient's head.

10. Apply localized sweeping on the front and back spleen chakra, then on the basic chakra.

11. Apply localized sweeping on the solar plexus chakra, liver, and navel chakra. Energize the solar plexus chakra and navel chakra with white prana.

12. Stabilize and release the projected pranic energy.

13. Repeat treatment once a day for the next several days.

DEAFNESS

Deafness manifests as a malfunctioning of the ear minor chakra(s). This is sometimes seen as muddy orange on the affected ear minor chakra. A normal ear chakra appears as light whitish-red. An affected ear may be depleted or congested or both simultaneously. In many cases, the back head minor chakra and jaw minor chakra are also affected. There are many possible physical causes of partial or complete deafness, such as earwax, glued ear or fluid in the middle ear, ruptured eardrum, and nerve deafness.

In general, apply localized sweeping on the affected ear. Energize it with light whitish-green prana, then with ordinary light whitish-violet prana. Apply localized sweeping on the back head minor chakra and on the jaw minor chakra of the affected ear. Energize them with white prana.

Most patients may experience immediate and substantial improvement with their hearing. Sometimes, the treated ear hears better than the other "normal ear," but this improvement is usually temporary. Pranic treatments have to be repeated. White prana is very safe but the improvement does not last as long as when color pranas are used.

I once encountered a strange case of a woman patient who suffered a bad fall on her basic chakra area when she was still a young child. When seen clairvoyantly, one half of her basic chakra was relatively normal, while the other half was quite depleted—such a case occurs very rarely. The root of the basic chakra was slightly off center. She was partially deaf in the right ear; the right eye was worse than the left eye; the right breast was smaller than the left one; and the right leg was shorter than the left one. The sex chakra was also malfunctioning. Obviously, if her ailments were to be gradually cured, the basic chakra had to be normalized. The basic chakra was cleansed and energized. By using the will, the root of the basic chakra was gradually centered. Spinal adjustment was also applied.

RUPTURED EARDRUM

1. Scan the patient, then rescan during pranic treatment.
2. Apply localized sweeping on the ear thoroughly and alternately with light whitish-green prana and ordinary light whitish-violet prana. Energize the ear with light whitish-green prana, then with more ordinary light whitish-violet prana.
3. Apply localized sweeping thoroughly on the back head minor chakra and on the jaw minor chakra below the affected ear. Energize them with light whitish-green, then with more ordinary light whitish-violet.
4. Apply localized sweeping on the front and back solar plexus chakra, navel chakra, and the basic chakra. Energize them with white prana. This is to further facilitate the healing process.
5. Stabilize and release the projected energy.
6. Repeat treatment three times a week.

GLUED EAR

Glued ear, or fluid in the middle ear, could be caused by a stuffy nose.

1. Scan the patient, then rescan during pranic treatment.
2. Apply localized sweeping on the affected ear thoroughly and alternately with light whitish-green prana and ordinary light whitish-violet prana. Energize the affected ear with light whitish-green prana, then with ordinary light whitish-violet prana.

3. The proficient, experienced, advanced pranic healers should energize the affected ear with light whitish-blue prana. Then apply localized sweeping alternately with light whitish-green prana and very light whitish-orange prana. Energize the affected ear with light whitish-blue, light whitish-green, and very light whitish-orange prana. This is to be done with caution since the ear is very near the brain.

4. Apply localized sweeping thoroughly on the back head minor chakra and on the jaw minor chakra below the affected ear. Energize them with light whitish-green prana, then with ordinary light whitish-violet prana.

5. Apply localized sweeping on the ajna chakra. Energize it with light whitish-green prana, then with ordinary light whitish-violet prana.

6. Apply localized sweeping on the throat chakra and on the secondary throat minor chakra. Energize them with light whitish-green prana, then with ordinary light whitish-violet prana.

7. Apply localized sweeping on the front and back heart chakra. Energize the back heart chakra with less light whitish-green prana and more ordinary light whitish-violet prana.

8. Apply localized sweeping on the lungs—front, side, and back. Energize the lungs directly through the back of the lungs with light whitish-green prana and light whitish-orange prana. When energizing the lungs with orange prana, the healer's fingers should be pointed away from the patient's head.

9. Apply localized sweeping on the front and back spleen chakra and on the basic chakra.

10. Apply localized sweeping on the solar plexus chakra, liver, and navel chakra. Energize the solar plexus chakra and navel chakra with white prana.

11. Stabilize and release the projected energy.

12. Repeat treatment three times a week.

NERVE DEAFNESS

Nerve deafness is usually connected with the aging process. Therefore, the major chakras have to be treated. Nerve deafness may also be caused by loud noise or prolonged listening to loud music, or could be a side effect of drugs.

1. Scan the patient, then rescan during pranic treatment.
2. Apply general sweeping twice.
3. Energize the affected ear with light whitish-blue prana. Then apply localized sweeping alternately with light whitish-green prana and very light whitish-orange prana. This is to be done only by proficient, experienced, advanced pranic healers. This step is to be done with caution.
4. Energize the affected ear with light whitish-green prana. Then energize with more ordinary light whitish-violet prana.
5. Apply localized sweeping thoroughly on the back head minor chakra and on the jaw minor chakra below the affected ear. Energize them with light whitish-green prana, then with ordinary light whitish-violet prana.
6. Apply localized sweeping thoroughly on the ajna chakra, forehead chakra, and crown chakra. Energize them with light whitish-green prana, then with ordinary light whitish-violet prana.
7. Apply localized sweeping on the front and back spleen chakra.
8. Apply localized sweeping on the throat chakra, secondary throat chakra, front and back heart chakra, front and back solar plexus chakra, navel chakra, sex chakra, and basic chakra. Energize them with white prana.
9. Stabilize and release the projected energy.
10. Repeat treatment three times a week for several months.

NOISE IN THE EAR OR TINNITUS

1. Scan the patient, then rescan during pranic treatment.
2. Apply localized sweeping on the affected ear thoroughly and alternately with light whitish-green prana and ordinary light whitish-violet prana. Energize it with light whitish-green prana; then use more ordinary light whitish-violet prana.
3. Apply localized sweeping thoroughly on the back head minor chakra, on the jaw minor chakra below the affected ear, and the throat chakra. Energize them with light whitish-green prana; then use more ordinary light whitish-violet prana.
4. Apply localized sweeping thoroughly on the ajna chakra, forehead chakra, and crown chakra. Energize them with light whitish-green prana; then use ordinary light whitish-violet prana.

5. Apply localized sweeping on the front and back heart chakra. Energize the back heart chakra with light whitish-green prana; then use more ordinary light whitish-violet prana.
6. Stabilize and release the projected pranic energy.
7. Repeat treatment three times a week.

VERTIGO

1. Scan the patient, then rescan during pranic treatment.
2. Apply localized sweeping thoroughly on the ears, jaw minor chakras, and on the back head minor chakra. Energize them with light whitish-green prana, then use more ordinary light whitish-violet prana.
3. Apply localized sweeping on the ajna chakra, forehead chakra, and crown chakra. Energize them with light whitish-green prana; then use more ordinary light whitish-violet prana.
4. Apply localized sweeping on the throat chakra and secondary throat chakra. Energize them with light whitish-green prana; then use more ordinary light whitish-violet prana.
5. Apply localized sweeping on the front and back heart chakra. Energize the back heart chakra with light whitish-green prana; then use more ordinary light whitish-violet prana.
6. Stabilize and release the projected energy.
7. Repeat treatment three times a week.

SORE THROAT, LARYNGITIS, MUMPS, AND TONSILLITIS

1. Scan the patient, then rescan during pranic treatment.
2. Apply general sweeping several times.
3. Apply localized sweeping thoroughly on the jaw minor chakras, the throat chakra, and secondary throat chakra. This is very important. Energize them with light whitish-green, light whitish-blue, and ordinary light whitish-violet prana. With sore throat and laryngitis, the emphasis is on the throat chakra and the secondary throat chakra. With mumps and tonsillitis, the emphasis of the treatment is on the jaw minor chakras. The affected parts can be

cleansed and energized several times a day to further accelerate the healing process.

4. Apply localized sweeping on the ajna chakra, forehead chakra, crown chakra, and back head minor chakra. Energize them with light whitish-green prana; then use more ordinary light whitish-violet prana.

5. Apply localized sweeping on the front and back heart chakra. Energize the back heart chakra with less light whitish-green prana and more ordinary light whitish-violet prana.

6. Apply localized sweeping on the lungs—front, side, and back. Energize the lungs directly through the back of the lungs with light whitish-green prana and light whitish-orange prana. When energizing the lungs with orange prana, the healer's fingers should be pointed away from the patient's head.

7. Apply localized sweeping on the front and back spleen chakra and the basic chakra.

8. Apply localized sweeping thoroughly on the front and back solar plexus chakra, liver, and navel chakra. The solar plexus chakra has to be cleansed thoroughly. Energize the solar plexus chakra and navel chakra with light whitish-green, light whitish-blue, and ordinary light whitish-violet prana.

9. Stabilize and release the projected pranic energy.

10. Repeat the entire treatment once or twice a day for the next several days.

Skin Disorders

SKIN

The skin is controlled and energized by the basic chakra. Patients with chronic or severe skin ailments usually have a dirty basic chakra. The navel and the solar plexus chakras control the digestive, assimilative, and eliminative system; therefore, they affect the health of the skin. The solar plexus chakra (through the liver), the spleen chakra (through the physical spleen), and the meng mein chakra (through the kidneys) purify the blood; therefore, they substantially affect the health of the skin. In many cases, the malfunctioning of the solar plexus chakra due to emotional factors may adversely affect the basic chakra manifesting as skin disease. The ajna chakra, which is the master chakra, controls the basic chakra; therefore, it also influences the health of the skin.

ITCH

1. Scan the patient, then rescan during pranic treatment.
2. Apply localized sweeping alternately with light whitish-green prana and light whitish-orange prana on the affected part. Do not

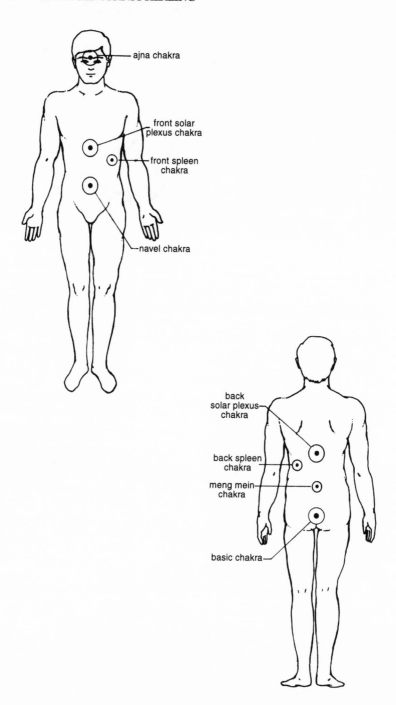

Figure 8-1. Chakras affecting the skin.

use orange prana on or near the head, heart, and spleen. If sweeping is done properly, the patient will usually be partially or completely relieved.

3. Energize the affected part with light whitish-green, light whitish-blue, then ordinary light whitish-violet.
4. Apply localized sweeping thoroughly on the front and back solar plexus chakra and the liver. Energize the solar plexus chakra with light whitish-green, light whitish-blue, and ordinary light whitish-violet prana.
5. Apply localized sweeping thoroughly on the basic chakra, then energize it with light whitish-red prana.
6. Stabilize and release the projected pranic energy.

ECZEMA OR DERMATITIS

1. Scan the patient, then rescan during pranic treatment.
2. Apply localized sweeping alternately with light whitish-green prana and light whitish-orange prana on the affected part. Do not use orange prana on the head, heart, and spleen or near them. Cleansing has to be done thoroughly.
3. Energize the affected part with a little light whitish-blue prana for a localizing effect, then with light whitish-orange, and light whitish-red prana.
4. Apply localized sweeping thoroughly on the front and back solar plexus chakra, the liver, and the spleen chakra. Energize them with light whitish-green then with more of light whitish-violet. The spleen chakra has to be energized with caution.
5. Apply localized sweeping thoroughly on the navel and basic chakras. Energize them with light whitish-red prana.
6. Stabilize and release the projected pranic energy.
7. Repeat treatment three times a week for as long as necessary.

MILD PIMPLES

1. Scan the patient, then rescan during pranic treatment.
2. Apply localized sweeping thoroughly with light whitish-green prana on the entire face with emphasis on the affected parts.
3. Energize the affected parts with light whitish-green, light whitish-blue, then with ordinary light whitish-violet prana.

4. Apply localized sweeping on the ajna chakra, throat chakra, and jaw minor chakras. Energize them with a little light whitish-green, then with more ordinary light violet prana.
5. Apply localized sweeping on the basic chakra, then energize it with light whitish-red prana.
6. Stabilize and release the projected pranic energy.
7. Repeat treatment if necessary.

CHRONIC SEVERE PIMPLES

With chronic severe pimple cases, the basic chakra, the sex chakra, the solar plexus chakra, the liver, the throat chakra, and the jaw minor chakras are usually quite dirty and affected. The ajna chakra is partially affected.

1. Scan the patient, then rescan during pranic treatment.
2. Apply general sweeping twice.
3. Apply localized sweeping thoroughly with light whitish-green prana on the entire face with emphasis on the affected parts.
4. Energize the affected parts with light whitish-green, light whitish-blue, then with ordinary light whitish-violet prana.
5. Apply localized sweeping thoroughly on the ajna chakra and energize it with a little light whitish-green; then use more ordinary light whitish-violet prana.
6. Apply localized sweeping thoroughly on the jaw minor chakras and on the throat chakra. Energize them with a little light whitish-green; then use more ordinary light violet prana.
7. Apply localized sweeping thoroughly on the front and back solar plexus chakra, the liver, and the spleen chakra. Energize them with light whitish-green; then use more light whitish-violet prana. The spleen chakra has to be energized with caution.
8. Apply localized sweeping thoroughly on the navel, sex, and basic chakras. Energize them with white prana.
9. Stabilize and release the projected pranic energy.
10. Repeat treatment three times a week for as long as necessary.

CHRONIC BOILS

In many instances, chronic boils are due to stress. The solar plexus chakra and liver are usually congested and dirty. The spleen chakra and the basic chakra are affected.

1. Scan the patient, then rescan during pranic treatment.
2. Apply localized sweeping alternately with light whitish-green prana and light whitish-orange prana on the affected part. Do not use orange prana on or near the head, heart, and spleen. Thorough cleansing is very important.
3. Energize the affected part with light whitish-green, light whitish-blue, then ordinary light whitish-violet prana.
4. Apply localized sweeping thoroughly on the front and back solar plexus chakra and the liver. This is very important. Energize the solar plexus chakra with light whitish-green, light whitish-blue, then with ordinary light whitish-violet prana.
5. Apply localized sweeping on the spleen chakra, then energize it with light whitish-green; then use ordinary light whitish-violet prana. This has to be done with caution.
6. Apply localized sweeping thoroughly and alternately on the basic chakra with light whitish-green prana and light whitish-orange prana. Energize it with light whitish-red.
7. Stabilize and release the projected pranic energy.
8. Repeat treatment three times a week for as long as necessary.

SKIN ALLERGY

1. Scan the patient, then rescan during pranic treatment.
2. To rapidly relieve the patient, apply localized sweeping on the affected parts with light whitish-green; then use light whitish-orange prana. Do not use orange prana on the head, heart, spleen, or anywhere near these areas.
3. Energize the affected part with light whitish-green, light whitish-orange, and light whitish-red prana. By cleansing and energizing the affected part, the patient will be rapidly relieved.
4. Apply localized sweeping on the lungs. Energize the lungs through the back of the lungs with light whitish-green, light whitish-orange, then with light whitish-red prana. This is to clean and strengthen the blood. When energizing the lungs with orange prana, the healer's fingers should be pointed away from the patient's head.
5. Apply localized sweeping thoroughly on the ajna chakra. Energize it with a little light whitish-green; then use more ordinary light whitish-violet prana.

6. Apply localized sweeping thoroughly on the front and back solar plexus chakra, and the liver. Energize the solar plexus chakra with light whitish-green; then use ordinary light whitish-violet prana.

7. Experienced, proficient, advanced pranic healers can apply localized sweeping on the front and back solar plexus chakra and the liver. Energize the front solar plexus chakra with light whitish-green, then use light whitish-orange prana.

8. Apply localized sweeping thoroughly on the front and back spleen chakra then energize it with white prana.

9. Apply localized sweeping on the basic chakra thoroughly and alternately with light whitish-green prana and light whitish-orange prana. Energize the basic chakra with light whitish-red prana.

10. Stabilize and release the projected pranic energy.

11. Repeat treatment several times a week.

PSORIASIS

Psoriasis patients have dirty solar plexus, meng mein, and basic chakras. The grayish red energy from the solar plexus chakra and the basic chakra goes to the meng mein chakra. From the meng mein chakra, the dirty grayish red energy is spread to other parts of the body. In general, psoriasis is emotional in origin.

1. Scan the patient, then rescan during pranic treatment.

2. Apply general sweeping twice.

3. To rapidly relieve the patient, apply localized sweeping on the affected parts alternately with light whitish-green prana and light whitish-orange prana. Do not use orange prana on or near the head, heart, or spleen.

4. Apply localized sweeping thoroughly on the front and back solar plexus chakra and the liver. Energize the solar plexus chakra with light whitish-green, light whitish-blue, then with ordinary light whitish-violet prana. Experienced, proficient, advanced pranic healers can apply the "cleansing the solar plexus chakra technique" (see pp. 87–88).

5. Apply localized sweeping thoroughly on the meng mein chakra. This is very important.

6. Apply localized sweeping thoroughly on the basic chakra alternately with light whitish-green prana and light whitish-orange prana. Energize the basic chakra with light whitish-red prana. The emphasis of the treatment includes Steps 3 to 6.

7. Apply localized sweeping on the ajna chakra, then energize it with light whitish-green, then with more ordinary light whitish-violet prana.
8. To activate the heart chakra, apply localized sweeping on the front and back heart chakra. Energize the back heart chakra with light whitish-green, and then use more ordinary light whitish-violet prana. Simultaneously, visualize the front heart chakra becoming bigger. This is to produce an inner sense of peace.
9. Stabilize and release the projected pranic energy.
10. Repeat treatment three times a week for as long as necessary.

THINNING HAIR

A person may have very healthy crown and forehead chakras but still have falling or thinning hair. This is because the scalp is depleted. Clairvoyantly, this is seen as light gray or light yellowish-gray on the scalp area.

The health of the scalp depends on the health of the back head minor chakra, jaw minor chakras, and throat chakra since these chakras affect the carotid arteries which supply blood to the head and the scalp.

In many, if not in most cases, the solar plexus chakra, the sex chakra, and the basic chakra are also affected. The basic chakra controls and energizes the skin and the hair. Depletion of the sex chakra will cause the throat chakra to become partially depleted. Extreme stress will cause the solar plexus chakra, basic chakra, throat chakra, and jaw minor chakras to malfunction which may manifest as rapid thinning of the hair.

1. Scan the patient, then rescan during pranic treatment.
2. Apply localized sweeping thoroughly on the affected area(s) of the scalp. Energize the affected part with light whitish-blue prana for a localizing effect. To stimulate rapid hair growth, energize the affected part with more light whitish-red; then use a little light whitish-yellow. The pranic proportion is 95% light whitish-red prana, and 5% light whitish-yellow prana. Red and yellow prana are projected one after the other. They are never projected simultaneously, as the effect will be quite adverse.
3. Apply localized sweeping on the ajna chakra, then energize it with a little light whitish-green followed by more ordinary light whitish-violet prana.
4. Apply localized sweeping thoroughly on the back head minor chakra, jaw minor chakras, and throat chakra. Energize them with

light whitish-green, and ordinary light whitish-violet prana. The purpose of this step is to improve the microcirculation of the blood in the scalp.

5. Apply localized sweeping thoroughly on the front and back solar plexus chakra and the liver. Energize the solar plexus chakra with light whitish-green, light whitish-blue, then with ordinary light whitish-violet prana.

6. Apply localized sweeping on the navel, sex, and basic chakras. Energize them with light whitish-red prana.

7. Stabilize and release the projected pranic energy.

8. Repeat treatment several times a week for as long as necessary.

Heart and Circulatory Ailments

CIRCULATORY SYSTEM

The heart is controlled and energized by the front and back heart chakra. Since the physical heart is basically made up of muscles, it is substantially energized and affected by the basic chakra. The physical heart is also affected by the solar plexus chakra which usually causes it to malfunction. In many, if not in most cases, stress or negative emotion is a major factor in heart ailments. Many, if not almost all, heart patients have malfunctioning solar plexus chakras. Part of the dirty congested energy from the solar plexus chakra goes to the heart chakra, thereby causing the physical heart to malfunction. Also, malfunctioning of the solar plexus chakra causes the liver to malfunction which adversely affects the cholesterol level of the body, and in the long run causes the physical heart to become diseased. In many instances, the malfunctioning of the solar plexus chakra causes the throat chakra to malfunction which causes the heart to malfunction.

The blood vessels are controlled and energized primarily by the heart chakra and the basic chakra. The other major and minor chakras also affect the blood vessels.

The heart has two minor chakras: the left heart minor chakra and the right heart minor chakra.

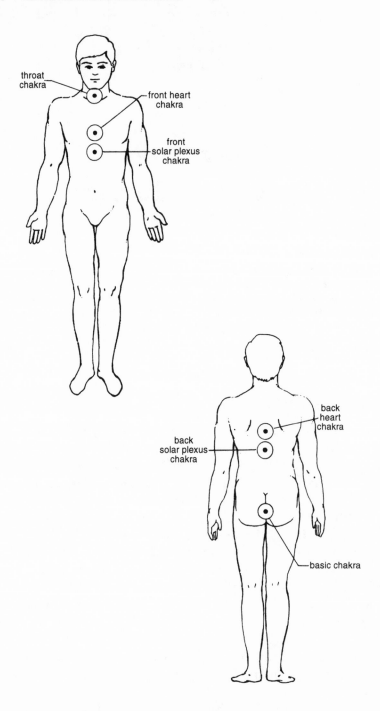

Figure 9-1. Chakras affecting the heart.

There are many types of heart ailments. Heart ailments may manifest as heart muscle failure due to obstruction or clotting in the heart arteries, heart infection, heart enlargement and malfunctioning of the heart valves, congenital hole or holes in the dividing wall between the left and the right sides of the heart, and as irregular beating of the heart. In treating heart ailments, the following chakras and organs have to be treated:

A) Front and back heart chakra;
B) Physical heart;
C) Front and back solar plexus chakra;
D) Liver;
E) Throat chakra;
F) Basic chakra.

In patients with heart ailments, the heart is either congested, or depleted, or both. Thorough cleansing of the solar plexus chakra is very important since it is usually the main cause of the ailment. The liver is affected and is grayish red. The basic chakra is depleted or partially depleted.

Light whitish-green prana is used for cleansing and dissolving. Light whitish-red prana is used for dilating and strengthening. Light whitish-blue prana is used for disinfecting and disinflaming effects. It is also necessary for the pliability of the heart muscles and is used for treating heart enlargement. Ordinary light whitish-violet prana has multipurpose effects.

The heart must be scanned thoroughly, with one or two fingers, to locate the small troubled spots. To help you locate them, ask the patient which specific spots hurt. The small spots with pranic depletion must be cleansed thoroughly using your finger (or fingers) alternating light whitish-green prana and ordinary light whitish-violet prana.

Cleansing the solar plexus chakra thoroughly is very important. For experienced, proficient, advanced pranic healers, it is better to use the "cleansing the solar plexus chakra technique" (page 87) to thoroughly and rapidly clean the solar plexus chakra and the liver. The overactivated solar plexus chakra has to be inhibited with light whitish-blue prana.

Experienced, proficient, advanced pranic healers may use light whitish-green and light whitish-orange alternately for cleansing the heart. Apply localized sweeping with light whitish-red to dilate the arteries. If cleansing is done properly, the relief is usually very fast. It is important that the orange prana used is light whitish-orange, not medium or dark orange prana. Orange prana is not usually used on the heart except by proficient, advanced pranic healers because of the possible adverse effects on weak hearts if the projected shade of the orange prana is incorrect.

In general, it is safer not to stabilize the projected pranic energy in the heart. This is because healers who are not proficient have a tendency to overstabilize the projected energy which may cause a slight congestion which will be felt as a discomfort. Should this happen, just apply localized sweeping on the heart.

In general, patients with heart problems are expected to stop smoking, to regulate their emotions, and to watch their diets.

PARTIAL HEART BLOCK— CORONARY ARTERY DISEASE

In patients with partial heart block or coronary artery disease parts of the heart are congested and certain parts are very depleted. Green prana is used for its cleansing and dissolving effects. Red prana is used for strengthening the physical heart and dilating the blood vessels, thereby allowing more blood to flow to the heart muscle. The solar plexus chakra is dirty and over-activated. The liver is partially affected.

1. Scan the patient, then rescan during pranic treatment.
2. Apply general sweeping.
3. Apply localized sweeping thoroughly on the front and back solar plexus chakra and on the liver. This is very important.
4. Apply localized sweeping thoroughly on the front heart chakra and on the physical heart. Apply localized sweeping on the small affected part(s) alternately with light whitish-green prana and light whitish-violet prana with one or two fingers. The lower left part of the heart should be thoroughly cleansed.
5. Apply localized sweeping thoroughly on the back heart chakra. Energize the physical heart with light whitish-green prana, then light whitish-red prana through the back heart chakra. Green prana has cleansing arid dissolving effects. Red prana has strengthening and dilating effects.
6. Apply more localized sweeping on the front heart chakra and on the physical heart.
7. Energize the front solar plexus chakra with light whitish-green prana, light whitish-blue prana, then light whitish-violet prana. This is to normalize the solar plexus chakra and the liver. Light whitish-blue prana has an inhibiting effect on the overactivated solar plexus chakra. Do not use dark blue since it has a constricting effect and may affect the heart.

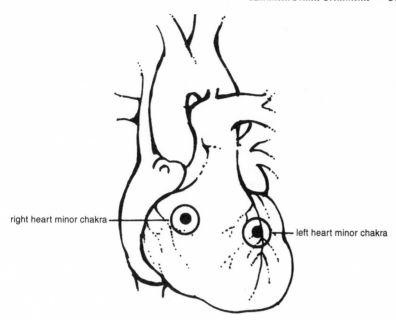

right heart minor chakra

left heart minor chakra

Figure 9-2. Left and right heart minor chakras.

8. Apply more localized sweeping on the front and back solar plexus chakra and on the liver.
9. Apply localized sweeping on the lungs. Energize them through the back of the lungs with light whitish-green, light whitish-orange, and light whitish-red. This has cleansing, dissolving, and dilating effects on the arteries. When energizing the lungs with orange prana, the healer's fingers should be pointed away from the patient's head.
10. Apply localized sweeping on the basic and navel chakras, and energize them with light whitish-red prana to further strengthen the physical heart and the body.
11. Apply localized sweeping on the crown, forehead, ajna, and throat chakras. Energize them with a little light whitish-green prana, then with more ordinary light whitish-violet prana.
12. Stabilize and release the projected pranic energy.
13. Repeat treatment three times a week.

If treatment is done properly, usually the patient will experience relief after the first treatment. There will be substantial improvement within a week or two, but pranic treatment may have to be continued for about two to three months or until the patient is fully healed. There is a strong possibility that the patient will feel quite good after a few treatments and may preterminate the pranic treatment. This is a serious mistake that should be avoided.

Experienced, proficient, advanced pranic healers can apply localized sweeping on the heart alternately with light whitish-green, light whitish-orange, and light whitish-red prana. Apply localized sweeping on the back heart chakra. Energize the heart through the back heart chakra with light whitish-green, light whitish-orange, and light whitish-red. Apply the "cleansing the solar plexus chakra technique." This has a rapid cleansing effect on the solar plexus chakra and on the liver. If treatment is done properly, the patient is likely to be relieved instantaneously and the recovery will be very fast.

The patient is expected to eat a proper diet. Stressful or irritating situations should be avoided. Patients should be instructed to regulate their emotions and not to overwork.

IRREGULAR HEARTBEAT OR CARDIAC ARRHYTHMIAS

Patients with irregular heartbeats have problems with their heart and solar plexus chakras. Both the heart chakra and the solar plexus chakra are filled with dirty red energy. The internal cause is basically emotional in origin. The right upper part of the heart, where the pacemaker of the heart is located, must be cleansed thoroughly since it is congested with dirty red energy. The throat chakra is also affected and has to be thoroughly treated.

1. Scan the patient, then rescan during pranic treatment.
2. Apply general sweeping.
3. Apply localized sweeping thoroughly on the front and back solar plexus chakra and on the liver. This is very important.
4. Apply localized sweeping thoroughly on the front heart chakra and the physical heart. The emphasis is on the right upper part of the heart. When sweeping, use light whitish-green then ordinary light whitish-violet alternately to facilitate the removal of dirty red prana.
5. Apply localized sweeping on the back heart chakra. Energize the heart through the back heart chakra with light whitish-green prana, light whitish-blue prana, then ordinary light whitish-violet prana.
6. Apply more localized sweeping on the front heart chakra and the physical heart, especially on the right upper part of the heart.

7. Energize the solar plexus chakra with light whitish-green prana, light whitish-blue prana, then ordinary light whitish-violet prana.
8. Apply more localized sweeping on the front and back solar plexus chakra and on the liver.
9. Apply localized sweeping thoroughly on the throat chakra, and secondary throat minor chakra. This is important. Energize them with light whitish-green, light whitish-blue, and ordinary light whitish-violet.
10. Apply localized sweeping on the basic and navel chakras, and energize them with light whitish-red prana.
11. Apply localized sweeping on the crown, forehead, and ajna chakras. Energize them with a little light whitish-green prana; then use more ordinary light whitish-violet prana.
12. Stabilize and release the projected pranic energy.
13. Repeat treatment three times a week.

If treatment is applied properly, there will be a significant improvement within a week or two. It may take about two to three months of persistent treatment for the patient to be substantially or fully healed. The patient is expected to regulate his or her emotions. Worries and apprehensions should be minimized. Stressful situations are to be avoided as much as possible.

Experienced, proficient, advanced pranic healers can apply localized sweeping on the heart alternately with light whitish-green and light whitish-orange with emphasis on the right upper part of the heart. Apply localized sweeping on the right upper part of the heart with light whitish-blue to help normalize the heartbeat. Energize the heart through the back heart chakra with light whitish-green, light whitish-blue, and ordinary light whitish-violet. This technique is very effective in treating an irregular heartbeat.

INFLAMMATION OF THE HEART OR RHEUMATIC HEART

The treatment for inflammation of the heart or rheumatic heart is almost the same as cardiac arrhythmia treatment. The defense mechanism of the body must be enhanced.

1. Scan the patient, then rescan during pranic treatment.
2. Apply general sweeping.
3. Apply localized sweeping thoroughly on the front and back solar plexus chakra and on the liver. This is very important.

4. Apply localized sweeping on the front heart chakra and the physical heart thoroughly and alternately with light whitish-green prana and ordinary light whitish-violet prana.
5. Apply localized sweeping on the back heart. Energize the heart with light whitish-green prana, light whitish-blue prana, then ordinary light whitish-violet prana.
6. Apply more localized sweeping on the front heart chakra and the physical heart.
7. Energize the front solar plexus chakra with light whitish-green prana, light whitish-blue prana, then ordinary light whitish-violet prana.
8. Apply more localized sweeping on the front and back solar plexus chakra and on the liver.
9. Apply localized sweeping on the front and back spleen chakra. Energize the spleen chakra with light whitish-green; then use more ordinary light whitish-violet. This has to be done with care.
10. Apply localized sweeping thoroughly on the basic chakra and the navel chakra and energize them with white prana. If the patient has a fever, do not energize the basic chakra.
11. Apply localized sweeping on the sole minor chakras and hand chakras, and energize them with ordinary light whitish-violet prana. This is to enhance the defense mechanism of the body.
12. Apply localized sweeping on the crown, forehead, ajna, and throat chakras. Energize them with a little light whitish-green prana; then use more ordinary light whitish-violet prana.
13. Stabilize and release the projected pranic energy.
14. Repeat treatment three or more times a week until the patient is substantially or fully healed.

There will be noticeable or substantial improvement after a few pranic treatments.

ENLARGED HEART—DEFECTIVE VALVE

In patients with enlarged hearts or defective valves the heart chakra and the solar plexus chakra are congested with dirty red pranic energy. The solar plexus chakra is overactivated. The liver is also filled with a lot of dirty red pranic energy. In many instances, the patients have long-standing resentments which cause the solar plexus chakra to be congested with too much red pranic energy. Part of the dirty red pranic energy goes to the heart chakra which, in the long run, causes the physical heart to become enlarged since red prana is expansive. The emphasis in treatment is on thorough cleansing of the front heart chakra, the physical heart, the front and back solar plexus chakra, and the liver. The affected chakras and parts are just like springs. After cleansing and energizing them, more dirty red energy will spring out. Therefore, more sweeping has to be done.

1. Scan the patient, then rescan during pranic treatment.
2. Apply general sweeping.
3. Apply localized sweeping thoroughly on the front and back solar plexus chakra and on the liver. This is very important.
4. Apply localized sweeping thoroughly on the front heart chakra and on the physical heart.
5. Apply localized sweeping on the back heart chakra. Energize the heart through the back heart chakra with light whitish-green prana, light whitish-blue prana, light whitish-yellow, then ordinary light whitish-violet prana. Green prana is for cleansing. Blue prana is needed for the pliability of the heart muscles. Yellow prana is needed for strong healthy heart tissue. Violet prana has strengthening and regenerating effects.
6. Apply more localized sweeping on the front heart chakra and the physical heart.
7. Energize the front solar plexus chakra with light whitish-green prana, light whitish-blue prana, then ordinary light whitish-violet prana.
8. Apply more localized sweeping on the front and back solar plexus chakra and on the liver.
9. Apply localized sweeping thoroughly on the basic chakra and the navel chakra, and energize them with light whitish-red prana.
10. Apply localized sweeping on the crown, forehead, ajna, and throat chakras. Energize them with some light whitish-green prana, followed by more ordinary light whitish-violet prana.
11. Stabilize and release the projected pranic energy.
12. Repeat treatment three times a week.

If treatment is done properly, the patient will usually experience improvement after a few treatments. But the pranic treatment has to be continued for several months. If the ailment is emotional in origin, it is advisable for the patient to release the hurt feelings and to forgive. This will facilitate the healing process.

Experienced, proficient, advanced pranic healers can apply localized sweeping alternately on the heart with light whitish-green and light whitish-orange. Apply the "cleansing the solar plexus chakra technique" to rapidly and thoroughly decongest the solar plexus chakra.

CONGENITAL HEART AILMENT

1. Scan the patient, then rescan during pranic treatment.
2. Apply general sweeping.
3. Apply localized sweeping on the front and back heart chakra. Energize the heart through the back heart chakra with light whitish-green then with light whitish-red prana. Experienced, proficient, advanced pranic healers may energize the heart through the back heart chakra with light whitish-green, with light whitish-orange, then with light whitish-red.
4. Apply more localized sweeping on the front heart chakra.
5. Apply localized sweeping thoroughly on the front and back solar plexus chakra and energize it with light whitish-green then with ordinary light whitish-violet.
6. Apply localized sweeping on the basic and navel chakras and energize them with light whitish-red prana.
7. Apply localized sweeping on the crown, forehead, ajna, and throat chakras. Energize them with less light whitish-green prana, then with more ordinary light whitish-violet prana.
8. Stabilize and release the projected pranic energy.
9. Repeat treatment several times a week for as long as necessary.

ARTERIOSCLEROSIS OR ATHEROSCLEROSIS

1. Scan the patient, then rescan during pranic treatment.
2. Apply general sweeping twice with light whitish-green prana.
3. Apply localized sweeping on all the major chakras and all the vital organs with light whitish-green prana.
4. Apply localized sweeping on the ajna, forehead, crown, and back head chakras. Energize them with light whitish-green, then with ordinary light whitish-violet.
5. Apply localized sweeping thoroughly on the jaw minor chakras, on the throat chakra, and on the secondary throat chakra. This is important. Energize them with light whitish-green, then with ordinary light whitish-violet.
6. Apply localized sweeping on the front and back heart chakra. Energize the heart through the back heart chakra with light whitish-

green prana, then with light whitish-red. Experienced, proficient, advanced pranic healers may use light whitish-orange.

7. Apply localized sweeping thoroughly on the lungs (front, side, and back). Energize them through the back of the lungs with light whitish-green, light whitish-orange, and light whitish-red.

This step is quite important since the light whitish-green prana and light whitish-orange prana will be absorbed by the blood passing through the lungs which will have a cleansing effect on the blood vessels throughout the body. The amount of light whitish-green and light whitish-orange prana that will be absorbed by the blood passing through the lungs will automatically be regulated by the body.

8. Apply localized sweeping thoroughly on the front and back solar plexus chakra and on the liver. Energize the solar plexus chakra with light whitish-green prana, light whitish-blue, then ordinary light whitish-violet.

Experienced, proficient, advanced pranic healers can apply the "cleansing the internal organs technique" (page 86). This has a rapid cleansing effect on the solar plexus chakra, the liver, and the other internal organs.

9. Apply localized sweeping thoroughly on the basic chakra, sex chakra, and navel chakra. Energize them with light whitish-red prana.
10. Apply localized sweeping on the arms and legs with light whitish-green and light whitish-orange. Energize the minor chakras in the arms and legs with light whitish-red.
11. Stabilize and release the projected pranic energy.
12. Repeat treatment twice a week for as long as necessary.

VARICOSE VEINS

The basic chakra is partially depleted. The legs and the minor chakras are quite dirty. The solar plexus chakra is usually affected.

1. Scan the patient, then rescan during pranic treatment.
2. Apply general sweeping twice.
3. Apply localized sweeping on the navel, sex and basic chakras. Energize them with light whitish-red prana.
4. Apply localized sweeping on the entire legs especially on the hip, knee, the minor chakras of the soles of the feet, and on the affected parts alternately with light whitish-green and light whitish-orange.

5. Energize the hip chakra, knee chakra, sole chakras, and the affected parts with light whitish-green then with ordinary light whitish-violet.

6. Apply localized sweeping thoroughly on the front and back solar plexus chakra and on the liver. Energize the solar plexus chakra with light whitish-green, light whitish-blue, then ordinary light whitish-violet.

7. Apply localized sweeping on the front and back heart chakra. Energize the back heart chakra with light whitish-green, then use more light whitish-red.

8. Stabilize and release the projected pranic energy.

9. Repeat treatment several times a week.

HYPERTENSION

The meng mein chakra controls the blood pressure. Its normal size is about 1/2 to 2/3 the average size of the other major chakras. Patients with hypertension have an overactivated meng mein chakra. If the size of the meng mein chakra is about 1:1 to the average size of the other chakras, then the patient is likely to have mild hypertension. If the ratio is more than 1:2, then the hypertension is rather severe. In other words, if the meng mein chakra is more than six inches and the other major chakras are about three inches in diameter, then the hypertension is severe. The meng mein chakra may be congested or depleted.

Patients with hypertension usually have a congested and overactivated solar plexus chakra which causes the meng mein chakra to become overactivated. The solar plexus chakra and the meng mein chakra are filled with dirty red pranic energy. To heal hypertension, the solar plexus chakra and the meng mein chakra must first be cleansed thoroughly and then inhibited by using light blue prana. Thorough localized sweeping has a gradual normalizing effect on the overactivated solar plexus and meng mein chakras. Inhibiting with blue prana without cleansing will not produce a lasting result. This is because, after a short period, the chakras will tend to overactivate again.

The spine and the head areas must also be treated since they are filled with dirty red pranic energy.

The spleen chakra is very closely connected with the meng mein chakra. If the spleen chakra is activated, then the meng mein chakra will become partially more activated. This is why it is not advisable to energize the spleen chakra of a hypertensive patient. The navel chakra of a hypertensive patient should not be overenergized since it is also closely connected to the spleen chakra and the meng mein chakra.

Hypertension may be physically caused by malfunctioning kidneys or by other external factors. In most cases, the cause or causes are not medically known; these are called essential hypertension. It can be controlled but is supposed to be "medically incurable." From the pranic healing viewpoint, essential hypertension is caused by the overactivation of the meng mein chakra which is usually caused by the overactivation of the solar plexus chakra. In other words, essential hypertension is predominantly of emotional origin. Through repeated pranic treatments, the patient's blood pressure can be normalized.

1. Scan the patient, then rescan during treatment. Scan the meng mein chakra frontally to determine the degree of pranic congestion, and then scan it sideways to determine the size or degree of overactivation. Apply the same scanning procedure on the solar plexus chakra. Scan the other chakras for comparison.
2. Apply general sweeping two or three times.
3. Apply localized sweeping on the entire head area, especially the back part and the spine. These areas are grayish-red.
4. Apply localized sweeping thoroughly on the front and back solar plexus chakra and the meng mein chakra. Rescan them frontally and sideways. By cleansing these two chakras thoroughly, blood pressure will gradually normalize. This step is very important.
5. Inhibit the meng mein chakra by energizing with light blue prana and simultaneously will the meng mein chakra to become smaller to about 1/2 the average size of the other chakras. Rescan the meng mein chakra. Once the meng mein chakra has been successfully inhibited, blood pressure will rapidly drop.
6. Inhibit the solar plexus chakra by energizing it with light blue prana and simultaneously will it to become smaller to about the average size of the other chakras. The solar plexus chakra should not be overinhibited since it will weaken the patient. Rescan the solar plexus chakra.
7. Steps 4 to 6 may have to be repeated after one or two hours since there is a possibility that the solar plexus chakra and meng mein chakra may overactivate again.
8. Apply localized sweeping on the front and back heart chakra. Energize the back heart chakra with light whitish-green, then with more ordinary light whitish-violet. Simultaneously visualize the

heart chakra becoming bigger. This will help normalize blood pressure and will also induce a sense of inner peace.

9. Apply more localized sweeping on the head area. To ensure that the blood vessels in the brain area remain pliable and strong, slightly energize the crown chakra, forehead chakra, ajna chakra, and back head minor chakra with light whitish-green prana, light whitish-blue prana, then light whitish-violet prana. Green is for cleansing, blue is for pliability, and ordinary violet is for strengthening. Do not overenergize the head. Rescan the head area and apply more sweeping.

10. Apply localized sweeping thoroughly on the jaw minor chakras, throat chakra, and secondary throat minor chakra. This is important. Energize them with less light whitish-green and with more ordinary light whitish-violet.

11. The basic chakra is partially affected. Apply localized sweeping thoroughly and energize it slightly with white prana.

12. Stabilize and release the projected pranic energy.

13. Repeat treatment several times a week if necessary. Instruct the patient to consult his or her physician to determine whether medication can be reduced or stopped.

HYPOTENSION

1. Scan the patient, especially on the meng mein, basic, solar plexus and ajna chakras. Rescan during treatment.

2. Apply general sweeping twice, with emphasis on the spine.

3. Apply localized sweeping on the meng mein chakra, and energize it with light whitish-red prana. Simultaneously, will the chakra to become bigger to about 1/2 to 2/3 the average size of the other major chakras. After several treatments, light red prana can be used on the meng mein chakra. Slightly stabilize it with very light whitish-blue. Stabilizing is necessary, otherwise the red prana will leak out and the meng mein chakra will become small again. Only a little light whitish-blue prana should be used, since too much blue prana will inhibit the meng mein chakra.

4. Apply localized sweeping on the basic chakra and energize it with white prana.

5. Apply localized sweeping on the solar plexus chakra, throat chakra, ajna chakra, and back head minor chakra. Energize them with light

whitish-green prana, then with more of ordinary light whitish-violet prana.

6. Stabilize and release the projected pranic energy.
7. Repeat treatment several times a week.

STROKE

Stroke could be caused by the blocking of a blood vessel in the brain due to progressive narrowing of the cerebral arteries, or by cerebral hemorrhage due to high blood pressure.

In cases of the progressive narrowing of cerebral arteries, the crown chakra, forehead chakra, ajna chakra, back head minor chakra, jaw minor chakras, throat chakra, solar plexus chakra, the liver, and basic chakra are affected. The emphasis is to thoroughly cleanse the back head minor chakra, jaw minor chakras, and throat chakra, since they affect the carotid arteries which supply blood to the brain. Malfunctioning of the solar plexus chakra may cause the throat chakra, jaw minor chakra(s), and the back minor chakra to malfunction. In other words, prolonged negative emotion may adversely affect the cerebral arteries.

It is important to clean thoroughly the affected part and the entire brain, especially the middle region of the brain where the motor area is located for it is usually affected. The affected part is congested and can be located by scanning. In some instances, just cleansing the affected part and the entire head area thoroughly, and cleansing and energizing the back head minor chakra, jaw minor chakras, and throat chakra will produce noticeable improvement.

Treatment for stroke due to the blocking of a cerebral blood vessel:

1. Scan the patient, especially on the crown chakra, forehead chakra, ajna chakra, back head minor chakra, jaw minor chakras, throat chakra, secondary throat minor chakra, solar plexus chakra, the liver, and the basic chakra. Rescan the patient during treatment.
2. Apply general sweeping two or three times.
3. Apply localized sweeping on the affected part and on the entire head area alternately with light whitish-green and ordinary light whitish-violet. Sweeping has to be done thoroughly. Rescan. Green prana has cleansing and dissolving effects.
4. Apply localized sweeping thoroughly on the crown chakra, forehead chakra, ajna chakra, and back head minor chakra. Energize them with whitish-green prana, then ordinary light whitish-violet

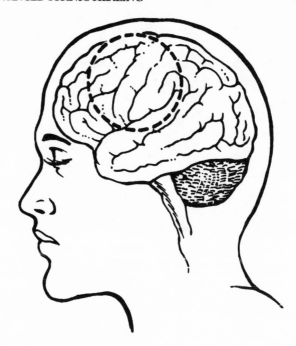

Figure 9-3. Middle region of the brain.

prana. Rescan and apply more localized sweeping. This step is quite important.

5. Apply localized sweeping on the entire neck area. Apply localized sweeping on the jaw minor chakras, throat chakra, and the secondary throat chakra. Energize them with light whitish-green prana, then with ordinary light whitish-violet prana. This step is quite important since the jaw minor chakras affect the left and right carotid arteries which supply blood to the brain and the head. The condition of the throat chakra and secondary throat chakras affect the health of the jaw minor chakras.

6. Apply localized sweeping on the spine alternately with light whitish-green and ordinary light whitish-violet. If the left side of the brain is affected, then the emphasis is on the right side of the spine. If the right side of the brain is affected, then the emphasis is on the left side of the spine.

7. Apply localized sweeping on the lungs. Energize them through the back of the lungs with light whitish-green, light whitish-orange, and light whitish-red. This has cleansing and dilating effects on the arteries. This step is important. When energizing the

lungs with orange prana, the healer's fingers should be pointed away from the patient's head.

8. Apply localized sweeping on the front and back heart chakra. Energize the heart through the back heart chakra with light whitish-green, then with ordinary light whitish-violet.

9. Apply localized sweeping thoroughly on the front and back solar plexus chakra, and on the liver. Cleansing the solar plexus chakra thoroughly is very important. Energize the solar plexus chakra with light whitish-green, light whitish-blue, then ordinary light whitish-violet.

10. Apply localized sweeping on the basic and navel chakra, and energize them with light whitish-red prana. This is to strengthen the body.

11. Apply localized sweeping on the sex chakra and energize it with light whitish-red prana. This will help strengthen the legs.

12. If the leg is affected, apply localized sweeping on the entire affected leg, the hip, knee, and sole minor chakras alternately with light whitish-green prana and light whitish-orange prana. Energize the hip, knee, and sole minor chakra with light whitish-green; then use more light whitish-red prana.

13. If the arm is affected, apply localized sweeping alternately with light whitish-green prana and light whitish-orange prana on the entire affected arm, the armpit, elbow, and hand minor chakras. Energize the armpit, elbow, and hand minor chakras with light whitish-green then with more light whitish-red prana for strengthening effects and for improving circulation.

14. Stabilize and release the projected pranic energy.

15. Repeat treatment three times a week. The patient is expected to undergo complementary physical therapy. The result is quite varied; some will improve very fast and some will improve slowly.

Steps 4 to 10 can be used as preventive treatment for this type of stroke.

Treatment for stroke caused by cerebral hemorrhage due to high blood pressure:

1. Scan the patient, then rescan during pranic treatment.

2. Apply general sweeping two or three times.

3. If blood pressure is still unstable, apply localized sweeping thoroughly on the meng mein chakra and the solar plexus chakra. Inhibit the meng mein chakra by energizing it with light blue prana, and simultaneously will it to become smaller to about 1/2 the average size of the other chakras.

4. Apply localized sweeping on the affected part and on the entire head area alternately with light whitish-green and ordinary light whitish-violet. Sweeping has to be done thoroughly. Rescan. Green prana has cleansing and dissolving effects. If the right part of the body is affected, then the left part of the brain should be treated and vice versa.

5. Apply localized sweeping thoroughly on the crown chakra, forehead chakra, ajna chakra, and back head minor chakra; and energize them with whitish-green prana, then ordinary light whitish-violet prana. Rescan and apply more localized sweeping.

6. Apply localized sweeping on the entire neck area. Apply localized sweeping on the jaw minor chakras, the throat chakra, and the secondary throat chakra. Energize them with light whitish-green prana, then with ordinary light whitish-violet prana.

7. Apply localized sweeping on the spine alternately with light whitish-green and ordinary light whitish-violet. If the left brain is affected, then the emphasis is on the right side of the spine. If the right side of the brain is affected, then the emphasis is on the left side of the spine.

8. Apply localized sweeping on the lungs. Energize them through the back of the lungs with light whitish-green, light whitish-orange, and light whitish-red. This has cleansing and dilating effects on the arteries. This step is important. When energizing the lungs with orange prana, the healer's fingers should be pointed away from the patient's head.

9. Apply localized sweeping on the front and back heart chakra. Energize the heart through the back heart chakra with whitish-green prana, then with light whitish-red.

10. Apply localized sweeping thoroughly on the front and back solar plexus chakra and on the liver. Energize the solar plexus chakra with light whitish-green, light whitish-blue, and ordinary light whitish-violet.

11. Apply localized sweeping on the basic and navel chakras, and energize them with light whitish-red prana. This is to strengthen the body. If the blood pressure is still not stabilized, it is safer not to energize them.

12. Apply localized sweeping on the sex chakra, and energize it with light whitish-red prana. This will help strengthen the legs.

13. If the leg is affected, apply localized sweeping on the entire affected leg, on the hip, knee, and sole minor chakras alternately with light whitish-green prana and light whitish-orange prana.

Energize the hip, knee, and sole minor chakras with light whitish-green; then use more light whitish-red prana.

14. If the arm is affected, apply localized sweeping on the entire affected arm, on the armpit, elbow, and hand minor chakras alternately with light whitish-green prana and light whitish-orange prana. Energize the armpit, elbow, and hand minor chakras with light whitish-green; then use more light whitish-red prana for strengthening effects and for improving circulation.

15. Stabilize and release the projected pranic energy.

16. Repeat treatment three times a week The patient is expected to undergo complementary physical therapy. With some patients, the effect is quite dramatic. But the result varies according to the condition and receptivity of the patient and the skill of the healer.

Respiratory Ailments

RESPIRATORY SYSTEM

The respiratory system is controlled and energized by the ajna chakra, the throat chakra, the back heart chakra and the solar plexus chakra. The ajna chakra controls and energizes the nose. The throat chakra and the secondary throat minor chakra control and energize the trachea or air tube. The back heart chakra controls and energizes the bronchial tubes and the lungs. The solar plexus chakra controls and energizes the diaphragm, which is in turn responsible for the movements of the lungs. It also substantially energizes the lower lungs. Emotional problems or stress may cause the solar plexus chakra to become congested, thereby adversely affecting the diaphragm and resulting in breathing difficulty.

The left lung has two minor chakras located at the back of the lung: the left upper lung minor chakra and the left lower lung minor chakra. The right lung has three minor chakras located at the back of the right lung: the right upper lung minor chakra, the right middle lung minor chakra and the right lower lung minor chakra.

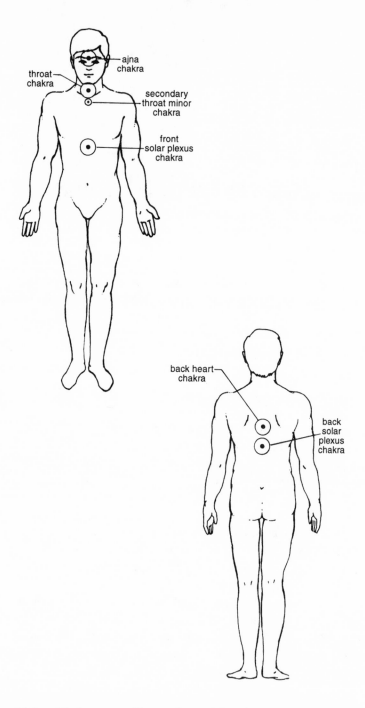

Figure 10-1.   Chakras controlling and energizing the respiratory system.

CHRONIC SINUSITIS

If sinusitis is chronic and acute, the solar plexus chakra is usually congested with dirty red energy and is overactivated. Part of the dirty congested red energy goes to the ajna chakra, causing the nasal sinuses to be susceptible to infection and inflammation. In many instances, if not in most cases, chronic sinusitis is partly or predominantly caused by negative emotions.

1. Scan the patient, then rescan during pranic treatment.
2. Apply general sweeping twice.
3. Apply localized sweeping thoroughly on the front and back solar plexus chakra and on the liver. The liver is also dirty.
4. Energize the solar plexus chakra with light whitish-green, light whitish-blue, and ordinary light whitish-violet. Steps 3 and 4 are quite important. Once the solar plexus chakra normalizes, the patient will be gradually healed of sinusitis.
5. Apply localized sweeping on the front and back heart chakra. Energize the back heart chakra with light whitish-green; then use ordinary light whitish-violet. Visualize the heart chakra becoming bigger. This is to produce a sense of inner peace and to help the patient regulate the lower emotions.
6. Apply localized sweeping thoroughly on the ajna chakra, on the forehead, and on the cheeks.
7. Energize the ajna chakra with light whitish-green, light whitish-blue, then ordinary light whitish-violet. Apply more localized sweeping. Repeat Steps 6 and 7 until the patient is substantially relieved.
8. Apply localized sweeping and energizing on the basic and navel chakras with white prana. This is to stimulate the body's defense mechanism and to strengthen the body.
9. Stabilize and release the projected pranic energy.
10. Repeat the treatment two to three times a week.
11. If the treatment is done properly, the patient will be relieved immediately. In general, chronic sinusitis can be cured through repeated pranic treatment.

CHRONIC COUGH

The solar plexus chakra, the throat chakra, and the secondary throat chakra are grayish-red. The basic chakra is partially depleted.

1. Scan the patient, then rescan during pranic treatment.
2. Apply general sweeping twice.

3. Apply localized sweeping thoroughly on the front and back solar plexus chakra and on the liver. Energize it with light whitish-green, light whitish-blue, then ordinary light whitish-violet prana.

4. Apply localized sweeping on the front and back heart chakra. Energize the back heart chakra with light whitish-green; then use ordinary light whitish-violet.

5. Apply localized sweeping thoroughly on the throat chakra, secondary throat minor chakra, and the jaw minor chakras. Energize them with light whitish-green, light whitish-blue, and ordinary light whitish-violet.

6. Apply localized sweeping on the ajna chakra. Energize it with light whitish-green, with light whitish-blue, then with ordinary light whitish-violet.

7. The lungs are usually affected to a certain degree. Apply localized sweeping thoroughly on the lungs and on the back heart chakra. Energize the lungs directly through the back of the lungs with light whitish-green and light whitish-orange. When energizing the lungs with orange prana, the healer's fingers should be pointed away from the patient's head.

8. Apply localized sweeping on the basic and navel chakras. Energize them with white prana or light whitish-red prana. This is to strengthen the immunity and defense system.

9. Stabilize and release the projected pranic energy.

10. Repeat treatment if necessary.

LUNG INFECTIONS: BRONCHITIS, INFLUENZA, AND PNEUMONIA

1. Scan the patient, then rescan during pranic treatment.

2. Apply general sweeping twice.

3. Apply localized sweeping thoroughly on the front and back solar plexus chakra and on the liver. Cleansing the solar plexus chakra is very important since it will facilitate bringing down the fever.

4. Energize the solar plexus chakra with light whitish-green prana then with light whitish-blue prana. Energizing the solar plexus chakra without cleansing it thoroughly may cause the fever to increase temporarily.

5. To facilitate the expelling of diseased energy, energize the front solar plexus chakra with light whitish-orange prana. This step is to be used by experienced, proficient, advanced pranic healers.

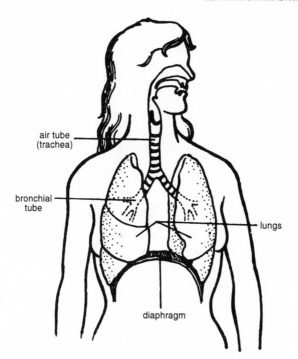

Figure 10-2. Respiratory system.

6. Apply localized sweeping on the front and back heart chakra. Energize the back heart chakra with light whitish-green then with ordinary light whitish-violet.

7. Apply localized sweeping thoroughly on the lungs and on the back heart chakra. Energize the lungs directly through the back of the lungs with light whitish-green, with light whitish-orange, then with ordinary light whitish-violet. When energizing the lungs with orange prana, the healer's fingers should be pointed away from the patient's head.

8. Apply localized sweeping on the ajna, throat, and secondary throat chakras. Energize them with light whitish-green, with light whitish-blue, then with ordinary light whitish-violet.

9. Apply localized sweeping on the front and back spleen chakra. Energize the spleen chakra with white prana. This should be done with caution.

10. Apply localized sweeping on the navel chakra and basic chakra. Energize the navel chakra with white prana.

11. Apply localized sweeping on the arms and legs. Apply localized sweeping on the hand and sole minor chakras, and energize them

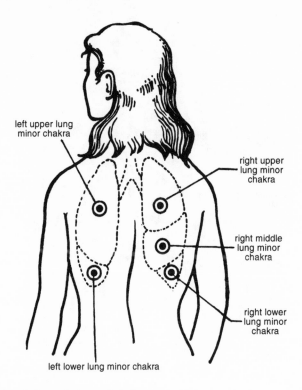

Figure 10-3. Minor chakras of the lungs.

with ordinary light whitish-violet prana. Visualize pranic energy going into the bones. This is to stimulate the defense system of the body. It is preferable not to energize the bones with ordinary violet prana more than once a day since it may have a reverse reaction.

12. Step 2 through Step 9 can be repeated several times a day if needed.
13. Stabilize and release the projected pranic energy.
14. Pneumonia is a serious ailment; therefore, the patient should have complementary medical treatment.

TUBERCULOSIS

1. Scan the patient, then rescan during pranic treatment.
2. Apply general sweeping twice.

3. Apply localized sweeping on the front and back heart chakra. Energize the back heart chakra with light whitish-green; then use ordinary light whitish-violet.
4. Apply localized sweeping on the lungs thoroughly and alternately with light whitish-green and light whitish-orange. Apply localized sweeping on the back heart chakra.
5. Energize the lungs directly through the back of the lungs with light whitish-green, light whitish-orange prana, and ordinary light whitish-violet. When energizing the lungs with orange prana, the healer's fingers should be pointed away from the patient's head.
6. Apply localized sweeping thoroughly on the front and back solar plexus chakra. Energize it with light whitish-green then with ordinary light whitish-violet.
7. Apply the Master Healing Technique to further hasten the rate of healing (see page 91).
8. Or, apply localized sweeping on the basic chakra and the navel chakra. Energize them with light whitish-red prana. Apply localized sweeping on the front and back spleen chakra and energize it with white prana.
9. Apply localized sweeping on the throat chakra and ajna chakra. Energize them with light whitish-green, then with ordinary light whitish-violet.
10. Stabilize and release the projected pranic energy.
11. Repeat treatment three times a week.

ASTHMA

In patients with asthma the throat chakra, the secondary throat chakra, the back heart chakra and the basic chakra are affected. The air tubes are constricted. Sometimes, asthma is caused by emotional factors. The solar plexus chakra is congested. If the patient is not able to express freely due to relationship problems, the trachea or the windpipe will most likely be constricted. If the ailment is emotional in origin, then the congested solar plexus chakra must be cleansed thoroughly.

If the cause of asthma is physical in origin, the rate of healing will usually be quite fast. If the cause of asthma is emotional in origin, then the rate of healing will usually take more time. There is a need for the patient to release pent-up emotions.

1. Scan the patient, then rescan during pranic treatment.
2. Apply general sweeping twice.

3. Apply localized sweeping thoroughly on the throat chakra and secondary throat minor chakra. The secondary throat minor chakra is located on the lower soft portion of the throat. Energize them with light whitish-green; then use light whitish-red. Red prana has a dilating effect on the air tube.

4. Apply localized sweeping on the lungs with light whitish-green then light whitish-orange. Energize the lungs directly through the back of the lungs with light whitish-green, with light whitish-orange, then with light whitish-red. Orange prana has an expelling effect which hastens the dilating and strengthening effects of the red prana. If Steps 3 and 4 are done properly, the patient will be quickly relieved.

5. Apply localized sweeping thoroughly on the front and back solar plexus chakra and on the liver. Energize them with light whitish-green, then with ordinary light whitish-violet prana. It is very important to clean the solar plexus chakra thoroughly if the cause of asthma is emotional in origin.

6. If the asthma is emotional in origin, activate the heart chakra. Apply localized sweeping on the front and back heart chakra. Energize the heart chakra through the back heart chakra with light whitish-green, and ordinary light whitish-violet. This is to produce a sense of inner peace and to help the patient regulate the lower emotions.

7. To gradually and permanently heal the patient, clean the basic chakra and energize it with light whitish-red prana. Clean the ajna chakra and energize it with light whitish-green; then use more ordinary light whitish-violet.

8. To further improve the quality of the blood produced, apply localized sweeping on the arms and legs. Energize the hand and sole minor chakras with light whitish-red prana. Visualize the pranic energy going inside the bones.

9. Stabilize and release the projected pranic energy.

10. Repeat treatment three times a week for about a month or two.

11. If treatment is applied properly, the patient will be relieved rapidly. Pranic healing is very effective in curing asthma.

EMPHYSEMA

1. Scan the patient, then rescan during pranic treatment.
2. Apply general sweeping twice.

3. Apply localized sweeping on the front and back heart chakra and energize the heart through the back heart chakra with light whitish-green; then use light whitish-red prana. This is to strengthen the physical heart.

4. Apply localized sweeping thoroughly on the lungs with light whitish-green then with light whitish-orange. The emphasis should be on the sides and the lower portions of the lungs.

5. Energize the lungs directly through the back of the lungs with light whitish-green, light whitish-orange, then light whitish-red. Green and orange pranas have cleansing effects. Orange facilitates the expelling of the old air in the lungs. The interaction of red prana with green and orange pranas has a regenerating effect. When energizing the lungs with orange prana, the healer's fingers should be pointed away from the patient's head.

6. Apply localized sweeping on the front and back solar plexus chakra thoroughly. Energize the front solar plexus chakra with white prana.

7. Apply localized sweeping on the basic and navel chakras, and energize them with light whitish-red. This is to strengthen the body and to facilitate the healing process.

8. Or use the Master Healing Technique (page 91) to greatly hasten the healing process. Since the patients are usually elderly, just use white prana on the basic chakra and the meng mein chakra.

9. Stabilize and release the projected pranic energy.

10. Treatment can be done several times for the first few days. Then repeat treatment at least three times a week for about five months or for as long as necessary.

11. If pranic treatment is applied properly, the patient will be partially relieved after a few treatments. In general, emphysema can be cured through prolonged pranic treatment.

Gastrointestinal Ailments

THE DIGESTIVE, ASSIMILATIVE, AND ELIMINATIVE SYSTEM

This system is controlled and energized by the throat chakra, solar plexus chakra, and navel chakra. The throat chakra, secondary throat chakra, and jaw minor chakras control and energize the mouth, salivary glands and esophagus. The solar plexus and navel chakras control and energize the gastrointestinal system. The solar plexus chakra controls and energizes the liver, pancreas, and stomach. The navel chakra controls and energizes the small and large intestines. Gastrointestinal ailments can be treated by just cleansing and energizing the solar plexus chakra and navel chakra. White prana or color pranas can be used when energizing.

The liver has three minor chakras: the upper right liver minor chakra, the upper left liver minor chakra, and the lower right liver minor chakra. The lower right liver minor chakra also controls and energizes the gall bladder, which has a corresponding gall bladder mini-chakra. The stomach has a corresponding stomach minor chakra. The pancreas has a corresponding pancreas minor chakra. The small intestine has a corresponding minor chakra, one small intestine mini-chakra for about every three feet. The large intestine has a corresponding minor chakra, one large intestine mini-chakra

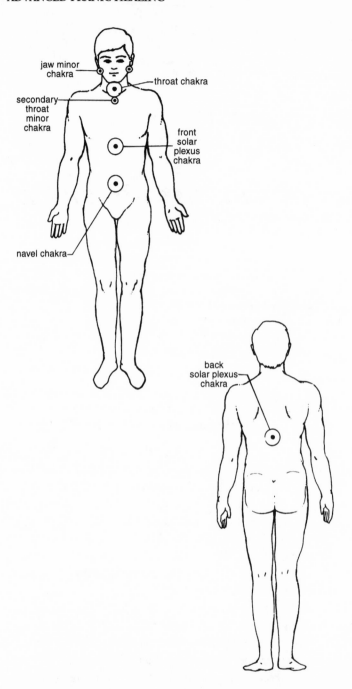

Figure 11-1. *Chakras controlling and energizing the gastrointestinal system.*

for about every three feet. The appendix has a corresponding appendix mini-chakra. The anus also has an anus minor chakra.

DIFFICULTY SWALLOWING

1. Scan the patient, then rescan during pranic treatment.
2. Apply localized sweeping thoroughly on the entire neck, the throat chakra, and the secondary throat chakra.
3. Energize the throat chakra and secondary throat chakra with light whitish-green then with ordinary light whitish-violet.
4. Apply localized sweeping thoroughly on the front and back solar plexus chakra and energize with light whitish-green, light whitish-blue, and ordinary light whitish-violet.
5. Stabilize and release the projected pranic energy.
6. Repeat treatment if necessary.

VOMITING AND DIARRHEA

Vomiting and loose bowel movements could be caused by infection or inflammation of the gastrointestinal system. Stress or fear may cause loose bowel movements.

1. Scan the patient, then rescan during pranic treatment.
2. Apply localized sweeping thoroughly on the front and back solar plexus chakra, the navel chakra, and on the upper and lower abdominal area. In many cases, the patient will be relieved by just receiving a thorough cleansing.
3. Energize the solar plexus chakra and the navel chakra with light whitish-green, light whitish-blue, and ordinary light whitish-violet. Apply more localized sweeping.
4. Stabilize and release the projected pranic energy.
5. Repeat treatment three to four times a day if necessary. Usually, one to two treatments will be enough.

With infants or small children, vomiting is sometimes caused by throat irritation; therefore, the throat chakra and the secondary throat minor chakra have to be treated.

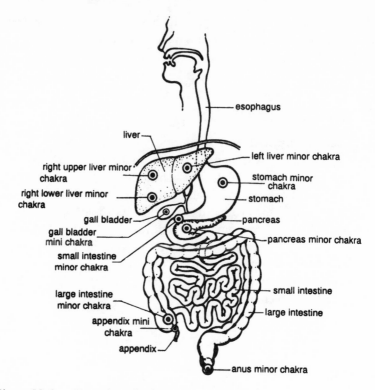

Figure 11-2.   Gastrointestinal system.

CONSTIPATION

1. Scan the patient, then rescan during pranic treatment.
2. Apply localized sweeping thoroughly on the front and back solar plexus chakra, the navel chakra, and on the abdominal area.
3. Energize the solar plexus chakra with light whitish green then with light whitish-red. Apply more localized sweeping.
4. Energize the navel chakra with light whitish-green, light whitish-orange, then light whitish-red. Apply more localized sweeping. Green has a cleansing effect. Orange has an eliminative effect. Red has a strengthening effect.
5. Apply localized sweeping on the basic chakra, and energize it with light whitish-red prana.
6. Stabilize and release the projected pranic energy.

ABDOMINAL PAIN

1. Scan the patient, then rescan during pranic treatment.
2. Apply localized sweeping thoroughly on the front and back solar plexus chakra, the navel chakra, and on the upper and lower abdominal areas. In many cases, the patient will be relieved by just thorough cleansing.
3. Energize the solar plexus chakra and the navel chakra with light whitish-green, light whitish-blue, and ordinary light whitish-violet. Apply more localized sweeping.
4. Stabilize and release the projected pranic energy.
5. One or two pranic treatments will usually be sufficient. If symptoms persist, instruct the patient to consult a medical doctor, and an advanced pranic healer.

INDIGESTION

Indigestion could be caused by physical or emotional factors. Shock, grief, or inability to cope with the stressful demands of life may cause indigestion.

1. Scan the patient, then rescan during pranic treatment.
2. Apply localized sweeping thoroughly on the front and back solar plexus chakra and on the navel chakra.
3. Energize the solar plexus chakra and navel chakra with light whitish-green then with ordinary light whitish-violet. Apply more localized sweeping.
4. Apply localized sweeping on the front and back heart chakra, energize the heart chakra through the back heart chakra with light whitish-green; then use more ordinary light whitish-violet.
5. Stabilize and release the projected pranic energy.

GASTROINTESTINAL ULCER

In patients suffering from gastrointestinal ulcers the solar plexus chakra is filled with diseased red energy. The navel chakra is partially affected. In many instances, if not in most cases, this is due to emotional factors.

A peptic ulcer is an ulceration of the stomach or of the duodenal lining. An ulceration of the stomach lining is called a gastric ulcer, while an ulceration of the duodenum lining is called a duodenal ulcer.

1. Scan the patient, then rescan during pranic treatment.
2. Apply general sweeping.

3. Apply localized sweeping thoroughly on the front and back solar plexus chakra, on the stomach and small intestine, and on the navel chakra. Cleansing has to be done thoroughly before energizing.
4. Energize the solar plexus chakra and navel chakra with light whitish-blue then with ordinary light whitish-violet. Apply alternately localized sweeping and energizing on the affected part until the patient is relieved.
5. Apply localized sweeping on the front and back heart chakra. Energize the heart chakra through the back heart chakra with light whitish-green prana then with ordinary light whitish-violet prana. This is to activate the heart chakra to produce a sense of inner peace.
6. Apply localized sweeping on the basic chakra, and energize it with light whitish-red prana. This is to further hasten the rate of healing.
7. Stabilize and release the projected energy.
8. Repeat treatment two to three times a week.

In more severe cases, and if the pain is quite intense, energize the solar plexus chakra and the stomach with light whitish-blue prana. Apply localized sweeping several times with light whitish-green, then use light whitish-orange. Then apply more localized sweeping with white prana. This will hasten the relief by facilitating the removal of the diseased red energy. Ordinary localized sweeping will take a long time just to remove the diseased red energy thoroughly. This step should be used only by experienced, proficient, advanced pranic healers, and only when it is really necessary.

HEMORRHOIDS

In patients suffering from painful hemorrhoids the solar plexus chakra and navel chakra are partially dirty and have too much red prana. The anus minor chakra is usually congested with grayish red prana. Red prana has an expansive or dilating effect. In many cases, painful hemorrhoids is a stress-related ailment.

1. Scan the patient, then rescan during pranic treatment.
2. Apply general sweeping.
3. Apply localized sweeping on the front and back solar plexus chakra, the navel chakra, and on the abdominal area, especially on the large intestines.

4. Energize the solar plexus chakra and the navel chakra with light whitish-green, light whitish-blue, then ordinary light whitish-violet. Apply more localized sweeping.
5. If the anus is affected, apply localized sweeping thoroughly on the anus. Energize it with light whitish-green prana then light whitish-blue prana.
6. Apply localized sweeping on the front and back heart chakra. Energize the heart chakra through the back heart chakra with some light whitish-green prana and follow with more ordinary light whitish-violet prana. This is to activate the heart chakra to produce a sense of inner peace.
7. Stabilize and release the projected pranic energy.
8. Repeat treatment twice or three times a week. The patient is expected to keep proper hygiene by washing the anus after bowel movements. Spicy foods should be avoided.

HERNIA

A hernia is a bulge or protrusion in the lower abdomen due to a weakened or ruptured abdominal wall. There are several types of hernia. In umbilical hernias, common in babies, the protrusion occurs in the navel area. In incisional hernias, the bulge occurs in the abdominal scar area. In inguinal hernias, the protrusion occurs in the area where the thigh joins the abdomen, and it may tend to go into the scrotum.

In patients with hernias, the navel and the sex chakras are partially affected. The affected part is dirty red.

1. Scan the patient, then rescan during pranic treatment.
2. Apply localized sweeping thoroughly on the navel, sex, and basic chakras. Energize them with white prana.
3. Apply localized sweeping thoroughly on the affected part. Energize the affected part with light whitish-green, light whitish-blue, light whitish-yellow, then with ordinary light whitish-violet. Green prana has cleansing effects. Blue prana has a contracting effect and gives pliability. Yellow prana is necessary for strong tissues. Violet prana has the properties of all the color pranas.
4. Stabilize and release the projected pranic energy.
5. Repeat treatment two to three times a week.

HIGH CHOLESTEROL

In patients with high cholesterol the solar plexus chakra is congested and the liver is grayish-red. The liver controls the cholesterol level of the body. The navel chakra is usually affected. In many cases, this ailment is also stress-related.

1. Scan the patient, then rescan during pranic treatment.
2. Apply general sweeping.
3. Apply localized sweeping thoroughly on the front and back solar plexus chakra and the liver. This is important.
4. Energize the solar plexus chakra with light whitish-green, light whitish-blue, then with ordinary light whitish-violet. The emphasis of the treatment is on Steps 3 and 4.
5. Apply localized sweeping on the basic and navel chakras. Energize them with light whitish-red.
6. Apply localized sweeping on the front and back heart chakra. Energize the heart chakra through the back heart chakra with less light whitish-green prana; then use more ordinary light whitish-violet prana. This is to activate the heart chakra to produce a sense of inner peace.
7. Apply localized sweeping on the crown chakra, forehead chakra, ajna chakra, back head minor chakra, and throat chakra. Energize them with light whitish-green; then use more ordinary light whitish-violet.
8. Stabilize and release the projected pranic energy.
9. Repeat treatment three times a week for as long as necessary.

GASTROINTESTINAL INFECTIONS

1. Scan the patient, then rescan during pranic treatment.
2. Apply general sweeping twice or more.
3. Apply localized sweeping thoroughly on the front and back solar plexus chakra, on the liver, on the navel chakra, and on the abdominal area. The solar plexus chakra has to be thoroughly swept. Thorough cleansing is very important before energizing. Otherwise, there will be a radical reaction. The fever may go up or the pain and the loose bowel movements may become worse.
4. Energize the solar plexus chakra and the navel chakra with light whitish-green, light whitish-blue, and ordinary light whitish-violet. Apply more localized sweeping. If there is intestinal bleeding,

it is preferable not to energize the solar plexus and navel chakra with green prana because if the energizing with green prana is not done properly, it may cause more bleeding. Energizing has to be done gently. If energizing is done too willfully, it may cause more bleeding. The emphasis of the treatment is from Steps 2 to 4.

5. Apply localized sweeping on the front and back heart chakra. Energize the thymus through the back heart chakra with light whitish-green; then use more ordinary light whitish-violet.
6. Apply localized sweeping thoroughly on the lungs. Energize them directly through the back of the lungs with light whitish-green then with light whitish-orange. It will facilitate the healing process since this has a cleansing effect on the blood and on the entire body. When energizing the lungs with orange prana, the healer's fingers should be pointed away from the patient's head.
7. Apply localized sweeping thoroughly on the spleen chakra, and energize it with white prana. The physical spleen helps fight infection. With infants, children, or patients with hypertension, just energize the spleen chakra slightly or do not energize it at all.
8. Apply localized sweeping on the crown chakra, forehead chakra, ajna chakra, back head minor chakra, and throat chakra. Energize them with light whitish-green; then use more ordinary light violet.
9. Apply localized sweeping thoroughly on the basic chakra.
10. Apply localized sweeping on the arms and legs, and their minor chakras. Energize the minor chakras of the hands and the soles of the feet with ordinary light whitish-violet. This is to enhance the defense system of the body. It is preferable not to repeat this treatment more than once a day because of a possible reverse reaction.
11. Stabilize and release the projected pranic energy.
12. Repeat pranic treatment three times a day if necessary.

ACUTE APPENDICITIS

In patients with acute appendicitis the solar plexus chakra and the navel chakra are both affected. The navel chakra controls and energizes the large intestine including the appendix. The appendix is dirty red and dirty green. The solar plexus chakra also affects and energizes the large intestine, including the appendix. This is why the pain may initially be felt on the solar plexus area before going down to the appendix. The spleen chakra is grayish. The basic chakra is depleted. The whole body is affected and grayish.

1. Scan the patient, then rescan during pranic treatment.
2. Apply general sweeping several times.
3. Apply localized sweeping thoroughly on the front and back solar plexus chakra, on the liver, on the navel chakra, on the abdominal area, and on the appendix with light whitish-green. The emphasis is on thorough sweeping on the appendix.
4. Energize the solar plexus chakra and the navel chakra with light whitish-green, light whitish-blue, then with ordinary light whitish-violet. Apply more localized sweeping. The solar plexus chakra has to be cleansed thoroughly. Otherwise the fever may go up.
5. Apply localized sweeping on the appendix thoroughly and alternately with light whitish-green and ordinary light whitish-violet. Energize it with light whitish-green, light whitish-blue, then with ordinary light whitish-violet. Apply localized sweeping and energizing alternately on the appendix until there is substantial relief. Do not use orange prana on the inflamed appendix since this may rupture the appendix.
6. Apply localized sweeping thoroughly on the lungs. Energize them directly through the back of the lungs with light whitish-green; then use light whitish-orange. This will facilitate the healing process and has a cleansing effect on the blood and on the entire body. When energizing the lungs with orange prana, the healer's fingers should be pointed away from the patient's head.
7. Apply localized sweeping thoroughly on the spleen chakra and energize it with light whitish-green; then use ordinary light whitish-violet. The physical spleen helps fight infection. With infants, children, or patients with hypertension, just energize the spleen chakra slightly or do not energize it at all.
8. Apply localized sweeping on the basic chakra. Do nor energize it since this may cause the fever to go up.
9. Apply localized sweeping on the arms and legs, and their minor chakras. Energize the hands and sole minor chakras with ordinary light whitish-violet. Visualize the pranic energy going inside the bones. This enhances the defense system of the body. Do not repeat this step more than once a day since it may result in a reverse reaction.
10. Apply localized sweeping on the crown chakra, forehead chakra, ajna chakra, back head minor chakra, and throat chakra. Energize them with light whitish-green then with ordinary light whitish-violet.
11. Stabilize and release the projected pranic energy.

12. The emphasis of the treatment is on Steps 3, 4, and 5. Repeat pranic treatment after two or three hours since the rate of pranic consumption is very fast. Pranic treatment should be done about three to four times in the first few days. The number of treatments can be reduced once the condition has improved and stabilized. Patients should preferably be hospitalized in case a surgical operation is needed. Not all acute appendicitis can be cured by pranic healing, especially if it is several days old.

Patients who have recently been healed should avoid heavy or strenuous exercises for the next few months. Heavy meals should also be avoided. They should have daily bowel movements and should go back for further treatment if they experience slight pain in the appendix area.

For chronic appendicitis, just apply localized sweeping thoroughly on the solar plexus chakra, navel chakra, and on the appendix. Energize them with light whitish-green, light whitish-blue, then ordinary light whitish-violet.

ACUTE PANCREATITIS

Acute pancreatitis is the severe inflammation of the pancreas. The patient feels intense pain on the solar plexus area and behind it. Fever, chill, cold sweat, vomiting, and headache are experienced. The patient is in a state of severe shock. This ailment is quite serious; the patient should receive proper medical treatment.

This manifests as a serious malfunctioning of the solar plexus chakra, and the entire etheric body is affected.

1. Scan the patient, then rescan during pranic treatment.
2. Apply general sweeping several times.
3. Apply localized sweeping thoroughly on the front and back solar plexus chakra, and on the pancreas. Energize the back solar plexus chakra with light whitish-blue then with ordinary light whitish-violet. Apply more localized sweeping. Blue prana soothes the pain and inhibits the pancreas from excreting more digestive juices. Avoid using yellow prana. This may further stimulate the pancreas to produce more juices, thereby making the patient worse.
4. Apply localized sweeping on the basic and navel chakras. Energize them with white prana to strengthen the body.
5. Apply localized sweeping on the crown chakra, forehead chakra, ajna chakra, back head minor chakra, and throat chakra. Energize them with ordinary light whitish-violet.

6. Stabilize and release the projected pranic energy.
7. Repeat treatment about three times a day for the next few days. The patient may experience substantial relief on the first day. The rate of healing is usually very fast.

GALLSTONES

1. Scan the patient, then rescan during pranic treatment.
2. Apply localized sweeping on the front and back solar plexus chakra, and on the liver. Energize the solar plexus chakra with light whitish-green, light whitish-blue, then with ordinary light whitish-violet.
3. Apply localized sweeping on the gall bladder alternately with light whitish-green and light whitish-orange. Sweeping has to be done thoroughly.
4. Energize the gall bladder with light blue, light green, then light orange prana. Green and orange pranas are used to dissolve gallstones. Blue prana is used to localize the green and orange pranas. The amount of blue prana projected should be about equal to the green and the orange prana projected.
5. Stabilize and release the projected pranic energy.
6. Repeat treatment three times a week for as long as necessary.

HEPATITIS

Inflammation of the liver, or hepatitis, can be caused by a virus or a prolonged period of excessive alcohol intake. Prolonged anger or stress causes the solar plexus chakra and the liver to malfunction and to become congested with dirty red energy which tends to make the liver susceptible to infection. Anger or stress tends to lower the body's pranic energy level and to cause some chakras to malfunction, thereby weakening the defense mechanism of the body.

1. Scan the patient, then rescan during pranic treatment.
2. Apply general sweeping several times.
3. Apply localized sweeping thoroughly on the front and back solar plexus chakra with whitish-green prana.

4. Apply localized sweeping on the liver (front, side and back) thoroughly and alternately with light whitish-green and light whitish-orange. This step will facilitate the cleansing and disinflaming of the liver. The orange prana used must be light whitish-orange or very light whitish-orange. Otherwise, it will cause loose bowel movements.

5. Energize the solar plexus chakra with light whitish-green, light whitish-blue, then ordinary light whitish-violet. Visualize the pranic energy going inside the liver.

6. Apply localized sweeping on the front and back heart chakra. Energize the thymus through the back heart chakra with light whitish-green then with ordinary light whitish-violet.

7. Apply localized sweeping thoroughly on the lungs. Energize them directly through the back of the lungs with light whitish-green; then use light whitish-orange. It will facilitate the healing process since this has a cleansing effect on the blood and on the entire body. When energizing the lungs with orange prana, the healer's fingers should be pointed away from the patient's head.

8. The spleen chakra is grayish and the physical spleen is partially affected. Apply localized sweeping on the front and back spleen chakra. Energize the spleen chakra with light whitish-green then with ordinary light whitish-violet. This has to be done with caution.

9. To further increase the pranic energy level of the body, clean and energize the navel chakra with white prana.

10. Apply localized sweeping on the basic chakra.

11. Apply localized sweeping on the arms and legs. Energize the hand and sole minor chakras with ordinary light whitish-violet. Do not repeat this step more than once a day since it may produce a reverse reaction.

12. Apply localized sweeping thoroughly on the crown chakra, forehead chakra, ajna chakra, throat chakra, and back head minor chakra. Energize them with light whitish-green; then use more ordinary light whitish-violet.

13. Stabilize and release the projected pranic energy.

14. For acute hepatitis, repeat Steps 2 to 5 three times a day for the next few days until the condition has improved and stabilized.

15. The whole treatment can be repeated three times or more a week until the patient is completely healed.

ASSIMILATION PROBLEMS

The solar plexus chakra controls and energizes the digestive organs. The navel chakra controls and energizes the small intestine which is responsible for the assimilation of nutrients.

1. Scan the patient, then rescan during pranic treatment.
2. Apply localized sweeping thoroughly on the solar plexus chakra, navel chakra, and on the abdominal area.
3. Energize the solar plexus chakra and the navel chakra with light whitish-green; then use more ordinary light whitish-violet.
4. Apply localized sweeping on the basic chakra. Energize it with light whitish-red. This is to strengthen the body.
5. Apply localized sweeping on the crown chakra, forehead chakra, ajna chakra, back head minor chakra, and throat chakra. Energize them with light whitish-green then ordinary light whitish-violet.
6. Stabilize and release the projected energy.
7. Repeat treatment several times a week.

Urinary Ailments

URINARY SYSTEM

The urinary system is controlled and energized by the meng mein chakra and the sex chakra. The meng mein chakra controls and energizes the kidneys and the ureter. It also controls blood pressure. The sex chakra controls and energizes the bladder and the urethra. Each kidney has a corresponding kidney minor chakra. The bladder has a corresponding bladder minor chakra. It is also affected by the basic chakra.

The kidneys are also affected by the solar plexus chakra. In certain cases, longstanding deep resentment in the form of congested red pranic energy from the solar plexus chakra goes down to the kidneys, thereby causing them to malfunction. This is why, in some instances, longstanding negative emotions may severely damage the kidneys. When this is the case, the back solar plexus chakra and the kidneys may be quite congested when scanned.

INFECTIONS OF THE
URINARY TUBE AND BLADDER

1. Scan the patient, then rescan during pranic treatment.
2. Apply general sweeping.

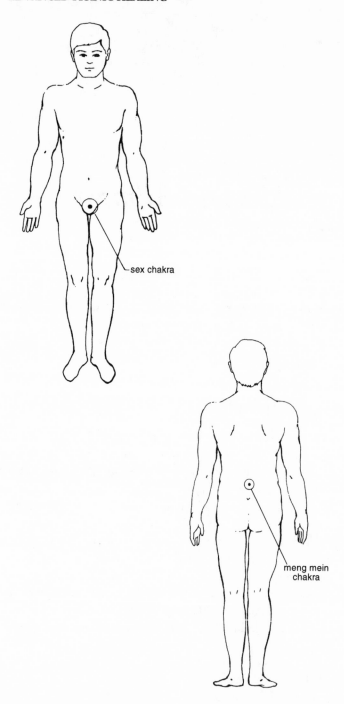

Figure 12-1. Chakras controlling and energizing the urinary system.

3. Apply localized sweeping on the sex chakra and the surrounding area thoroughly and alternately with light whitish-green prana and light whitish-orange prana.

4. Energize the sex chakra with light whitish-green, light whitish-blue, then ordinary light whitish-violet. Apply more localized sweeping. If Steps 3 and 4 are applied properly, the patient will be substantially relieved.

5. Apply localized sweeping on the lungs and energize them through the back with light whitish-green prana and light whitish-orange. This will facilitate the healing process since it has a cleansing effect on the blood and the entire body. When energizing the lungs with orange prana, the healer's fingers should be pointed away from the patient's head.

6. Apply localized sweeping on the front and back solar plexus chakra, the navel chakra, and the basic chakra. Energize them with white prana. This strengthens the body and enhances the body's immunity and defense system.

7. Stabilize and release the projected pranic energy.

8. Since the rate of pranic consumption is quite fast, repeat treatment about two to three times a day for the next several days if necessary.

Pranic healing is very effective in treating bladder and urinary tube infections. The rate of healing is very fast.

INFECTION AND INFLAMMATION OF THE KIDNEY

1. Scan the patient, then rescan during pranic treatment.

2. Apply general sweeping.

3. Apply localized sweeping thoroughly on the meng mein chakra. If the patient has high blood pressure, then inhibit the meng mein chakra by energizing it with blue prana. Simultaneously, will it to become smaller to about half the average size of the other chakras.

4. Apply localized sweeping on the kidney(s) thoroughly and alternately with light whitish-green and light whitish-orange.

5. To soothe and disinfect the kidney(s), energize the kidney(s) directly with light whitish-green, light whitish-blue, then ordinary light whitish-violet. Apply more localized sweeping on the kidney(s).

6. After energizing the kidney(s), the patient may experience slight pain on the back head area. Apply localized sweeping thoroughly

on the meng mein chakra, the back head minor chakra, and the entire spine until the patient is relieved. Steps 3, 4, 5, and 6 can be repeated several times a day if necessary.

7. Apply localized sweeping on the lungs and energize them through the back lungs with light whitish-green prana and light whitish-orange. This will facilitate the healing process it has a cleansing effect on the blood and the entire body. When energizing the lungs with orange prana, the healer's fingers should be pointed away from the patient's head.

8. Apply localized sweeping thoroughly on the front and back solar plexus chakra, and on the liver. Energize the solar plexus chakra with light whitish-green, with light whitish-blue, then with ordinary light whitish-violet.

9. Apply localized sweeping on the front and back spleen chakra. Do not energize it.

10. Apply localized sweeping on the basic chakra. Do not energize it.

11. Apply localized sweeping on the arms and legs. Energize the hand and sole minor chakras with ordinary light whitish-violet. Do not repeat this step more than once a day. By energizing the minor chakras on the soles of the feet, the basic chakra will be energized without being overenergized.

12. Apply localized sweeping on the throat chakra, ajna chakra, forehead chakra, and crown chakra. Energize them with light whitish-green, then with ordinary light whitish-violet.

13. Stabilize and release the projected pranic energy.

14. The emphasis of the treatment is on Steps 3, 4, and 5.

15. Repeat treatment until the patient is healed.

KIDNEY STONES

In many cases, the cause of kidney stones is medically unknown. The solar plexus chakra is usually congested. Part of the congested energy from the back solar plexus chakra goes to the kidney(s).

1. Scan the patient, then rescan during pranic treatment.

2. Apply localized sweeping thoroughly on the meng mein chakra.

3. Apply localized sweeping thoroughly on the front and back solar plexus chakra and energize it with light whitish-green; then use light whitish-blue.

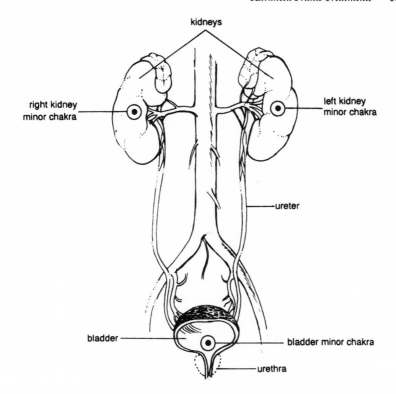

Figure 12-2. The urinary system.

4. Apply localized sweeping on the affected kidney thoroughly and alternately with light whitish-green and light whitish-orange. Apply localized sweeping on the ureter if it is affected.

5. To gradually disintegrate the stones, energize directly the affected kidney with light whitish-blue, light green, then light orange. Blue is for localizing. Green and orange are used for their dissolving or disintegrating effects. If the ureter is affected, apply the same treatment.

6. After energizing the kidney, the patient may experience slight pain in the back of the head. Apply localized sweeping thoroughly on the meng mein chakra, the back head minor chakra, and the entire spine until the patient is relieved. If necessary, inhibit the meng mein chakra with light whitish-blue prana.

7. If the urethra is affected, apply localized sweeping on the sex chakra with light whitish-green; then use light whitish-orange. Energize it with light whitish-blue, light green, then light orange.

8. Stabilize and release the projected pranic energy.

9. Repeat pranic treatment several times a day for the next few days.

If the treatment is done properly, the patient is likely to be substantially relieved and will be able to urinate better after the first treatment.

Since the problem is likely to recur, it will be better if the patient undergoes regular preventive pranic treatment.

1. Scan the patient, then rescan during pranic treatment.
2. Apply general sweeping twice.
3. Apply localized sweeping thoroughly on the front and back solar plexus chakra.
4. Energize the solar plexus chakra with light whitish-green then with light whitish-blue. Apply more sweeping on the solar plexus chakra.
5. Apply localized sweeping on the meng mein chakra.
6. Apply localized sweeping on the kidneys alternately with light whitish-green and with light whitish-orange.
7. Energize the kidneys directly with light whitish-green, light whitish-orange, then light whitish-red.
8. After energizing the kidneys, the patient may experience slight pain on the back head area. Apply localized sweeping thoroughly on the meng mein chakra, on the back head minor chakra and the entire spine until the patient is relieved. If necessary, inhibit the meng mein chakra with light whitish-blue prana.
9. Stabilize and release the projected pranic energy.
10. Repeat treatment once a month.

STIMULATING URINATION

1. Scan, then rescan the meng mein chakra and the kidneys.
2. Apply localized sweeping on the meng mein chakra.
3. Apply localized sweeping on the kidneys alternately with light whitish-green and light whitish-orange.
4. Energize the kidneys directly with light whitish-green, with light whitish-orange, then with light whitish-red.
5. After energizing the kidneys, the patient may experience slight pain in the back of the head. Apply localized sweeping thoroughly on the meng mein chakra, on the back head minor chakra, and on the entire spine until the patient is relieved. If necessary, inhibit the meng mein chakra with light whitish-blue prana.
6. Stabilize and release the projected pranic energy.

REGENERATING THE KIDNEYS

I have observed that many patients with gradual kidney failure have experienced longstanding resentment. The solar plexus chakra is congested. Part of the dirty red energy from the back solar plexus chakra goes to the kidneys. In the long run, this causes the kidneys to malfunction. The liver and the spleen are etherically dirty.

1. Scan the patient, then rescan during pranic treatment.
2. Apply general sweeping twice.
3. Apply localized sweeping on the lungs and energize them through the back lungs with light whitish-green prana, light whitish-orange, and light whitish-red. This has cleansing and strengthening effects on the blood and the entire body.
4. Apply localized sweeping thoroughly on the front and back solar plexus chakra, and on the liver. Energize it with light whitish-green, with light whitish-blue, then with ordinary light whitish-violet.
5. Apply localized sweeping on the front and back heart chakra and energize the back heart chakra with light whitish-green; then use more ordinary light whitish-violet. This is to induce a sense of inner peace.
6. Apply localized sweeping thoroughly on the meng mein chakra and on the entire spine. If the meng mein chakra is overactivated, inhibit it by energizing it with light blue prana and will it to become about half the average size of the other chakras.
7. Apply localized sweeping on the kidneys thoroughly and alternately with light whitish-green and light whitish-orange.
8. Energize the kidneys directly with light whitish-green, light whitish-orange, and light whitish-red. Apply more localized sweeping on the kidneys. This is to gradually regenerate them.
9. After energizing the kidneys, the patient may experience slight pain in the back of the head. Apply localized sweeping thoroughly on the meng mein chakra, the back head minor chakra and the entire spine until the patient is relieved. If necessary, inhibit the meng mein chakra with light whitish-blue prana.
10. Apply localized sweeping on the front and back spleen chakra with light whitish-green prana then with ordinary light whitish-violet. This has to be done with caution.
11. Apply localized sweeping thoroughly on the basic chakra and energize it with white prana.

12. Apply localized sweeping on the crown, forehead, ajna, and throat chakras. Energize them with light whitish-green then with light whitish-violet.
13. The emphasis of the treatment is on Steps 7 and 8.
14. Stabilize and release the projected pranic energy.
15. Repeat treatment three times a week for about six months to a year. The result varies. Some patients will improve and some will not improve.

Experienced, proficient, advanced pranic healers, can apply the "cleansing the internal organ technique" (page 86). This has a rapid cleansing effect on the solar plexus chakra, the liver, the kidneys, and other organs. This healing technique has a cleansing effect on pent-up negative emotions, the etheric body, and the physical body. Therefore, it will hasten the healing process.

If the ailment is emotional in origin, it is important that the patient tries to release the pent-up negative emotion by:

1. Mentally forgiving and blessing those who are responsible for the hurt(s)—real or imagined, intentional or unintentional.
2. Mentally asking for forgiveness from those who were hurt by the patient and blessing them.
3. The process has to be repeated over and over until the patient is emotionally cleansed.
4. The process of forgiving and asking for forgiveness and blessing can be externalized by writing letters addressed to the persons involved. The letters are not mailed, but are burned and the ash scattered. The act of burning and scattering symbolizes releasing.
5. Tithing is recommended.

Reproductive Ailments

REPRODUCTIVE SYSTEM

The reproductive system is controlled and energized primarily by the sex chakra. It is also controlled by the ajna chakra, which controls the endocrine system. The reproductive system is also affected by the throat chakra, which is the center for higher creativity, and by the basic chakra, which substantially energizes the sex chakra.

With men, the sex chakra controls and energizes the penis, testes, and prostate. The testes are also controlled and energized by the testes minor chakras. The prostate is controlled and energized by the prostate and the perineum minor chakras.

With women, the sex chakra controls and energizes the vulva, clitoris, vagina, uterus, fallopian tubes, and ovaries. The uterus is controlled and energized by the uterus minor chakra. The ovaries and the fallopian tubes are also controlled and energized by the ovary minor chakras.

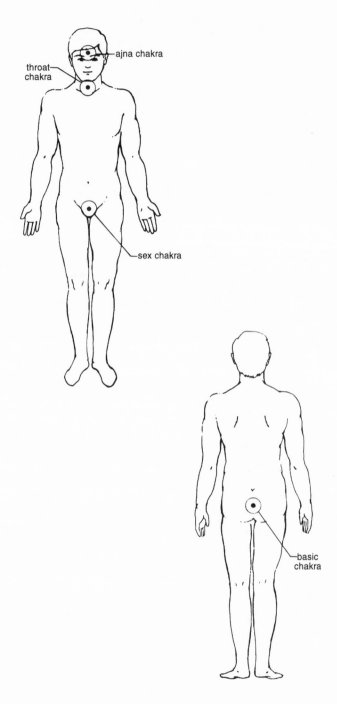

Figure 13-1.   Chakras affecting the reproductive system.

DYSMENORRHEA

1. Scan the patient, then rescan during pranic treatment.
2. Apply localized sweeping on the sex chakra alternately with light whitish-green prana and light whitish-orange prana. If cleansing is done properly, the patient can be relieved instantly.
3. Energize the sex chakra with white prana.
4. Apply localized sweeping on the basic and navel chakras and energize them with white prana.
5. If the patient is exhausted and has fainted, apply localized sweeping thoroughly on the solar plexus chakra and energize it with light whitish-red prana.
6. Stabilize and release the projected pranic energy.
7. Treatment can be applied three days before menstruation to prevent dysmenorrhea.

IRREGULAR MENSTRUATION OR NO MENSTRUATION

1. Scan the patient, then rescan during pranic treatment.
2. Apply localized sweeping on the sex chakra alternately with light whitish-green prana and light whitish-orange prana.
3. Energize the sex chakra with light whitish-green, light whitish-orange, then light whitish-red.
4. Apply localized sweeping on the basic and navel chakras and energize them with white prana.
5. Apply localized sweeping thoroughly on the ajna and throat chakras. Energize them with light whitish-green; then use more ordinary light whitish-violet.
6. Stabilize and release the projected pranic energy.
7. Repeat treatment three times a week. Stop and wait for the result. Repeat treatment if necessary.

VULVITIS, VAGINITIS, CERVICITIS

1. Scan the patient, then rescan during pranic treatment.
2. Apply general sweeping.
3. Apply localized sweeping on the sex chakra and the surrounding area alternately with light whitish-green and light whitish-orange.

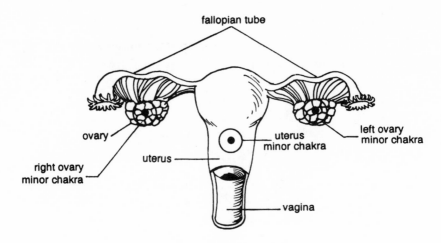

Figure 13-2. Female reproductive system.

The patient may experience substantial relief after thorough cleansing.

4. Energize the sex chakra with light whitish-green, light whitish-blue, and ordinary light whitish-violet prana. Apply more localized sweeping on the sex chakra and the surrounding area.

5. Apply localized sweeping on the lungs. Energize the lungs through the back lungs with light whitish-green, then with light whitish-orange. This will increase the rate of recovery since it has a cleansing effect on the blood and on the whole body. When energizing the lungs with orange prana, the healer's fingers should be pointed away from the patient's head.

6. Apply localized sweeping thoroughly on the basic, navel, and spleen chakras. Energize the basic and navel chakras with white prana. Part of the pranic energy from the navel chakra will automatically go to the spleen chakra.

7. Apply localized sweeping on the front and back solar plexus chakra and on the liver. Energize the solar plexus chakra with light whitish-green, light whitish-blue, then with ordinary light whitish-violet.

8. The emphasis of the treatment is on Step 3 and Step 4.

9. Stabilize and release the projected pranic energy.

10. Repeat treatment for the next few days.

OVARIAN CYST

In patients with ovarian cysts the sex chakra and the affected ovary are congested and filled with dirty red energy. The emphasis of the treatment is on thorough sweeping on the sex chakra and the affected ovary.

1. Scan the patient, then rescan during pranic treatment.
2. Apply general sweeping.
3. Apply localized sweeping on the sex chakra, the surrounding area, and the affected ovary alternately with light whitish-green and light whitish-orange.
4. Energize the sex chakra with light whitish-green. Apply more localized sweeping.
5. Apply more localized sweeping on the affected ovary alternately with light whitish-green and light whitish-orange. Cleansing is very important.
6. Energize the affected ovary with light whitish-blue; then use more light green. Blue is for localizing. Green is for decongesting and dissolving.
7. Apply localized sweeping thoroughly on the basic and navel chakras. Slightly energize them with white prana.
8. Apply localized sweeping thoroughly on the front and back solar plexus chakra. Energize it with light whitish-green and light whitish-blue; then use ordinary light whitish-violet.
9. Apply localized sweeping thoroughly on the crown, ajna, and throat chakras. Energize them with light whitish-green; then use more ordinary light whitish-violet.
10. The emphasis of the treatment is on Steps 3 to 6.
11. Stabilize and release the projected pranic energy.
12. Repeat treatment three times a week. The treatment may take three months or more.

MYOMA

In patients with myoma, the sex chakra is congested and filled with dirty red energy. Patients with myoma are usually sexually inhibited and have an improper attitude toward sex. The sex energy is not sufficiently released, even during intercourse. The sexual desire is excessively suppressed; sex energy is not able to flow freely to the other chakras as in normal healthy persons. This has an accumulating effect, manifesting as the development of myoma and its gradual growth. Women who have been sexually violated may develop a negative attitude toward sex, which, in the long run, may manifest as sexual ailment(s). With nuns, this is a result of sexual abstinence without consciously or subconsciously sublimating the sex energy.

It is not advisable to energize—even with just light orange prana—the sex chakra of a patient with myoma or an ovarian cyst. The sex chakra contains orange and red pranas in a certain mathematical proportion. Energizing the sex chakra with dark orange or medium orange will cause the sex chakra to produce more red prana in order to maintain the proportion. This will cause the sex chakra to become overactivated and more congested. This may cause the condition to deteriorate, or it may slow down the healing process.

1. Scan the patient, then rescan during pranic treatment.
2. Apply general sweeping.
3. Apply localized sweeping on the sex chakra and the surrounding area thoroughly and alternately with light whitish-green and light whitish-orange.
4. Energize the sex chakra with light blue; then use more light green. Blue is for localizing. Green is for decongesting and dissolving.
5. Apply localized sweeping thoroughly on the basic and navel chakras. Slightly energize them with white prana.
6. Apply localized sweeping thoroughly on the front and back solar plexus chakra. Energize it with light whitish-green, with light whitish-blue, then with ordinary light whitish-violet.
7. Apply localized sweeping thoroughly on the crown, ajna, and throat chakras. Energize them with light whitish-green; then use more ordinary light whitish-violet.
8. The emphasis of the treatment is on Step 3 and Step 4.
9. Stabilize and release the projected pranic energy.
10. Repeat treatment three times a week for as long as necessary. The treatment may take about three months.

PROLAPSED UTERUS

1. Scan the patient, then rescan during pranic treatment.
2. Apply general sweeping.
3. Apply localized sweeping on the sex chakra alternately with light whitish-green and light whitish-orange.
4. Energize the sex chakra with light whitish-green, light whitish-orange, and light whitish-red.

5. Apply localized sweeping thoroughly on the basic chakra and the navel chakra. Energize them with light whitish-red.
6. Apply localized sweeping thoroughly on the front and back solar plexus chakra. Energize it with light whitish-green, light whitish-blue, then with ordinary light whitish-violet.
7. Stabilize and release the projected pranic energy.
8. Repeat treatment three times a week.

ENLARGED PROSTATE

Enlarged prostate could be caused by congestion or depletion of the sex chakra. Congestion of the sex chakra occurs mostly among the celibate. Depletion of the sex chakra occurs mostly with older men.

1. Scan the patient, then rescan during pranic treatment.
2. Apply general sweeping.
3. Apply localized sweeping on the sex chakra alternately with light whitish-green and light whitish-orange.

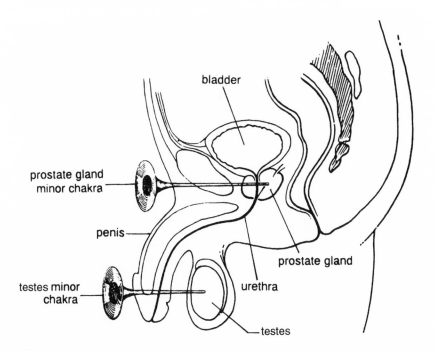

Figure 13-3. Male reproductive system.

4. Energize the sex chakra with white prana. Or, if the condition is due to congestion, energize the sex chakra with light whitish-green. If it is due to depletion, energize the sex chakra with light whitish-green; then use more light whitish-red prana.
5. Apply localized sweeping on the basic chakra and navel chakra. Energize them with white prana.
6. Apply localized sweeping on the front and back solar plexus chakra and energize it with white prana.
7. Stabilize and release the projected pranic energy.
8. Repeat treatment three times a week.

SEXUAL IMPOTENCE

1. Scan the patient, then rescan during pranic treatment.
2. Apply general sweeping.
3. Apply localized sweeping on the sex chakra alternately with light whitish-green and light whitish-orange. Energize the sex chakra with light whitish-red.
4. Apply localized sweeping on the basic chakra and the navel chakra. Energize them with light whitish-red.
5. If the problem is psychological in nature, apply localized sweeping thoroughly on the front and back solar plexus chakra. Energize it with light whitish-green, light whitish-blue, then ordinary light whitish-violet.
6. Apply localized sweeping on the front and back heart chakra. Energize the back heart chakra with light whitish-green; then use more ordinary light violet. Visualize the heart chakra becoming bigger.
7. Apply localized sweeping on the crown, ajna, and throat chakras. Energize them with light whitish-green; then use more ordinary light whitish-violet.
8. Stabilize and release the projected pranic energy.
9. Repeat treatment three times a week.

STERILITY

1. Scan the patient, then rescan during pranic treatment.
2. Apply general sweeping twice.
3. Apply localized sweeping on the sex chakra alternately with light whitish-green and light whitish-orange. Energize the sex chakra

with light whitish-green, light whitish-orange, then light whitish-red.

4. Apply localized sweeping on the basic chakra and the navel chakra. Energize them with light whitish-red.
5. Apply localized sweeping thoroughly on the front and back solar plexus chakra. Energize it with light whitish-green, light whitish-blue, then ordinary light whitish-violet.
6. Apply localized sweeping on the ajna, back head, and throat chakras with light whitish-green; then use more ordinary light whitish-violet.
7. Stabilize and release the projected pranic energy.
8. Repeat treatment three times a week for about a month. Stop treatment. Wait and observe for about two months.

VENEREAL DISEASE

In patients with venereal disease the sex chakra and the affected part(s) are extremely dirty. The use of ordinary localized sweeping will take too much time. Light whitish-green and light whitish-orange are used in cleansing. Medium or dark red prana should not be used on the basic chakra, the sex chakra, and the affected part(s) since it will stimulate the growth of germs. This is seen as more dirty energy rapidly springing out of the sex chakra. It is safer to avoid using red prana, even light red. The whole energy body is quite dirty.

1. Scan the patient, then rescan during pranic treatment.
2. Apply general sweeping two or three times with light whitish-green prana.
3. Energize the affected sex chakra and the affected part(s) with light blue. Blue prana is projected first for its localizing effect in order to minimize the possibility of spreading germs when the next step is applied.
4. Apply localized sweeping thoroughly and alternately with light whitish-green and light whitish-orange on the sex chakra and the affected parts.
5. Energize the sex chakra and the affected part(s) with light whitish-blue, light whitish-green, and ordinary light whitish-violet prana.
6. Apply localized sweeping thoroughly on the basic chakra. It is preferable not to energize it. Overenergizing the basic chakra of these patients may stimulate the venereal germs to grow.

7. Apply localized sweeping thoroughly on the arms and legs. Energize the hand and sole minor chakras with ordinary light whitish-violet. By energizing the sole minor chakras, the basic chakra will be energized without being overenergized. This is to stimulate the production of white blood cells. Do not repeat this step more than once a day since it may have a reverse reaction.

8. Apply localized sweeping on the lungs. Energize the lungs through the back of the lungs with light whitish-green, then with light whitish-orange. This will facilitate the rate of recovery since it has a cleansing effect on the blood and on the whole body.

9. The solar plexus chakra is partially affected. Apply localized sweeping thoroughly on the front and back solar plexus chakra and the liver. Energize the solar plexus chakra with light whitish-green, light whitish-blue, and ordinary light whitish-violet.

10. The spleen chakra is grayish. Apply localized sweeping thoroughly on the front and back spleen chakra. Energize it with light whitish-green, then with ordinary light whitish-violet. This has to be done with care. The spleen helps remove germs.

11. Apply localized sweeping thoroughly on the front and back heart chakra. Energize the thymus through the back heart chakra with a little light whitish-green; then use more ordinary light whitish-violet. This is to stimulate and strengthen the thymus, and to further stimulate the bone marrow in the spine, ribs, and the breast bone.

12. Apply localized sweeping on the throat chakra and energize it with light whitish-green, then ordinary light whitish-violet. The throat chakra controls and energizes the lymphatic system.

13. Apply localized sweeping on the crown, forehead, ajna, and back head chakras. Energize them with light whitish-green, then use more ordinary light whitish-violet.

14. Stabilize and release the projected pranic energy.

15. Repeat treatment three times a week.

PREGNANT WOMEN

Pregnant women should be treated gently. This means both sweeping and energizing must be done gently. In general, it is safer to use white prana than color pranas.

Do not use green or orange prana on pregnant women, especially on the navel and sex chakras. The effect could be quite destructive. There is a certain degree of risk, even if the green or orange pranic energy is directed to the legs, since part of it may go to the unborn child, especially if the healer is quite powerful. It is safer not to use green and orange in any part of the body of a pregnant woman.

Do not energize the spleen and the meng mein chakras of a pregnant woman since it may adversely affect the unborn child.

Healers should watch out for pregnant women who may pretend to have dysmenorrhea, irregular menstruation, or some other sickness, hoping that the treatment may cause abortion. Although such cases are relatively few, the healer should still be on guard.

Pregnant women usually have strong solar plexus, navel, sex, basic, and meng mein chakras. These chakras when scanned are usually bigger and thicker than the other chakras. If the woman is several months pregnant, these chakras are overactivated and the meng mein chakra is slightly smaller than the overactivated basic chakra. The ajna chakra is activated and reddish.

A healer is supposed to heal and save lives, not to hurt people. Therefore, healers should not get involved in the destruction of defenseless unborn infants. Misuse of power will result in severe negative karmic repercussions, so be very careful when working on pregnant women.

AVOIDING MISCARRIAGE

This treatment is for women who are not pregnant but have a history of miscarriages. The sex, navel, and basic chakras are affected.

1. Scan the patient, then rescan during pranic treatment.
2. Apply general sweeping.
3. Apply localized sweeping on the sex chakra alternately with light whitish-green prana and light whitish-orange prana.
4. Energize the sex chakra with light whitish-green, with light whitish-orange, and with light whitish-red.
5. Apply localized sweeping thoroughly on the basic and navel chakras. Energize them with light whitish-red.
6. Apply localized sweeping thoroughly on the front and back solar plexus chakra. Energize it with light whitish-green, light whitish-blue, then ordinary light whitish-violet.
7. Apply localized sweeping on the ajna and throat chakras. Energize them with light whitish-green, then use more light whitish-violet.
8. Stabilize and release the projected pranic energy.
9. Repeat treatment three times a week for about one month.

PREVENTING MISCARRIAGE

This treatment is for pregnant women who complain of lower abdominal pain with bleeding. Do not use the will when healing this condition.

1. Scan the patient, then rescan during pranic treatment.
2. Apply general sweeping gently.
3. Apply localized sweeping gently on the navel chakra, sex chakra, and the surrounding area.
4. Energize gently and slightly on the navel chakra and sex chakra with white prana.
5. Apply localized sweeping on the basic chakra. Energize it gently and slightly with white prana.
6. Apply localized sweeping gently on the front and back solar plexus chakra. Energize it gently with white prana.
7. Apply localized sweeping thoroughly on the ajna and throat chakras. Energize them with white prana.
8. Stabilize with a little very light whitish-blue prana and release the projected pranic energy.
9. Repeat treatment if necessary.

FACILITATING THE BIRTHING PROCESS

1. Scan the patient, then rescan during pranic treatment.
2. Apply localized sweeping very gently on the navel and sex chakras.
3. Gently energize the navel chakra with white prana or light whitish-blue prana to facilitate the muscular contraction of the womb.
4. Gently energize the sex chakra with white prana or light whitish-red prana to facilitate the dilation of the cervix.
5. Apply localized sweeping on the basic chakra, and gently energize it with white prana or light whitish-red prana.
6. If the back is painful, sweeping can be applied several times. Do not energize the meng mein chakra. This may cause stillbirth.
7. Apply localized sweeping on the ajna and throat chakras. Energize them gently with white prana.
8. Stabilize with a little very light whitish-blue prana, and release the projected pranic energy.
9. The entire procedure can be repeated after one or two hours.

The entire process can also be done three times a week, two weeks before the expected delivery date. *Use only white prana.*

HASTENING RECOVERY AFTER GIVING BIRTH

1. Scan the patient, then rescan during pranic treatment.
2. Apply general sweeping twice.
3. Apply localized sweeping on the sex chakra alternately with light whitish-green and light whitish-orange prana.
4. Energize the sex chakra with white prana or ordinary light whitish-violet.
5. Apply localized sweeping on the basic, navel, and solar plexus chakras. Energize them with white prana.
6. Stabilize and release the projected pranic energy.
7. Repeat treatment twice a day for about a week.

BIRTHING AT HOME

Based on my wife's description, the birthing process in the hospital, although medically efficient and effective, is unfortunately rather cold, if not almost inhuman. The option of birthing at home, where there is human warmth and the surrounding is natural, should be seriously considered. It is about time that would-be mothers assert their right to be treated as human beings who should be handled with sensitivity, dignity, and warmth—not just as mere bodies.

Endocrine Ailments

ENDOCRINE SYSTEM

The ajna chakra controls the endocrine system. The crown and forehead chakras control and energize the pineal gland. The ajna chakra controls and energizes the pituitary gland. The throat chakra controls and energizes the thyroid and parathyroid glands. The heart chakra controls and energizes the thymus gland. The solar plexus chakra controls and energizes the pancreas. The sex chakra controls and energizes the gonads. The throat chakra, which is the higher correspondence of the sex chakra, also affects the gonads. The meng mein and basic chakras control and energize the adrenal glands. The solar plexus chakra affects the meng mein and basic chakras; therefore, it also affects the adrenal glands.

The heart chakra and thymus gland help the ajna chakra regulate and harmonize the upper major and minor chakras and their corresponding organs. The thymus gland affects the heart, the blood pressure, throat, thyroid gland, parathyroid glands, and the organs inside the head. The upper chakras are those chakras above the solar plexus chakra.

Blood pressure can also be gradually lowered by cleansing and energizing the heart chakra and the thymus gland with light whitish-green, then

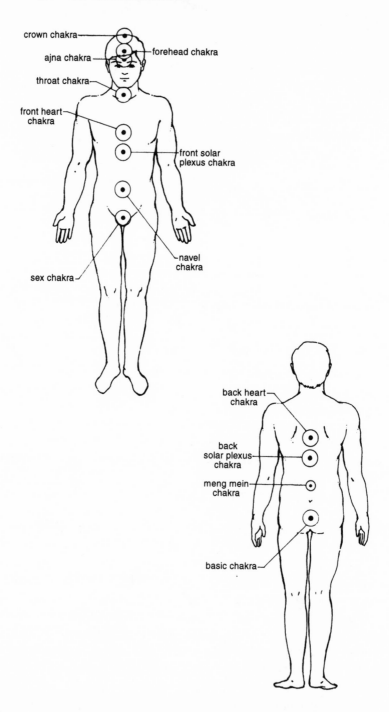

Figure 14-1. Chakras controlling and energizing the endocrine system.

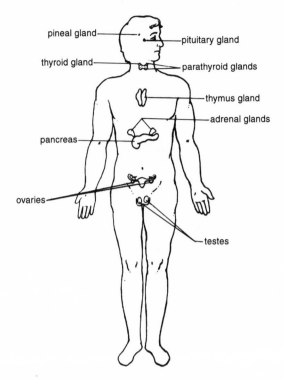

Figure 14-2. Endocrine system.

with ordinary light whitish-violet. Energizing is done through the back heart chakra. This gradually normalizes the solar plexus chakra and the meng mein chakra. A faster result is obtained by also cleansing and inhibiting the solar plexus chakra and the meng mein chakra.

Self-pranic healing for hypertension can be done by smiling at your front heart chakra and the thymus gland for several minutes, or by sending them happy and loving energy. In many instances, this will gradually normalize the solar plexus chakra and the meng mein chakra.

The navel chakra helps the ajna chakra regulate the lower major and minor chakras and their corresponding organs. The lower chakras are the meng mein chakra, sex chakra, basic chakra, and the lower minor chakras.

The pineal gland has a corresponding pineal minor chakra. The pituitary gland has a corresponding pituitary minor chakra. The thyroid gland has corresponding left and right thyroid minor chakras. The parathyroid glands have four parathyroid mini-chakras. The thymus gland has the thymus minor chakra with left and right thymus mini-chakras; the pancreas, the pancreas minor chakra with two mini-chakras on top of the pancreas;

the adrenal glands, the left and right adrenal minor chakras. The testes have the left and the right testes minor chakras, and the ovaries have the left and the right ovary minor chakras.

DIABETES CAUSED BY THE BODY'S INABILITY TO USE INSULIN

Pancreatic diabetes could be due to insulin deficiency or the inability of the body to make use of insulin. In most cases, it is due to the body's inability to utilize insulin. The solar plexus chakra is usually congested. In general, the pancreas is slightly inflamed. This is clairvoyantly seen as slightly grayish-red diseased energy on the pancreas. The liver and kidneys are partially affected. The ajna, navel, and basic chakras are also partially affected.

1. Scan the patient, then rescan during pranic treatment.
2. Apply general sweeping twice.
3. Apply localized sweeping thoroughly on the front and back solar plexus chakra, the liver, and the pancreas.
4. Energize the back solar plexus chakra and the pancreas with light whitish-green, light whitish-blue, then with ordinary light whitish-violet.
5. Apply localized sweeping thoroughly on the ajna chakra. Energize it with light whitish-green, then use more ordinary light whitish-violet. This step is important.
6. Apply localized sweeping thoroughly on the meng mein chakra.
7. Apply localized sweeping alternately on the kidneys with light whitish-green and light whitish-orange.
8. Apply localized sweeping on the basic and navel chakras. Energize them with light whitish-red. The emphasis of the treatment is Step 3 to Step 8.
9. Apply localized sweeping on the front and back heart chakra. Energize the back heart chakra with less light whitish-green, then use more ordinary light whitish-violet.
10. Apply localized sweeping on the throat chakra, forehead chakra, crown chakra, and back head minor chakra. Energize them with light whitish-green, then use more light whitish-violet.
11. Stabilize and release the projected pranic energy.
12. Repeat treatment twice a week.

PANCREATIC DIABETES
DUE TO INSUFFICIENT INSULIN

In patients with this kind of diabetes, the solar plexus chakra is depleted. The ajna, navel, and basic chakras are affected.

1. Scan the patient, then rescan during pranic treatment.
2. Apply general sweeping twice.
3. Apply localized sweeping thoroughly on the front and back solar plexus chakra, the liver, and the pancreas.
4. Energize the back solar plexus chakra and the pancreas with light whitish-green, then use more light whitish-red.
5. Apply localized sweeping thoroughly on the basic and navel chakras. Energize them with light whitish-red.
6. Apply localized sweeping on the ajna chakra. Energize it with less light whitish-green; then use more ordinary light whitish-violet. The emphasis of the treatment is from Step 3 to Step 6.
7. Apply localized sweeping on the front and back heart chakra. Energize the back heart chakra with light whitish-green, then use more ordinary light whitish-violet.
8. Apply localized sweeping on the throat chakra, forehead chakra, crown chakra, back head minor chakra, and base head minor chakra. Energize them with light whitish-green, then use more ordinary light whitish-violet.

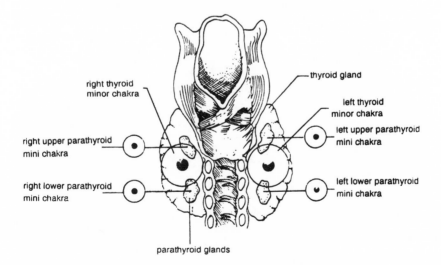

Figure 14-3. Thyroid and parathyroid glands.

9. Stabilize and release the projected pranic energy.
10. Repeat treatment three times a week.

HYPERTHYROIDISM

In patients with hyperthyroidism, the solar plexus chakra is congested and filled with dirty red energy. Part of this diseased energy goes to the throat chakra, causing the throat chakra to become reddish and overactivated. The ajna chakra is partially affected and contaminated with dirty red energy. Upon scanning the throat chakra, the healer may feel that it is relatively small and underactivated. This is because the patient has already taken medication for quite some time, which inhibits the throat chakra. This is why, sometimes, a patient with hyperthyroidism may end up having hypothyroidism.

1. Scan the patient, then rescan during pranic treatment.
2. Apply general sweeping twice.
3. Apply localized sweeping thoroughly on the front and back solar plexus chakra, and on the liver. Experienced, proficient, advanced pranic healers may apply the "cleansing the solar plexus chakra technique" (page 87). This is very important.
4. Energize the solar plexus chakra with light whitish-green, light whitish-blue, then ordinary light whitish-violet.
5. To activate the heart, apply localized sweeping on the front and back heart chakra. Energize the back heart with a little light whitish-green; then use more ordinary light whitish-violet. Visualize the heart chakra becoming bigger.
6. Energize the throat chakra with light blue prana to localize the light whitish-orange prana that will be used later.
7. Apply localized sweeping on the throat chakra alternately with light whitish-green and light whitish-orange. Ordinary localized sweeping would take a long time just to clean the throat chakra thoroughly.
8. Energize the throat chakra with light whitish-green, then with light blue. Simultaneously will it to become smaller.
9. Apply localized sweeping thoroughly on the ajna chakra, and energize it with light whitish-green, then use more ordinary light whitish-violet. The emphasis of the treatment is on Step 3 to Step 9.
10. Apply localized sweeping on the forehead, crown, and back head chakras. Energize them with light whitish-green, then use more ordinary light whitish-violet.

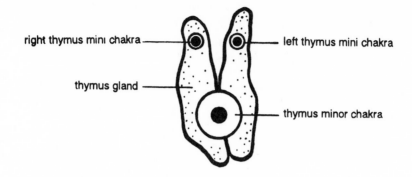

Figure 14-4. Thymus gland.

11. Apply localized sweeping on the basic and navel chakras. Energize them with white prana.
12. Stabilize and release the projected pranic energy.
13. Repeat treatment three times a week.

AILMENTS OF THE ENDOCRINE GLANDS

1. Scan the patient, then rescan during pranic treatment.
2. If the affected chakra is overactivated, apply localized sweeping thoroughly on the affected chakra. Energize it with light whitish-green, then use light blue. Simultaneously will it to become smaller.
3. If the affected chakra is underactivated, apply localized sweeping thoroughly on the affected chakra. If the affected chakra is on or below the solar plexus chakra, energize it with light whitish-green; then use more light whitish-red. Simultaneously will the chakra to become bigger. If the affected chakra is above the solar plexus chakra, energize it with light whitish-green; then use ordinary light whitish-violet. Simultaneously will the chakra to become bigger.
4. The ajna chakra has to be treated since it controls the endocrine system. Apply localized sweeping thoroughly on it, and energize it with light whitish-green; then use more ordinary light whitish-violet.
5. In general, the solar plexus chakra has to be treated since it is usually not functioning properly or is the cause of the ailment.
6. The heart chakra and the navel chakra have to be treated, since the heart chakra helps regulate the upper chakras and their endocrine

glands. The navel chakra helps regulate the lower chakras and the corresponding endocrine glands.

7. Stabilize and release the projected pranic energy.
8. Repeat treatment three times a week.

Skeletal and
Muscular Disorders

SKELETAL AND MUSCULAR SYSTEM

The skeletal and muscular system is controlled and energized primarily by the basic chakra, and by the minor chakras on the arms and legs. The proper functioning of the basic chakra is dependent to a substantial degree on the ajna chakra.

This system is also affected by the solar plexus chakra (through the liver), and by the spleen chakra (through the spleen), which affects the quality of blood. Prolonged improper emotion can cause the basic chakra to malfunction, thereby resulting in a disorder of the skeletal and muscular system.

The navel chakra also affects the skeletal and muscular system since it substantially controls and energizes the digestive, assimilative, and eliminative system. It also helps regulate and harmonize the lower chakras including the basic chakra. Arthritic patients in general have weak navel chakras.

LOWER BACK PAIN—
SCIATICA AND HERNIATED DISK

Lower back pain can be caused by a kidney problem or spinal disorder. The basic chakra controls and energizes the spine. In spinal disorders, the basic

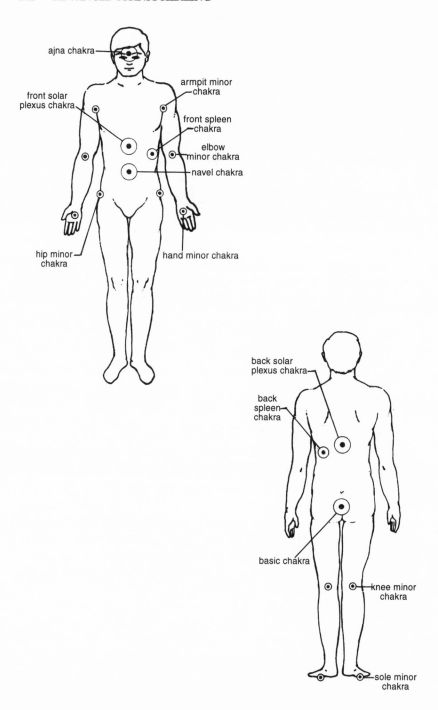

Figure 15-1.   Chakras affecting the skeletal and muscular system.

chakra is affected. In many instances, lower back pain could be emotional in origin. The solar plexus chakra is congested with dirty red prana. Part of the dirty red pranic energy goes to the lower portion of the spine, causing the disk in the long run to become herniated. Too much congested red pranic energy has expansive and weakening effects.

1. Scan the patient, then rescan during pranic treatment.
2. Apply general sweeping.
3. Apply localized sweeping on the spine with whitish-green prana.
4. Apply localized sweeping thoroughly on the front and back solar plexus chakra and on the liver. This is important.
5. Energize the solar plexus chakra with light whitish-green, light whitish-blue, then ordinary light whitish-violet. Apply more localized sweeping.
6. To induce a sense of inner peace, activate the heart chakra. Apply localized sweeping on the front and back heart chakra. Energize the back heart chakra with light whitish-green; then use more ordinary light whitish-violet. Visualize the heart chakra becoming bigger.
7. Apply localized sweeping on the affected lower portion of the spine alternately with light whitish-green and light whitish-orange. Thorough cleansing is important.
8. Energize the affected part in the spine with light whitish-green, light whitish-blue, then light whitish-yellow. This will have contracting and firming effects on the affected fibrous ring.
9. Apply localized sweeping and energizing on the basic chakra with light whitish-red. The emphasis of the treatment is on Steps 4, 7, 8, and 9. If treatment is done properly, the patient will be partially relieved, and in some cases may even be completely relieved.
10. Apply localized sweeping on the navel chakra and energize it with white prana.
11. Stabilize and release the projected pranic energy.
12. Treatment can be repeated two to three times a day for the first few days, especially on the affected part.

SCOLIOSIS

In patients with scoliosis, the solar plexus chakra is congested. The basic chakra is partially depleted. The upward straight flow of the pranic energy from the basic chakra is obstructed by the dirty solar plexus chakra, causing the pranic energy to swerve to the right or to the left of the spine. Based on the "law of correspondence," the spine will curve sideways, in the long run, to follow the flow of the pranic energy.

1. Scan the patient, then rescan during pranic treatment.
2. Apply general sweeping twice.
3. Apply localized sweeping thoroughly on the front and back solar plexus chakra and on the liver. This is important.
4. Energize the solar plexus chakra with light whitish-green, light whitish-blue, then ordinary light whitish-violet. Apply more localized sweeping on it.
5. Apply localized sweeping on the spine thoroughly and alternately with light whitish-green and light whitish-orange. Do not apply orange prana near the head or beyond the neck.
6. Apply localized sweeping on the affected part thoroughly and alternately with light whitish-green and light whitish-orange. Energize it with light whitish-red. Apply more sweeping on it after energizing. Whitish-red has a relaxing effect on the surrounding muscles.
7. Apply localized sweeping thoroughly on the basic chakra. Energize it with light whitish-red. Visualize the spine becoming straight.
8. Stabilize and release the projected pranic energy.
9. Repeat treatment three times a week. The patient will usually be substantially relieved after the first treatment.

ARTHRITIS OR RHEUMATISM

Although there are many types of arthritis, there are certain common denominators. With patients suffering from severe arthritis, the basic chakra is depleted. The basic chakra controls and energizes the skeletal and muscular system. This includes the joints. The navel chakra, the solar plexus chakra, the liver, the spleen chakra, and the physical spleen are usually affected. In other words, most of the lower chakras are affected.

In general, the following chakras are usually affected in arthritic cases:

1. Solar plexus chakra;
2. Spleen chakra;
3. Navel chakra;
4. Basic chakra.

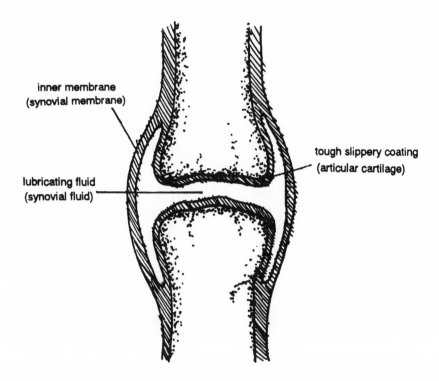

inner membrane
(synovial membrane)

tough slippery coating
(articular cartilage)

lubricating fluid
(synovial fluid)

Figure 15-2. Anatomy of a joint.

In many instances, a malfunctioning of the solar plexus chakra due to pro-longed negative emotions tends to cause the basic, navel, and spleen chakras to malfunction, which manifests as severe arthritis.

In general, the application of the "super healing technique" (see p. 95), is very effective in healing minor and severe arthritis. The solar plexus chakra has to be cleansed thoroughly. If it is ovcractivated, it has to be inhibited. If the patient is elderly, it is safer to use white prana when ap-plying the Master Healing Technique (p. 91).

From a medical viewpoint, arthritis could be caused by:

a) Inflammation of the muscles and tendons;
b) Degeneration of the joints due to old age;
c) Inflammation of the joints' membrane;
d) Inflammation of the joints due to excess uric acid and urates.

INFLAMMATION OF MUSCLES AND TENDONS

1. Apply localized sweeping on the affected part thoroughly and alternately with light whitish-green and light whitish-orange prana.
2. Energize the affected part with light whitish-green, light whitish-blue, then light whitish-violet.
3. Repeat treatment if necessary. Usually, the patient may be partially or completely relieved after the first treatment.

STIFF NECK

Stiff necks can be caused by wrong sleeping habits, heart ailments, hypertension, and other factors. In many instances, stiff necks may be due to emotional factors. Usually, the patient is not able to verbally express his or her negative emotions. The solar plexus chakra is congested with pent-up emotions (dirty red energy). Since the patient is not able to verbalize his or her negative emotions, the pent-up emotion (dirty red energy) gets stuck in the throat chakra and in the affected jaw minor chakra, which eventually manifests as a stiff neck. In many instances, the shoulders are also affected. This type of patient is also susceptible to throat infections. In more severe cases, the throat chakra, secondary throat chakra, and the basic chakra may become so affected that the patient may develop bronchial asthma.

1. Scan the patient, then rescan during pranic treatment.
2. Apply general sweeping.
3. Apply localized sweeping thoroughly on the front and back solar plexus chakra and the liver. This is important.
4. Energize the solar plexus chakra with light whitish-green, light whitish-blue, then light whitish-violet. Apply more localized sweeping.
5. Apply localized sweeping thoroughly on the spine.
6. Apply localized sweeping thoroughly on the meng mein chakra.
7. Apply localized sweeping on the throat chakra, secondary throat chakra, affected jaw minor chakra, and on the affected part alternately with light whitish-green and ordinary light whitish-violet. Cleansing has to be done thoroughly.
8. Energize the throat chakra, secondary throat minor chakra, and the jaw minor chakra with light whitish-green, light whitish-blue, and ordinary light whitish-violet.

9. Energize the affected part with light whitish-green, light whitish-blue, then ordinary light whitish-violet. Apply more localized sweeping.
10. Apply localized sweeping on the basic and navel chakras. Energize them with light whitish-red.
11. Stabilize and release the projected pranic energy.

PAINFUL SHOULDER

1. Scan the patient, then rescan during pranic treatment.
2. Apply localized sweeping on the armpit and the affected part thoroughly and alternately with light whitish-green and light whitish-orange. Avoid using orange prana near the head area. If cleansing is done properly, the patient will usually feel substantial or complete relief.
3. Energize the armpit and the affected part with whitish-green, light whitish-blue, then ordinary light whitish-violet.
4. Sometimes shoulder pain can be caused by tension or emotional problems which affect the solar plexus chakra and the throat chakra. The malfunctioning of the throat chakra may affect the armpit minor chakra which manifests as shoulder pain. Apply localized sweeping thoroughly on the solar plexus chakra. Energize it with light whitish-green, with light whitish-blue, then with ordinary light whitish-violet.
5. Apply localized sweeping thoroughly on the throat chakra. Energize it with light whitish-green, light whitish-blue, and ordinary light whitish-violet. The emphasis of the treatment is on Steps 2 to 5.
6. Apply localized sweeping on the meng mein chakra.
7. Apply localized sweeping on the basic and navel chakras, then energize them with light whitish-red.
8. Shoulder pain can also be caused by a heart ailment or hypertension.
9. Stabilize and release the projected pranic energy.
10. Repeat treatment if necessary.

GOUT

In patients with gout the basic and navel chakras are depleted. The solar plexus chakra is also affected. The large intestine is etherically dirty. The kidneys are partially affected. The affected parts are inflamed. The treatment is divided into two parts: a) relieving the patient, and b) healing the gout by normalizing the affected basic, navel, and solar plexus chakras.

1. Scan the patient, then rescan during pranic treatment.
2. Apply general sweeping.
3. Apply localized sweeping on the leg and the affected part thoroughly and alternately with light whitish-green and light whitish-orange. The minor chakras on the legs have to be cleansed thoroughly.
4. Energize the hip, knee, and sole minor chakras on the leg with white prana.
5. Energize the affected part with light whitish-green, light whitish-blue, then light whitish-orange. Steps 3 and 5 have to be repeated several times a day until the patient is substantially or completely relieved.
6. Apply localized sweeping thoroughly on the front and back solar plexus chakra. Energize it with light whitish-green, with light whitish-blue, then with ordinary light whitish-violet.
7. Apply localized sweeping thoroughly on the basic and navel chakras. Energize them with light whitish-red.
8. Apply localized sweeping on the meng mein chakra. Apply localized sweeping on the kidneys alternately with light whitish-green and light whitish-orange. Energize the kidneys with white prana.
9. If the patient experiences pain or discomfort in the back of the head, apply localized sweeping thoroughly on the back of the head, on the spine, and on the meng mein chakra.
10. To make the treatment more thorough, the upper chakras can also be treated. Apply localized sweeping on the front and back heart chakra. Energize it through the back heart chakra with light whitish-green; then use more ordinary light whitish-violet.
11. Apply localized sweeping on the throat, ajna, forehead, crown, and back head chakras. Energize them with light whitish-green; then use more ordinary light whitish-violet.
12. Stabilize and release the projected pranic energy.
13. Repeat the entire treatment once a day for the next several days.

DEGENERATIVE ARTHRITIS — OSTEOARTHRITIS

The basic chakra controls and energizes the skeletal system. This includes the joints. With aging, the basic chakra (as well as the other chakras) loses its flexibility and gradually becomes depleted. This manifests as the curving of the spine and deterioration of the joint cartilage. This is also why, among older people, broken bones require a longer time to heal. The basic, navel, solar plexus, and spleen chakras are usually affected.

1. Scan the patient, then rescan during pranic treatment.
2. Apply general sweeping.
3. Apply localized sweeping on the affected leg or arm, and on the affected part with light whitish-green; then use light whitish-orange.
4. Energize the affected part with light whitish-green, light whitish-blue; then use more ordinary light whitish-violet. Or energize the affected part with light whitish-green, light whitish-blue, then light whitish-orange-yellow to rapidly regenerate the worn-out cartilage.
5. Apply localized sweeping on the minor chakras of the affected arm or leg and energize them with light whitish-red.
6. Apply localized sweeping on the basic and navel chakras. Energize them with light whitish-red.
7. Apply localized sweeping thoroughly on the front and back solar plexus chakra and energize it with white prana.
8. Apply localized sweeping on the spleen chakra and energize it with white prana. This has to be done with care.
9. To make the treatment more thorough, the upper chakras can also be treated. Apply localized sweeping on the front and back heart chakra. Energize it through the back heart chakra with light whitish-green; then use more ordinary light whitish-violet.
10. Apply localized sweeping on the throat, ajna, forehead, crown, and back head chakras. Energize them with light whitish-green; then use more ordinary light whitish-violet.
11. Stabilize and release the projected pranic energy.
12. Repeat treatment thrice a week.

RHEUMATOID ARTHRITIS

In patients with rheumatoid arthritis, the basic, navel, spleen, and solar plexus chakras are affected. The liver and spleen are etherically dirty. In many cases, it seems that rheumatoid arthritis is emotional in origin. The solar plexus chakra malfunctions, affecting the basic chakra, the liver, and the spleen. From a medical viewpoint, rheumatoid arthritis is basically an inflammation of the inner membrane (synovium) of the joint which in the long run will damage the joint cartilage.

1. Scan the patient, then rescan during pranic treatment.
2. Apply general sweeping.
3. Apply localized sweeping thoroughly on the front and back solar plexus chakra and on the liver. Energize the solar plexus chakra with light whitish-green, light whitish-blue, then ordinary light whitish-violet.
4. Apply localized sweeping on the affected leg or arm, and on the affected joint, thoroughly and alternately with light whitish-green and light whitish-orange. If cleansing is done thoroughly, the patient will be partially relieved.
5. Energize the affected joint with light whitish-green, light whitish-blue, then light whitish-violet.
6. Energize the minor chakras on the affected arm or leg with white prana or light whitish-red prana.
7. Apply localized sweeping thoroughly on the basic and navel chakras. Energize them with light whitish-red.
8. Apply localized sweeping thoroughly on the spleen chakra, then energize it with white prana. Do not energize the spleen if the patient has hypertension.
9. To make the treatment more thorough, the upper chakras can also be treated. Apply localized sweeping on the front and back heart chakra. Energize it through the back heart chakra with light whitish-green; then use more ordinary light whitish-violet.
10. Apply localized sweeping on the throat, ajna, forehead, crown, and back head chakras. Energize them with light whitish-green; then use more ordinary light whitish-violet.
11. Stabilize and release the projected pranic energy.
12. Repeat treatment three times a week.

SYSTEMIC LUPUS ERYTHEMATOSUS

This etheric condition is similar to rheumatoid arthritis, but the condition is more severe. Etherically, the whole body is affected and depleted. The basic chakra is very depleted. The navel, spleen, and solar plexus chakras are also affected. The solar plexus chakra is congested and quite dirty. The liver and spleen are etherically dirty. The ajna chakra, the heart chakra, and the throat chakra are affected. The throat chakra controls and energizes the lymphatic system. The throat chakra and the heart chakra control and energize the thymus.

If part of the dirty congested energy from the back solar plexus chakra goes to the kidney(s), then the kidney(s) may become affected. The kidney(s) when scanned is congested. The blood, when seen clairvoyantly, is quite dirty.

The joints are painful and the condition is usually accompanied by skin rashes all over the body. The patient is quite depleted. Unless the healer is relatively powerful, there is a possibility that the healer may become partially depleted due to the rapid absorption of pranic energy by the patient.

1. Scan the patient, then rescan during pranic treatment.
2. Apply general sweeping twice.
3. Apply localized sweeping thoroughly on the front and back solar plexus chakra and on the liver. Energize the solar plexus chakra with light whitish-green, light whitish-blue, then light whitish-orange. Do not use dark orange prana; just use light whitish-orange, which is safe. Apply more localized sweeping on the front and back solar plexus chakra, and on the liver. This step has cleansing effects throughout the whole body. The patient is likely to sweat.
4. Apply localized sweeping thoroughly on the lungs. Energize the lungs directly through the back of the lungs with light whitish-green, light whitish-orange, and light whitish-red. This has cleansing and strengthening effects on the blood. When energizing the lungs with orange prana, the healer's fingers should be pointed away from the patient's head.
5. Apply localized sweeping on the legs and arms and on the affected parts thoroughly and alternately with light whitish-green and light whitish-orange. The minor chakras on the arms and legs have to be cleansed thoroughly. If cleansing is done properly, the pain will be reduced and the rashes will become lighter.
6. Energize the affected joints with light whitish-green, light whitish-blue, then light whitish-orange. After several treatments or after several weeks when the condition has improved, energize the affected joints with light whitish-green; then use more light whitish-violet.
7. Energize the remaining minor chakras of the arms and legs with light whitish-red.
8. Apply localized sweeping on the kidneys alternately with light whitish-green and light whitish-orange. Energize them directly with white prana.
9. Apply localized sweeping thoroughly on the basic and navel chakras. Energize them with light whitish-red.

10. Apply localized sweeping thoroughly on the spleen chakra, then energize it with white prana. Do not energize the spleen if the patient has hypertension.
11. Apply localized sweeping on the front and back heart chakra. Energize the thymus through the back heart chakra with light whitish-green; then use more ordinary light whitish-violet.
12. Apply localized sweeping thoroughly on the throat chakra and the secondary throat minor chakra. Energize them with light whitish-green, light whitish-blue, then use ordinary light whitish-violet.
13. Apply localized sweeping thoroughly on the ajna chakra, forehead chakra, crown chakra, and back head minor chakra. Energize them with light whitish-green; then use more ordinary light whitish-violet.
14. Stabilize and release the projected pranic energy.
15. Repeat treatment three times a week. The pranic treatment may last from several months to about a year.

The treatment of lupus requires a relatively powerful, proficient, advanced pranic healer. If treatment is done properly, there will usually be noticeable or substantial improvements after several treatments. The patient has to cooperate by minimizing negative emotions and thoughts. It is advisable to become a vegetarian.

SPORTS INJURIES

Pranic healing is very effective in treating sports injuries. If the treatment is done by an expert advanced pranic healer and the patient is receptive, in many instances, the results can be miraculous from a layman's viewpoint.

Someday all major sport teams will have pranic healers specializing in sports injuries. This will be a tremendous advantage over teams without pranic healers. In China, some of the national sports teams have pranic healers or medical chi kung practitioners to treat athletes with sport injuries right on the spot, or just to give them a boost of pranic energy if required.

MUSCLE CRAMPS

1. Scan the patient, then rescan during pranic treatment.
2. If the affected part is on the leg, then apply localized sweeping on the entire leg, especially on the hip, knee, and sole minor chakras alternately with light whitish-green and light whitish-orange.

3. Energize the hip, knee, and sole minor chakras with light whitish-red.
4. Apply localized sweeping on the affected part alternately with light whitish-green and light whitish-orange.
5. Energize the affected part with light whitish-green, light whitish-orange; then use more light whitish-red.
6. Apply localized sweeping on the basic and navel chakras. Energize them with light whitish-red prana.
7. Stabilize and release the projected pranic energy.

BURSITIS

Apply treatment for the inflammation of muscles and tendons (see page 216).

STRAINS

1. Scan the patient, then rescan during pranic treatment.
2. Apply localized sweeping on the affected part alternately with light whitish-green and light whitish-orange. It is important to clean the affected part thoroughly.
3. Energize the affected part with light whitish-blue for soothing and localizing effects then with more light whitish-orange-red for accelerating the healing process. Usually, the relief is instantaneous if Step 2 and Step 3 are done properly.
4. Apply localized sweeping on the basic and navel chakras, then energize them with light whitish-red.
5. Stabilize and release the projected pranic energy.
6. Preferably, the patient should rest the treated part and not overexert it immediately.

SPRAINS

1. Scan the patient, then rescan during pranic treatment.
2. Apply localized sweeping on the affected part alternately with light whitish-green and light whitish-orange. It is important to clean the affected part thoroughly.

3. Energize the affected part with light whitish-blue for soothing and localizing effects.

4. To accelerate the healing process, energize the affected part with light whitish-orange-red; then use light whitish-orange-yellow. Usually, the relief is instantaneous if Step 2 to Step 4 are done properly.

5. Apply localized sweeping on the basic and navel chakras, then energize them with light whitish-red.

6. Stabilize and release the projected pranic energy.

7. Preferably, the patient should rest the treated part and not overexert it immediately.

HERNIA

1. Scan the patient, then rescan during pranic treatment.

2. Apply localized sweeping on the affected part alternately with light whitish-green and light whitish-orange.

3. Energize the affected part with light whitish-green, light whitish-blue, then light whitish-yellow.

4. Apply localized sweeping on the basic, navel, and solar plexus chakras. Energize them with white prana.

5. Stabilize and release the projected pranic energy.

TORN TENDONS

If the tendon has been completely torn, then it is advisable to have it sewn together. Pranic healing can be applied to accelerate the healing process.

1. Scan the patient, then rescan during pranic treatment.

2. Apply localized sweeping on the affected part alternately with light whitish-green and light whitish-orange. Cleansing has to be done thoroughly.

3. Energize the affected part with light whitish-blue for soothing and localizing effects.

4. To accelerate the healing process, energize the affected part with light whitish-orange-red then with light whitish-orange-yellow.

5. Apply localized sweeping on the basic and navel chakras, then energize them with light whitish-red.

6. Apply localized sweeping on the front and back solar plexus chakra. Energize it with white prana.

7. Stabilize and release the projected pranic energy.
8. Repeat treatment three times a week.

DISLOCATION

1. Scan the patient, then rescan during pranic treatment.
2. To reduce the pain or to anesthetize, apply localized sweeping on the affected part alternately with light whitish-green and light whitish-orange. Energize the affected part with light whitish-green; then use lots of light whitish-blue prana.
3. The bones have to be manipulated to restore them to normal position. This is to be done by a specialist or an expert.
4. To accelerate the healing process, energize the affected part with light whitish-orange-yellow; then use light whitish-orange-red.
5. Apply localized sweeping on the basic and navel chakras, then energize them with light whitish-red.
6. Apply localized sweeping on the front and back solar plexus chakra and energize with white prana.
7. Stabilize and release the projected pranic energy.
8. Repeat treatment three times a week.

Blood Disorders

BLOOD

The basic chakra controls and energizes the skeletal system, including the bone marrow, which produces blood cells. Therefore, the basic chakra also controls and energizes the production of blood cells. Proper functioning of the basic chakra depends on the ajna chakra through the pituitary gland. The basic chakra through its subchakras on the arms and legs—the armpit, elbow, hand, hip, knee, and sole minor chakras—controls and energizes the bone marrow in the arms and legs. The bone marrow in the spine is controlled by the basic chakra. The bone marrow in the ribs, breastbone, and scapula is controlled by the basic chakra through the heart chakra. The bone marrow in the skull is controlled and energized by the basic chakra through the back head minor chakra. Before adulthood, blood cells are produced in the marrow in all the bones. With adults, the production of blood cells takes place mainly in the marrow of the hipbones, spine, ribs, and breastbone.

The quality of the blood is affected by the solar plexus chakra primarily through the liver and the stomach, by the spleen chakra through the physical spleen, by the meng mein chakra through the kidneys, and by the navel chakra through the small and large intestines. The liver, spleen, kidneys, and large intestines purify the blood.

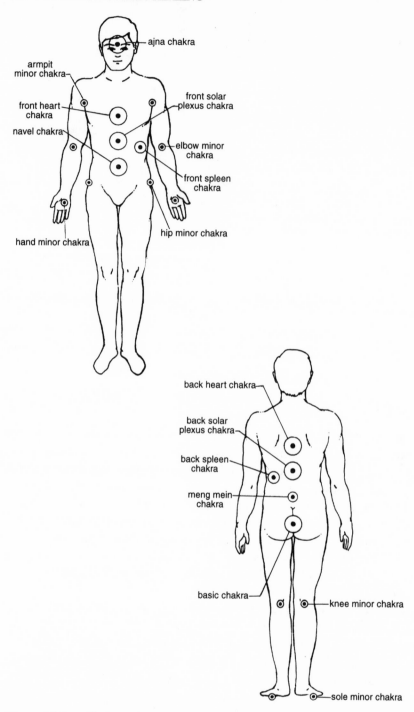

Figure 16-1. Chakras affecting the blood.

ANEMIA

Anemia is usually caused by menstrual bleeding or by intestinal bleeding. This is remedied by the intake of iron supplements. Anemia can also be caused by other factors. The following chakras have to be treated:

a) The basic chakra—for the production of red blood cells;
b) The spleen chakra—for the destruction of old worn-out blood cells;
c) The solar plexus and navel chakras—for digestion and assimilation;
d) The ajna chakra—to control the other chakras.

1. Scan the patient, then rescan during pranic treatment.
2. Apply general sweeping twice.
3. Apply localized sweeping on the basic chakra thoroughly and alternately with light whitish-green and light whitish-orange prana. Energize the basic chakra with light whitish-red prana.
4. Apply localized sweeping on the arms and legs with an emphasis on their minor chakras. Energize the minor chakras of the arms and legs with light whitish-red prana.
5. Apply localized sweeping on the front and back heart chakra. Energize the back heart chakra with light whitish-green, then with light whitish-red prana.
6. Apply localized sweeping on the navel chakra and the lower abdominal area. Energize the navel chakra with light whitish-green; then use more light whitish-red prana.
7. Apply localized sweeping thoroughly on the front and back solar plexus chakra, then on the liver. Energize the solar plexus chakra with light whitish-green; then use more ordinary light whitish-violet prana.
8. Apply localized sweeping on the front and back spleen chakra. Energize the spleen chakra with light whitish-green, then with ordinary light whitish-violet prana. This has to be done with caution.
9. Apply localized sweeping on the ajna chakra. Energize it with a little light whitish-green; then use more ordinary light whitish-violet prana.
10. Stabilize and release the projected pranic energy.
11. Repeat treatment three times a week for as long as necessary.

ACUTE ALLERGY

All types of pranas can relieve allergies to a certain degree. But the best color pranas for allergies are orange and red prana. There are certain types of acute or severe allergy that can be relieved only by using these two pranas.

Orange prana is essential for its expelling or cleansing effect. Red prana has a strengthening effect.

The treatment is divided into two parts: to relieve the patient and to gradually heal the ailment. The "cleansing the blood technique" (see page 88) has to be applied to produce fast relief. The ajna chakra, the solar plexus chakra, the liver, and the basic chakra have to be treated.

1. Scan the patient, then rescan during pranic treatment.
2. Apply general sweeping twice.
3. Apply localized sweeping on the lungs. Directly energize the back of the lungs with light whitish-green, light whitish-orange, and light whitish-red prana. Green and orange pranas have cleansing effects on the blood. Red prana has a strengthening effect. When energizing the lungs with orange prana, the healer's fingers should be pointed away from the patient's head.
4. Apply localized sweeping on the affected parts alternately with light whitish-green and light whitish-orange prana. As you continue to cleanse, the affected parts will become lighter. Energize them with light whitish-red. Do not apply sweeping with light whitish-orange on the head, on the heart, on the spleen, or very near them.
5. If the affected part is on the head or near a delicate organ, apply localized sweeping alternately with light whitish-green and ordinary light whitish-violet prana. Energize it with ordinary light whitish-violet. Steps 3 to 5 are applied to relieve the patient.
6. Apply localized sweeping on the ajna chakra. Energize it with a little light whitish-green, then with more ordinary light whitish-violet prana. The ajna chakra is the master chakra; therefore it has to be treated.
7. Apply localized sweeping on the basic chakra thoroughly and alternately with light whitish-green and light whitish-orange. Energize it with light whitish-red prana.
8. Apply localized sweeping on the arms and legs with emphasis on their minor chakras. Energize the minor chakras of the arms and legs with light whitish-red prana.
9. Apply localized sweeping on the front and back heart chakra. Energize the heart chakra through the back heart chakra with light whitish-green, then use more ordinary light whitish-violet prana.
10. Apply localized sweeping thoroughly on the front and back solar plexus chakra, and the liver. Energize the solar plexus chakra with light whitish-green, then use more ordinary light whitish-violet prana.

11. For experienced, advanced pranic healers, apply localized sweeping on the front and back solar plexus chakra and on the liver alternately with light whitish-green and light whitish-orange prana. Energize the solar plexus chakra with white prana. Steps 6 to 11 are applied to gradually heal the patient of the allergy.
12. Stabilize and release the projected pranic energy.

AUTOIMMUNE AILMENTS

In patients with an autoimmune ailment the whole body is etherically quite dirty. The basic chakra, the heart chakra, the thymus gland, and the ajna chakra are adversely affected. The basic chakra and the minor chakras in the arms and legs are depleted. The solar plexus chakra and the liver are usually, if not always, congested and filled with grayish red energy. The spleen chakra and the spleen are etherically quite dirty. Because of the proximity of the kidneys to the congested back solar plexus chakra and the liver, the kidneys are likely to be affected.

1. Scan the patient, then rescan during pranic treatment.
2. Apply general sweeping several times.
3. Apply localized sweeping on the lungs. Directly energize the back of the lungs with light whitish-green, light whitish-orange, and light whitish-red prana. This has cleansing and strengthening effects on the blood. When energizing the lungs with orange prana, the healer's fingers should be pointed away from the patient's head.
4. Apply localized sweeping on the basic chakra thoroughly and alternately with light whitish-green and light whitish-orange prana. Energize it with light whitish-red prana.
5. Apply localized sweeping on the arms and legs with emphasis on their minor chakras thoroughly and alternately with light whitish-green and light whitish-orange prana. Energize the minor chakras of the arms and legs with light whitish-red.
6. Apply localized sweeping on the front and back heart chakra. Energize the heart chakra through the back heart chakra with light whitish-green, then with more of ordinary light whitish-violet prana.
7. Apply localized sweeping thoroughly on the front and back solar plexus chakra. Energize it with light whitish-green, then with more of ordinary light whitish-violet prana.

8. For experienced, advanced pranic healers, apply localized sweeping on the front and back solar plexus chakra, and on the liver alternately with light whitish-green and light whitish-orange prana. Energize the solar plexus chakra with light whitish-blue, light whitish-green, and light whitish-orange.

9. Apply localized sweeping on the front and back spleen chakra with light whitish-green prana. Energize the spleen chakra with light whitish-green, then with ordinary light whitish-violet. This has to be done with caution.

10. Apply localized sweeping on the kidneys thoroughly and alternately with light whitish-green and light whitish-orange prana. Energize them with light whitish-red prana.

11. Apply localized sweeping thoroughly on the meng mein chakra.

12. Apply localized sweeping thoroughly on the throat chakra and ajna chakra. Energize them with a little of light whitish-green prana; then use more ordinary light whitish-violet.

13. Stabilize and release the projected pranic energy.

14. Repeat treatment three times a week for as long as necessary.

LEUKEMIA

The following chakras are affected in leukemia:

a) The basic chakra is depleted, overactivated, and filled with dirty yellow-red diseased energy.

b) The ajna chakra is depleted, underactivated, and filled with dirty yellow-red diseased energy.

c) The heart chakra is depleted, underactivated, and filled with dirty yellow-red diseased energy.

Patients suffering from leukemia have a malfunctioning basic chakra, heart chakra, and ajna chakra. The physical spleen is severely affected by the leukemia cells, and the spleen chakra is adversely affected. These four chakras have to be cleansed and energized thoroughly. The other major chakras and the minor chakras on the arms and legs are also affected.

The difference between chronic leukemia and acute leukemia is in the degree of overactivation of the basic chakra and the amount of dirty yellow diseased energy contained in the basic chakra, heart chakra, and ajna chakra. In acute cases, the basic chakra is overactivated by 2-1/2 to 3 times relative to the normal size, and the dirty yellow diseased energy is as high as 40–60%. The prognosis for acute leukemia is poor. In chronic leukemia, the basic chakra is not so overactivated and the dirty yellow diseased energy could range from 5–10%. In not so acute cases, the dirty yellow diseased energy could range from 10–40%.

1. Scan the patient, then rescan during pranic treatment.
2. Apply general sweeping several times with light whitish-green prana.
3. Apply localized sweeping on the crown, forehead, ajna, back head, and throat chakras alternately with light whitish-green prana and ordinary light whitish-violet prana. Energize them with light electric-violet pranic energy. The emphasis of the treatment is on the ajna chakra which has to be cleansed and energized thoroughly.
4. Apply localized sweeping on the front and back heart chakra thoroughly and alternately with light whitish-green prana and ordinary light whitish-violet prana. Energize the heart chakra through the back heart chakra with light electric-violet pranic energy. This step is very important.
5. Apply localized sweeping on the lungs. Energize the lungs through the back of the lungs with light whitish-green prana and light whitish-orange prana. This has a cleansing effect on the blood. When energizing the lungs with orange prana, the healer's fingers should be pointed away from the patient's head.
6. Apply localized sweeping on the front and back spleen chakra alternately with light whitish-green prana and ordinary light whitish-violet. Energize the spleen chakra with light electric-violet, with the intention of disintegrating the leukemia cells. This has to be done with caution. Rescan the spleen chakra and the meng mein chakra. If they are overactivated, apply localized sweeping and inhibit with light blue prana. This step is quite important. The not so proficient, advanced pranic healers should just energize the spleen chakra with ordinary light whitish-violet.
7. Apply localized sweeping on the spine thoroughly and alternately with light whitish-green and light whitish-orange. Do not apply orange prana near the head or beyond the neck
8. Apply localized sweeping on the basic chakra thoroughly and alternately with light whitish-green and light whitish-orange prana. Apply localized sweeping 50 to 100 times. Thorough cleansing is very important. Inhibit the basic chakra by energizing it with light blue prana. Rescan the basic chakra.
9. Apply localized sweeping alternately with light whitish-green and light whitish-orange prana on the arms and legs, with emphasis

on their minor chakras. Energize the minor chakras of the arms and legs with light whitish-red prana.

10. Energize the basic chakra with light electric-violet pranic energy with the intention of disintegrating the leukemia cells. Visualize electric-violet pranic energy going into the entire skeletal system: the spine, ribs, chest bone, hip bones, and the bones in the arms and legs. The healer has to exert a certain degree of willpower when energizing, since the basic chakra is usually not responsive to electric-violet pranic energy. When energizing, the healer should also form an intention that the basic chakra will not become overactivated. Rescan the basic chakra. This step is very important. An experienced, proficient, advanced pranic healer is required to perform this step properly.

11. The less proficient pranic healer can just energize the basic chakra with light whitish-red. Energizing this chakra will take quite some time since it is very depleted. This step is very important.

12. Apply localized sweeping thoroughly on the front and back solar plexus chakra and the liver thoroughly and alternately with light whitish-green and light whitish-orange. Energize the solar plexus chakra with light whitish-red prana.

13. Apply localized sweeping thoroughly on the meng mein chakra, sex chakra, and navel chakra. Energize the sex chakra and navel chakra with white prana.

14. Stabilize and release the projected pranic energy.

15. Repeat treatment three times a week for as long as necessary.

It is advisable to encourage the patient to become a pure vegetarian. Aside from the health benefits derived from a vegetarian diet, being a vegetarian is also an act of mercy toward the animal kingdom. Based on the law of karma, a person who shows mercy will also receive mercy. This helps in the faster healing of the patient's illness. Furthermore, instruct the patient to practice tithing, and to do the Meditation on Twin Hearts regularly to generate more positive karma. It is also advisable to utilize the law of forgiveness, by forgiving others and asking for divine forgiveness.

Disorders of the Brain and Nervous System

BRAIN AND NERVOUS SYSTEM

The brain and nervous system are controlled and energized by the crown and forehead chakra. The ajna chakra also affects and energizes the brain and the nervous system. The back head minor chakra controls and energizes the internal carotid arteries which supply blood to the brain, eyes, ears, and other organs inside the head. It also controls and energizes the external carotid arteries which supply blood to the scalp and the face. The back head minor chakra energizes the entire head area. The jaw minor chakras, the throat chakra, and the secondary throat minor chakra affect and energize the carotid arteries going to the head. The heart chakra and thymus gland help regulate and harmonize the upper chakras and their corresponding organs.

Portions of the pranic energy from the basic chakra, sex chakra, and navel chakra are transmuted and utilized by the head chakras and the brain. Therefore, the health of the head chakras, the brain, and the organs inside the head depends on the health of the lower chakras. The human body is just like a tree. Nutrients from the ground must go up for the tree to be healthy.

The eyes and ears are controlled and energized by the crown, forehead, and ajna chakras. The eyes have corresponding eye minor chakras. The ears

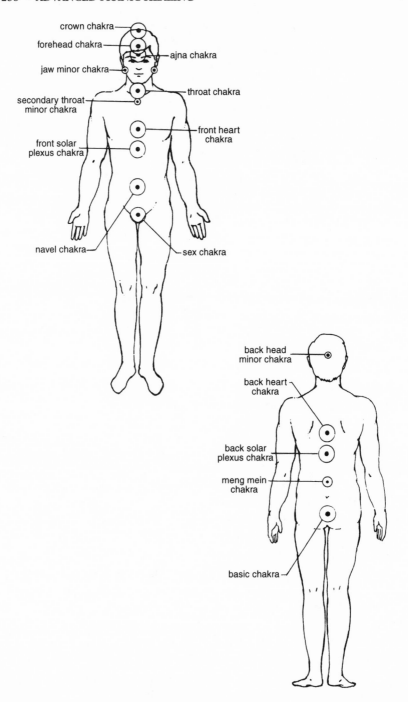

Figure 17-1. Chakras affecting the brain.

have corresponding ear minor chakras. The back head chakra and the jaw minor chakras affect and energize the entire head including the eyes and ears. The sense of smell is controlled and energized by the crown, forehead, and ajna chakras. It is also controlled and energized by the nostril minor chakras. The sense of taste is controlled by the crown and forehead chakras. It is also controlled and energized by the throat chakra and the jaw minor chakras. The sense of touch is controlled and energized by the crown chakra, forehead chakra, and the basic chakra.

BELL'S PALSY

The following chakras are adversely affected in Bell's palsy:

1. Solar plexus chakra;
2. Forehead chakra;
3. Ajna chakra;
4. Temple minor chakra;
5. Jaw minor chakra.

The crown chakra, the back head chakra, ear minor chakra, and the throat chakra are partially affected.

1. Scan the patient, then rescan during pranic treatment.
2. Apply general sweeping once or twice.
3. Apply localized sweeping thoroughly on the front and back solar plexus chakra, and the liver. Energize the solar plexus chakra with light whitish-green, light whitish-blue, and ordinary light whitish-violet prana.
4. Apply localized sweeping on the front and back heart chakra. Energize the heart chakra through the back heart chakra with light whitish-green; then use more ordinary light whitish-violet.
5. Apply localized sweeping on the ajna chakra, forehead chakra, crown chakra, back head minor chakra, the affected temple minor chakra, the affected ear minor chakra, and the affected jaw minor chakra thoroughly and alternately with light whitish-green prana and ordinary light whitish-violet prana. It is important that cleansing be done thoroughly. Energize them with light whitish-green, then use more ordinary light whitish-violet.
6. Apply localized sweeping on the affected part thoroughly and alternately with light whitish-green prana and ordinary light whitish-violet prana. Energize the affected part with light

whitish-green prana; then use more ordinary light whitish-violet prana.

7. Apply localized sweeping on the throat chakra alternately with light whitish-green prana and ordinary light whitish-violet prana. Energize it with light whitish-green prana; then use more ordinary light whitish-violet prana.

8. To further accelerate the healing process, apply localized sweeping on the navel chakra and the basic chakra. Energize them with white prana.

9. Stabilize and release the projected pranic energy.

10. Repeat the treatment once a day for as long as necessary.

FACIAL TICS

In patients with facial tics the forehead chakra, ajna chakra, eye minor chakra, and the temple minor chakra are affected. The crown chakra, back head minor chakra, jaw minor chakra, and throat chakra are partially affected. If it is emotional in origin, then the solar plexus chakra is affected.

1. Scan the patient, then rescan during pranic treatment.

2. Apply general sweeping once or twice.

3. Apply localized sweeping on the front and back heart chakra. Energize the back heart chakra with light whitish-green prana, then with more ordinary light whitish-violet prana. Visualize the heart chakra becoming bigger.

4. Apply localized sweeping thoroughly on the front and back solar plexus chakra and the liver. Energize the solar plexus chakra with light whitish-green prana, ordinary light whitish-violet prana, and light whitish-blue prana.

5. Apply localized sweeping on the crown chakra, forehead chakra, ajna chakra, back head minor chakra, the affected eye minor chakra, and the affected temple minor chakra thoroughly and alternately with light whitish-green prana and ordinary light whitish-violet prana. Energize them with light whitish-green, then use more ordinary light whitish-violet.

6. Apply localized sweeping on the jaw minor chakras, throat chakra, and secondary throat minor chakra. Energize them with light whitish-green prana, then use more ordinary light whitish-violet prana.

7. Apply localized sweeping on the navel chakra and basic chakra. Energize them with white prana.

8. Stabilize and release the projected pranic energy.
9. Repeat treatment three times a week.

NUMBNESS

Numbness could be due to many possible causes. It could be due to a vitamin deficiency manifesting as pranic depletion of the basic chakra, of the arms, and of the legs. The basic chakra, the arms, the legs, and their minor chakras have to be cleansed thoroughly and alternately with light whitish-green prana and light whitish-orange prana. Then energize the basic chakra, the minor chakras of the arms and legs, and the affected parts with light whitish-green prana, light whitish-orange prana, then use more light whitish-red prana. In many instances, the numbness will disappear almost instantly if the treatment is done properly.

Numbness could also be due to pancreatic diabetes. The treatment for diabetes and the treatment for numbness have to be combined (see page 207).

Numbness could also be due to a stroke, an accident, and other factors. The pranic treatment will have to be based on the cause and the finding from scanning the patient. Or you may just clean and energize all the chakras, except the spleen chakra and the meng mein chakra, which may or may not be energized depending upon the situation.

EPILEPSY

In patients with epilepsy the solar plexus chakra is congested and overactivated. The forehead, ajna, and back head chakras are adversely affected. The crown chakra, the jaw minor chakras, and the throat chakra are partially affected. The left and right brain are not balanced. One side of the brain is depleted. The other side is congested. The area between the left brain and the right brain is filled with grayish energy. The grayish energy of the head is connected to the dirty energy from the solar plexus chakra. An epileptic attack is likely to occur when the patient is emotionally upset.

1. Scan the patient, then rescan during pranic treatment.
2. Apply general sweeping twice.
3. Apply localized sweeping on the front and back heart chakra. Energize the heart chakra through the back heart chakra with less light whitish-green prana and more light whitish-violet prana.

4. Apply localized sweeping on the front and back solar plexus chakra and the liver. The "solar plexus chakra cleansing technique" (page 87) can be applied by experienced, proficient, advanced pranic healers. Energize the solar plexus chakra with light whitish-green prana and light whitish-blue prana. When energizing with blue prana, simultaneously will the overactive solar plexus chakra to become smaller.

5. Apply localized sweeping on the entire head, on the back head minor chakra, crown chakra, forehead chakra, ajna chakra, jaw minor chakras, the throat chakra, and secondary throat minor chakra thoroughly, and alternately use light whitish-green prana and light whitish-violet prana. The grayish energy between the left and right brain must be cleansed thoroughly.

6. Energize the crown chakra, forehead chakra, ajna chakra, back head chakra, jaw minor chakras, throat chakra, and secondary throat minor chakra with light whitish-green prana; then use more ordinary light whitish-violet prana. The emphasis of the treatment is on the ajna chakra, forehead chakra, and the back head minor chakra.

7. Apply localized sweeping on the navel chakra and the basic chakra. Energize them with white prana.

8. Stabilize and release the projected pranic energy.

9. Repeat treatment three times a week.

PARKINSON'S DISEASE

In patients with Parkinson's disease, the following chakras are affected:

a) The basic chakra is depleted, underactivated, and filled with dirty red diseased energy;

b) The solar plexus chakra is congested, overactivated, and filled with dirty red diseased energy;

c) The back head minor chakra is depleted, overactivated, and filled with dirty red diseased energy;

d) The ajna chakra is depleted, overactivated, and filled with dirty red diseased energy.

The spine and the sides of the spine are clogged by dirty red diseased energy. The body is very depleted. The other chakras are also affected. The healer has to be relatively powerful, otherwise, there is a tendency to become depleted. The root cause is the malfunctioning of the basic chakra. In healthy persons, the pranic energy rises to the upper chakras, including the back head minor chakra, providing them with the necessary pranic energy. In Parkinson's disease, the patient's basic chakra is filled with dirty red diseased energy clogging the spine, the sides of the spine, and the solar plexus chakra. The ajna chakra and the back head minor chakra are clogged and deprived of the necessary transmuted pranic energy from the basic chakra. This is why they are depleted, but also overactivated. The ajna chakra and the back head chakra are overactivated since they have to work harder in order to compensate for the lack of pranic energy from the basic chakra. The malfunction of the back head minor chakra gradually manifests as degeneration of certain nerve cells in the brain which are responsible for producing dopamine, resulting in its deficiency.

1. Scan the patient, then rescan during pranic treatment.
2. Apply general sweeping several times with light whitish-green prana.
3. Apply localized sweeping on the spine and the sides of the spine thoroughly and alternately with light whitish-green prana, light whitish-orange prana, and ordinary light whitish-violet prana. Light whitish-orange should not be used near the head or beyond the neck. This step is very important.
4. Apply localized sweeping on the basic chakra thoroughly and alternately with light whitish-green and light whitish-orange. This has to be done 50 to 100 times. Energize the basic chakra with light whitish-red prana. This step is very important.
5. Apply localized sweeping thoroughly on the meng mein chakra.
6. Apply localized sweeping on the sex and navel chakras, and energize them with light whitish-red prana.
7. Apply localized sweeping on the front and back solar plexus chakra and on the liver thoroughly and alternately with light whitish-green and light whitish-orange. Energize the solar plexus chakra with light whitish-green, light whitish-orange, and light whitish-red. This has to be done by an experienced advanced pranic healer.
8. Apply localized sweeping on the lungs. Energize the lungs through the back of the lungs directly with light whitish-green, light whitish-orange, and light whitish-red prana. This has cleansing and strengthening effects on the blood and on the whole body. When energizing, the healer's fingers should be pointed away from the patient's head.
9. Apply localized sweeping on the front and back heart chakra. Energize the back heart chakra with less of light whitish-green, then

with more of ordinary light whitish-violet prana. The heart chakra helps regulate and harmonize the upper chakras.

10. Apply localized sweeping on the spleen chakra. Energize the spleen chakra with white prana. This has to be done with caution.

11. Apply localized sweeping on the throat chakra, secondary throat minor chakra, and jaw minor chakras alternately with light whitish-green and ordinary light whitish-violet. Energize them with ordinary light whitish-violet.

12. Apply localized sweeping on the entire head, crown chakra, forehead chakra, ajna chakra, and back head minor chakra thoroughly and alternately with light whitish-green and ordinary light whitish-violet. Energize them with light electric-violet pranic energy. Inhibit the back head minor chakra and the ajna chakra by energizing them with light whitish-blue prana. The emphasis is on the back head minor chakra and on the ajna chakra which have to be cleansed and energized thoroughly. This step is very important.

13. Apply localized sweeping on the arms, legs, and on their minor chakras alternately with light whitish-green prana and light whitish-orange prana. Energize the minor chakras on the arms and legs with light whitish-red prana.

14. Stabilize and release the projected pranic energy.

15. Repeat pranic treatment every day for the first few weeks. Later, repeat pranic treatment three times a week for as long as necessary. In general, there will be a noticeable improvement after a few weeks of pranic treatment. The treatment has to be continued for at least several months.

It is advisable for the patient to become a vegetarian, to generate good karma by tithing, and to use the Law of Forgiveness by forgiving others and by asking for divine forgiveness.

ENCEPHALITIS AND MENINGITIS

1. Scan the patient, then rescan during pranic treatment.
2. Apply general sweeping twice.
3. Apply localized sweeping thoroughly and alternately with light whitish-green prana and ordinary light whitish-violet prana on the entire head, crown chakra, forehead chakra, ajna chakra, back head minor chakra, and jaw minor chakras. Energize them with light whitish-green, light whitish-blue, and ordinary light

whitish-violet. This step is very important and can be repeated several times a day.

4. Apply localized sweeping on the throat chakra and secondary throat minor chakra. Energize them with light whitish-green prana and ordinary light whitish-violet prana. This stimulates the lymphatic system.

5. Apply localized sweeping on the front and back heart chakra. Energize the thymus through the back heart chakra with light whitish-green prana, then use more ordinary light whitish-violet prana.

6. Apply localized sweeping thoroughly on the spine.

7. Apply localized sweeping on the lungs. Energize the lungs through the back of the lungs with light whitish-green prana, and light whitish-orange prana. This has a cleansing effect on the blood. When energizing with orange prana, the healer's fingers should be pointed away from the patient's head.

8. Apply localized sweeping thoroughly on the front and back solar plexus chakra. This is very important. Energize the front solar plexus chakra with light whitish-green, light whitish-blue, and ordinary light whitish-violet prana.

9. Apply localized sweeping on the front and back spleen chakra. Energize the spleen chakra with light whitish-green prana, then use more ordinary light whitish-violet prana. This has to be done with caution.

10. Apply localized sweeping on the navel and sex chakras. Energize them with white prana.

11. Apply localized sweeping on the meng mein chakra and on the basic chakra.

12. Apply localized sweeping on the arms and legs. Energize the sole and hand chakras with ordinary light whitish-violet prana.

13. Stabilize and release the projected pranic energy.

14. Repeat treatment once a day for as long as necessary.

MENTAL RETARDATION

In patients with mental retardation, the crown chakra, forehead chakra, ajna chakra, back head minor chakra, and throat chakra are grayish and underactivated. The basic chakra and the sex chakra are affected and have to be treated, since the transmuted basic pranic energy and sex pranic energy are needed and utilized by the upper chakras.

1. Scan the patient, then rescan during pranic treatment.
2. Apply general sweeping twice.
3. Apply localized sweeping alternately with light whitish-green prana and ordinary light whitish-violet prana on the entire head, crown chakra, forehead chakra, ajna chakra, back head minor chakra, jaw minor chakras, throat chakra, and secondary throat minor chakra. This has to be done thoroughly.
4. Energize the crown chakra, forehead chakra, ajna chakra, and throat chakra with light whitish-green prana, then use more ordinary light whitish-violet prana. When energizing with ordinary light whitish-violet, simultaneously will the chakras to become bigger.
5. Energize the back head minor chakra, jaw minor chakras, and secondary throat minor chakra with light whitish-green prana then use more ordinary light whitish-violet prana.
6. Apply localized sweeping on the front and back heart chakra. Energize the back heart chakra with light whitish-green prana, then use more ordinary light whitish-violet prana.
7. Apply localized sweeping on the front and back solar plexus chakra. Energize the front solar plexus chakra with white prana.
8. Apply localized sweeping on the navel chakra. Energize with light whitish-red prana.
9. Apply localized sweeping on the sex chakra and basic chakra thoroughly and alternately with light whitish-green and light whitish-orange prana. Energize them with light whitish-red prana.
10. Apply localized sweeping on the arms and legs alternately with light whitish-green and light whitish-orange prana. Energize the minor chakras of the arms and legs with light whitish-red.
11. Stabilize and release the projected energy.
12. Repeat treatment three times a week for the next several years. Pranic treatment has to be complemented with special education.

This procedure can be applied once or twice a week on older people as a corrective or preventive treatment for senility.

Tumors and Cancer

BENIGN TUMORS

Tumors are either benign or malignant. Cancer is any malignant tumor. The multiplication of cells requires pranic energy. If an organ or a part is congested with dirty red pranic energy for a prolonged period, this may tend to manifest as abnormal cell growth or a tumor. An affected part or organ with a tumor is clairvoyantly seen as congested with dirty red energy. In benign tumors, the following chakras are affected:

a) The ajna chakra is overactivated, congested, and filled with dirty red diseased energy;

b) The solar plexus chakra is overactivated, congested, and filled with dirty red diseased energy;

c) The basic chakra is overactivated, congested or depleted, and filled with dirty diseased energy.

Tumors could be physical, etheric, or emotional in origin. In rare cases, the improper practice of advanced chi kung may manifest as a tumor. This is an example of a tumor of etheric origin. Prolonged harboring of negative emotions will manifest as pranic congestion in certain parts of the body. This may manifest as abnormal cell growth.

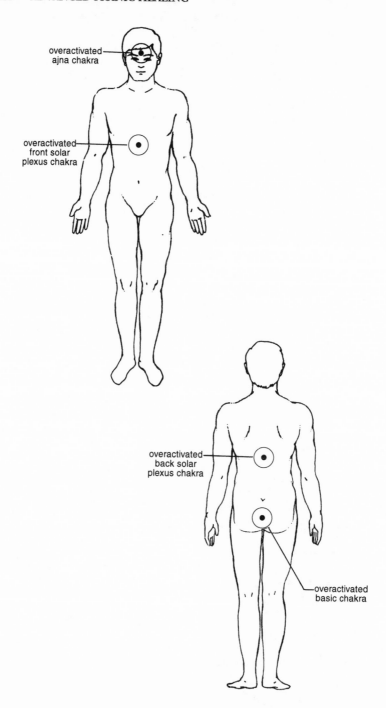

Figure 18-1. Chakral condition of patient with a benign tumor.

1. Scan the patient, and rescan during treatment.
2. Apply general sweeping twice.
3. Apply localized sweeping on the ajna chakra alternately with light whitish-green and ordinary light whitish-violet. Energize the ajna chakra with light electric-violet pranic energy.
4. Apply localized sweeping on the front and back heart chakra. Energize the back heart chakra with light electric-violet pranic energy.
5. Apply localized sweeping on the front and back solar plexus chakra, and on the liver thoroughly and alternately with light whitish-green and light whitish-orange. Energize the solar plexus chakra with light whitish-green, ordinary light whitish-violet, and light whitish-blue.
6. Apply localized sweeping on the basic chakra alternately with light whitish-green and light whitish-orange. Energize the basic chakra with white prana.
7. Apply localized sweeping on the affected part thoroughly and alternately with light whitish-green and light whitish-orange. Energize the affected part with light blue for a localizing effect. Then energize it with light green prana, and light orange prana. If the affected part is delicate, then just use light electric-violet pranic energy for cleansing and energizing.
8. Stabilize and release the projected pranic energy.
9. Repeat treatment twice or thrice a week for as long as necessary.

CANCER

In cancer cases, the following chakras are affected:

a) The basic chakra is overactivated, depleted, and filled with dirty yellow-red diseased energy or with dirty red diseased energy;
b) The meng mein chakra is overactivated, depleted, and filled with dirty yellow-red diseased energy or with dirty red diseased energy;
c) The solar plexus chakra is overactivated, congested, and filled with dirty yellow-red diseased energy or dirty red diseased energy;
d) The heart chakra is underactivated, depleted, and filled with dirty yellow-red diseased energy or dirty red diseased energy;
e) The ajna chakra is underactivated, depleted, and filled with dirty yellow-red diseased energy or dirty red diseased energy.

In general, the upper chakras are underactivated and depleted. If the ajna chakra and the heart chakra are normalized, then the other affected chakras will also gradually become normalized. The corresponding chakra of the af-

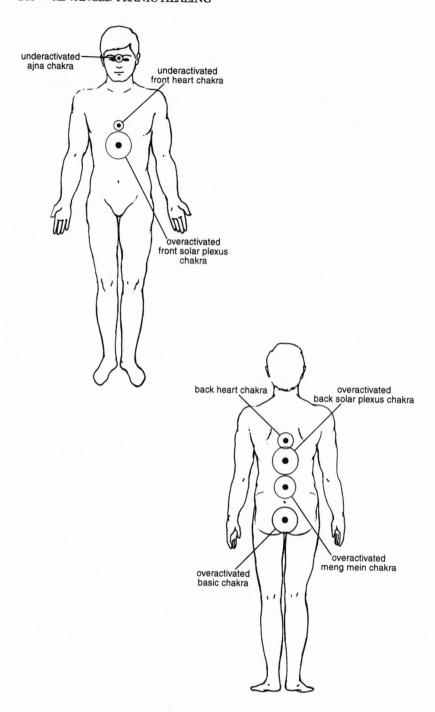

Figure 18-2.   Chakral condition of patient with cancer.

fected organ is overactivated and filled with dirty yellow-red diseased energy or dirty red diseased energy. If the lungs are affected, the back heart chakra is overactivated. If the brain is affected, the ajna chakra and back head chakra are overactivated.

A cancerous organ or part is clairvoyantly seen as congested with dirty red diseased energy or with dirty yellow-red diseased energy. There is too much dirty red diseased energy and dirty yellow diseased energy in the affected area, resulting in the rampant growth of cancerous cells. The more dirty yellow diseased energy, the faster is the growth. If the affected part contains only a little dirty yellow diseased energy or none at all, then the growth of cancer cells is slow. The differences between acute cancer and mild cancer are: a) in acute cases, the affected chakras and parts contain a lot of dirty yellow diseased energy ranging from 40–60%, while in mild cases, the affected chakras and parts contain less dirty yellow diseased energy or none at all ranging from 0–20% (if the range is between 20–40%, the cases are partially acute); b) in acute cases, the basic, meng mein, and solar plexus chakras are very overactivated, while in mild cases, they are not so overactivated. The prognosis for acute cancer is poor.

Cancer could be physical, etheric, emotional, or karmic in origin, or a combination of these. Negative emotions, such as anger, resentment, or hatred overactivate the solar plexus chakra. The overactivated solar plexus chakra in turn activates the meng mein and basic chakras. This in the long run may manifest as cancer. For example, heavy smoking for a long period combined with prolonged harboring of negative emotions may manifest as lung cancer. It seems that negative emotions in the form of longstanding anger, resentment, or hatred is a major contributing cause of cancer.

If the cancer is due to negative karma, then it is difficult to heal. The nature of the negative karma is that of physical cruelty.

For healing to take place, there is a need to forgive others for actual or "apparent" hurts. Forgiving releases the longstanding negative emotions; therefore, it is therapeutic. There is a need to change one's attitude toward others, oneself, and life in general from that of hating to that of being sweet and loving; from being too critical to tolerance and appreciativeness; from being greedy and too selfish to being more sensitive and giving; from resentfulness and vindictiveness to understanding and forgiveness; from pessimism and depression to happiness and hopefulness.

The treatment of cancer requires a combination of several approaches:

1. Proper medical treatment. What constitutes proper medical treatment will be left to scientists, medical doctors, and patients to decide. Each patient has the right to choose the type of treatment.

Artificial legal impediments preventing the patient from exercising this right should be removed.
2. Proper pranic treatment.
3. Proper diet.
4. Proper emotion.
5. The utilization of the law of forgiveness and the law of mercy.

PROPER PRANIC TREATMENT

The approach in treating cancer is as follows:

1. Cleansing;
2. Normalizing the chakras;
3. Stimulating the defense system;
4. Disintegrating the cancerous cells.

By cleansing or removing the dirty or muddy yellowish-red diseased energy from the affected part and the affected chakras, the cancer cells will be deprived of necessary diseased energy for rampant growth. This will help the body heal itself or at least reduce the rate of deterioration.

Cancer patients have underactivated upper chakras, especially the ajna chakra and heart chakra, which normally do not contain dirty yellow-red diseased energy. The solar plexus chakra, meng mein chakra, and basic chakra are overactivated and filled with dirty yellow-red diseased energy. The upper chakras have to be cleansed and activated; and the affected lower chakras have to be cleansed and inhibited. By normalizing the ajna chakra and the heart chakra, it will be easier to normalize the affected lower chakras. Whether the affected chakras can be permanently normalized depends on the karmic factor.

The healing process is further hastened by stimulating the defense system of the body.

The cancer cells can also be gradually disintegrated by using medium or dark green prana and orange prana. Dark electric-violet pranic energy can also be used by more advanced pranic healers. Medium or dark blue prana is projected first to localize the destructive pranic energies that will be projected. In using destructive pranic energies, it is more important that the patient should be receptive. Otherwise, the projected destructive pranic energies may bounce back to the healer. The use of destructive pranic energies is optional. They should not be used on delicate organs like the brain, eyes, and the pancreas (except for medium electric-violet prana).

PROPER DIET

A proper diet is very important. The body of the patient is very grayish and its ability to expel diseased and used-up energy is adversely affected. Eating meat which contains a lot of grayish-red energy, sometimes also grayish-yellow energy, will only worsen the condition. Pork definitely should be avoided. Hot spicy food is to be avoided, since it contains a lot of red prana. In general, fish is cleaner than meat, but it is still to be avoided.

It is important that the patient become a vegetarian. This will substantially lessen the burden of the body in expelling used-up diseased energy. Intake of "yang" fruits and vegetables are to be minimized or avoided since they contain a lot of red prana. Yang fruits and vegetables are those that tend to make the body feel "hot."

PROPER EMOTION

Irritability, anger, resentment, a sense of hopelessness, and other negative emotions are to be avoided for the following reasons:

1. Prolonged negative emotions are a major contributing factor in cancer.
2. Negative emotions have a depleting effect on the already very depleted body, thereby worsening the condition.
3. Negative emotions cause the major chakras to malfunction, which adversely affects the immune and defense system.
4. Negative emotions cause the major chakras to malfunction, thereby making recovery very unlikely. A healthy body requires healthy chakras.

Tolerance, forgiveness, peace, happiness or joy, warmth, kindness, cordiality, love, hope, and other positive emotions are to be encouraged. Many positive emotions produce pink prana which is a type of emotional pranic energy. Pink prana has a cleansing effect on the chakras and on the meridians. This is clairvoyantly seen as dirty red energy being dispersed and transmuted by the pink prana from the chakras and the meridians. The cleansing of the chakras and meridians allows the free flow of pranic energy and causes the chakras to normalize, thereby enhancing the body's ability to normalize itself.

Musk and rose oil contain a lot of pink prana. They can be taken internally. Since many ailments are emotional in origin, it is likely in the future that musk and rose oil will be widely used to normalize emotions, as well as for medication. Another source of pink prana comes from rose quartz. Water can be energized with pink prana by putting a "clean" rose quartz in a bottle of water for several hours. It is not advisable for cancer patients to wear crystals, including diamonds, or be near large crystals since crystals tend to activate the lower chakras, thereby making the condition worse.

Avoiding negative emotions, and feeling positive emotions is essential in the treatment of cancer, as well as for the treatment of other severe ailments. Doing the Meditation on Twin Hearts regularly or daily will be extremely helpful, since this meditation produces a sense of inner peace, harmony, and happiness. It also stimulates kindness and love in the meditator if done persistently. The Meditation on Twin Hearts has powerful healing effects for the following reasons:

1. The meditator feels happiness, peace, loving-kindness, and other positive emotions during and after meditation. This has cleansing and normalizing effects on the affected chakras and meridians.
2. A tremendous flow of divine energy or electric-violet energy pours down during the Meditation on Twin Hearts. This divine energy has cleansing, energizing, normalizing, and regenerating effects.

The assimilation of the divine healing energy can be enhanced by repeating the following affirmation three times after the meditation. The excess energy has to be released and physical exercise has to be done.

My mind, emotion, and body are being cleansed. They are assimilating the divine healing energy. My chakras, meridians, and every particle in my body are being cleansed, energized, and healed. I am being made whole. I am being healed. I willingly and gratefully accept the divine healing energy with thanks and in full faith.

LAW OF FORGIVENESS AND LAW OF MERCY

Negative karma can be neutralized by utilizing the "law of forgiveness" and the "law of mercy." It is necessary to forgive and bless those who have hurt you. This is done by making a list of these people. Visualize them. Mentally forgive each one of them and bless them with good health, happiness, success, abundance, and divine protection. For one's negative karma to be forgiven, it is necessary to forgive others. "For if ye forgive men their trespasses, your heavenly Father will also forgive you; but if ye forgive not men their trespasses, neither will your Father forgive your trespasses" (Matthew 6:14-15).

The law of mercy simply means to receive mercy, one must be merciful. "Blessed are the merciful: for they shall obtain mercy" (Matthew 5:7). It is advisable to tithe every month and to do charitable acts. These acts of mercy will generate good karma which will entitle you to receive mercy. Being a vegetarian is an act of mercy toward the animal kingdom; therefore, it is highly recommended, especially for those with severe ailments. Acts of cruelty, injurious words, and critical negative thoughts must be avoided. How can one receive mercy when one is causing so much pain for others? "God cannot be mocked. A man reaps what he sows" (Galatians 6:7).

GENERAL PRANIC PROCEDURE FOR TREATING CANCER

1. Scan the patient, then rescan during pranic treatment.
2. Apply general sweeping several times with light whitish-green prana. Many cancer patients have blackish or dark gray auras. The outer, health, and inner auras are all badly affected.
3. Apply localized sweeping on the lungs. Energize the lungs directly through the back of the lungs with light whitish-green and light whitish-orange prana. This has cleansing effects on the blood and on the whole body. The blood, under normal conditions, is very light whitish-orange-red. In many cancer cases, the blood is dirty yellow-red.
4. Apply localized sweeping on the front and back heart chakra alternately with light whitish-green and ordinary light whitish-violet. Energize the front heart chakra and the thymus gland through the back heart chakra with electric-violet prana. Simultaneously will the heart chakra to become bigger. Rescan the front and back heart chakra. By cleansing and energizing the heart chakra, the thymus gland will be strengthened which will stimulate the defense system. It will also help normalize the upper chakras and enable the patient to experience a sense of inner peace.
5. Apply localized sweeping alternately with light whitish-green prana and ordinary light violet prana on the entire head area, on the crown chakra, forehead chakra, ajna chakra, and on the back head minor chakra. The ajna chakra has to be cleansed thoroughly by applying localized sweeping 30 to 50 times. Energize them with electric-violet prana. Simultaneously will the crown chakra, forehead chakra, and ajna chakra to become bigger. Rescan the treated chakras. The emphasis is on the ajna chakra.

6. When energizing the ajna chakra with electric-violet prana, gently but firmly instruct the ajna chakra to normalize and to harmonize all the chakras and all the internal organs. This has cleansing and normalizing effects on the other affected chakras. The solar plexus chakra, meng mein chakra, and basic chakra will be partially or substantially cleansed and inhibited.

7. Apply localized sweeping thoroughly on the jaw minor chakras, throat chakra, and secondary throat minor chakra alternately with light whitish-green prana and ordinary light whitish-violet prana. Energize them with electric-violet prana. When energizing the throat chakra, simultaneously will it to become bigger.

8. The solar plexus chakra is overactivated and filled with dirty yellow-red diseased energy. The solar plexus chakra and the liver have to be cleansed thoroughly. This is very important. Energize the front and back solar plexus chakra and the liver with light blue prana for a localizing effect. Apply localized sweeping on the front and back solar plexus chakra and the liver alternately with light whitish-green prana and light whitish-orange prana 30 to 50 times.

9. Energize the front solar plexus chakra with light whitish-green prana and light whitish-orange prana. This has a cleansing effect on the internal organs and the body. Wait for a few minutes before inhibiting the solar plexus chakra. Energize the solar plexus chakra with light blue; simultaneously will it to become smaller. Do not overinhibit since it has a weakening effect. Rescan the solar plexus chakra.

10. After several weeks or months, when the patient has substantially improved, energize the solar plexus chakra with light whitish-green, light whitish-violet, and light blue prana instead of light whitish-green, light whitish-orange, and light blue.

11. The meng mein chakra is overactivated and filled with grayish-yellowish-red energy. The meng mein chakra has to be cleansed thoroughly and inhibited. Energize the meng mein chakra with light blue for localizing effects. Apply sweeping on the meng mein chakra alternately with light whitish-green prana and light whitish-orange prana 20 to 30 times.

12. Inhibit the meng mein chakra by energizing it with light blue prana and simultaneously will it to become smaller. Rescan the meng mein chakra. The normal size of the meng mein chakra is about 1/2 to 2/3 the average size of the major chakras. This step is very important.

13. The basic chakra is overactivated and filled with dirty yellow-red diseased energy. The basic chakra has to be cleansed thoroughly

and inhibited. Energize the basic chakra with light blue prana for a localizing effect. Apply localized sweeping on the basic chakra with light whitish-green prana and light whitish-orange prana 50 times.

14. Energize thoroughly the basic chakra with white prana. This is very important since the basic chakra is very depleted. Inhibit the basic chakra by energizing it with light blue prana and simultaneously will it to become smaller. Rescan the basic chakra.

15. Apply sweeping thoroughly on the front and back spleen chakra with light whitish-green prana. Energize the spleen chakra with light whitish-green and ordinary light whitish-violet. This has to be done with caution.

16. Apply localized sweeping on the navel chakra with light whitish-green prana. Energize it with white prana.

17. Apply localized sweeping on the sex chakra and energize it with white prana.

18. Apply localized sweeping on the arms and legs with light whitish-green and light whitish-orange prana. The armpit, elbow, hand, hip, knee, and sole minor chakras must also be cleansed. Energize the hand and sole minor chakras with ordinary light whitish-violet.

19. The affected part is very congested and filled with dirty yellow-red diseased energy. Energize the affected part with light blue prana for localizing effects. Apply localized sweeping on the affected organ thoroughly and alternately with light whitish-green and light whitish-orange 100 to 200 times. Light whitish-green and light whitish-orange are used only on affected organs which are not delicate. Light whitish-green is used in cleansing delicate organs. Electric-violet can be used to clean both delicate and nondelicate organs. By cleansing the affected part thoroughly, the cancer cells will be starved of dirty yellow-red diseased energy which is necessary for their chaotic growth. If cleansing is done properly, the patient will be partially, substantially, or completely relieved. This step is very important.

20. Cancer cells can be gradually disintegrated by energizing with medium or dark green prana and orange prana. Energize the affected part with medium blue prana for localizing effects for several minutes then energize with medium or dark green prana then medium or dark orange prana. More proficient, pranic healers can also project dark electric-violet prana. Visualize the pranic energy coming out as laser-like and as thin as the tip of a ballpoint pen.

The destructive pranic energies have to be projected in a very concentrated form to give them sufficient potency to partially and gradually disintegrate the cancer cells. This is to be used only on non-delicate organs. Do not energize the sex organ with medium or dark orange prana.

21. When projecting the medium or dark green prana and orange prana, simultaneously visualize the cancer as shrinking or becoming smaller and smaller until it disappears completely.

22. If the cancer cells have metastasized, project electric-violet prana on the ajna chakra, and instruct the electric-violet light to seek and destroy all cancer cells in the body.

23. For delicate organs like the eyes, brain, and pancreas, just clean and energize with light electric-violet pranic energy.

24. The corresponding chakra of the affected organ is overactivated; therefore, it has to be cleansed and inhibited. Apply localized sweeping on the corresponding chakra thoroughly and alternately with light whitish-green prana and light whitish-orange prana. Do not use orange on or near the head, or the spleen. Energize it with light blue, and simultaneously will it to become smaller. Rescan.

25. Stabilize and release the projected pranic energy.

26. Repeat the treatment three times a week for as long as necessary. Some cancer patients undergo pranic treatment for more than a year.

Unless the healer is sufficiently powerful, he or she may become exhausted during the treatment since the patient is very depleted. The treatment of cancer patients requires a proficient, powerful, advanced pranic healer.

Since the energy body of the cancer patient is very dirty, it is advisable that healers wash their hands and the arms with water and salt (or alcohol) regularly during sweeping and energizing to minimize contamination. Please flick your hand regularly when energizing to minimize contamination. If the healer has been contaminated, he or she may experience arthritis of the fingers. If the basic chakra and spleen chakra are contaminated, the healer may experience severe general weakness lasting for several months unless treated regularly by another pranic healer.

Encourage the patient to become a vegetarian. Aside from the benefits derived from a vegetarian diet, being a vegetarian is an act of mercy toward the animal kingdom. Based on the law of karma, a person who shows mercy will in turn also receive mercy. This helps in the faster healing of the patient's illness. All forms of negative emotions are to be minimized or avoided. It is necessary to forgive, since this releases the accumulated pent-up negative emotions. Furthermore, instruct the patient to practice tithing and to do the Meditation on Twin Hearts regularly to help generate more positive karma.

In general, the following are the benefits derived by cancer patients from this form of healing:

1. The intense pain will be gradually reduced after several treatments.
2. The energy level of the patient will be increased, and the patient will feel much stronger after several treatments.
3. The appetite will improve.
4. The growth of cancer cells will be reduced, if not stopped.
5. Cancer cells will be gradually and partially destroyed.
6. For terminal cancer patients, pranic healing will enable them to die in peace and with dignity.

Many cancer patients cannot be healed for the following reasons:

1. The patient's body has already been badly damaged by potent drugs;
2. Cancer cells have already spread;
3. The body of the patient is already extremely weak and its capacity to absorb and retain pranic energy has greatly diminished;
4. Some of the organs have already been badly damaged and are beyond repair;
5. The ailment could be of karmic origin.

Because of these factors, many cancer patients will be partially or completely relieved, their health improved and their life prolonged, but only some will be substantially or completely cured.

LUNG CANCER

With lung cancer, the back heart chakra is overactivated and filled with grayish-yellowish-red energy. The lung minor chakras are also overactivated.

Energize the lungs with light whitish-blue prana for a localizing effect. Apply localized sweeping on the front, side, and back of the lungs thoroughly and alternately with light whitish-green and light whitish-orange. The affected parts have to be cleansed thoroughly.

To partially and gradually disintegrate the cancer cells, energize the lungs directly through the back of the lungs with light blue prana for localizing effects. Then energize with medium or dark green prana and orange prana. When energizing, simultaneously visualize the cancer shrinking, becoming smaller, and gradually disappearing.

Apply localized sweeping thoroughly on the back heart chakra with light green prana. Energize it with light green prana then light whitish-blue prana. When energizing with light whitish-blue, simultaneously will the back heart chakra to become smaller. Rescan.

Energize the affected lung minor chakras with light blue and simultaneously will them to become smaller.

BREAST CANCER

The sex chakra is affected. Apply localized sweeping on the sex chakra thoroughly and alternately with light whitish-green prana and whitish-orange prana. Energize the sex chakra with light whitish-green, then with light blue. When energizing with light blue, simultaneously will the sex chakra to become smaller. Rescan.

Energize the affected breast with light blue prana for a localizing effect. Apply localized sweeping on the affected nipple chakra and on the affected breast thoroughly and alternately with light whitish-green prana and light whitish-orange prana.

Energize the affected breast with light blue for several minutes then with light green prana and light orange prana. When energizing, simultaneously visualize the cancer shrinking, becoming smaller, and gradually disappearing.

Energize the affected nipple chakra with light blue prana and simultaneously will it to become smaller. Rescan.

LIVER CANCER

Energize the liver with light blue prana for a localizing effect. Apply localized sweeping on the entire liver, with emphasis on the affected parts, thoroughly and alternately with light whitish-green prana and light whitish-orange prana.

Energize the liver directly with light or medium blue prana for several minutes. Then energize with medium or dark green prana and orange prana. When energizing, simultaneously visualize the cancer as shrinking, becoming smaller, and gradually disappearing.

Energize the liver minor chakras with light blue prana and simultaneously will them to become smaller.

COLON CANCER

Energize the colon with light blue prana for a localizing effect. Apply localized sweeping on the colon and on the affected part thoroughly and alternately with light whitish-green prana and light whitish-orange prana.

Energize the affected part with light or medium blue prana for several minutes. Energize the affected part with medium or dark green prana and orange prana. When energizing, simultaneously visualize the cancer as shrinking, becoming smaller, and gradually disappearing.

Apply localized sweeping thoroughly on the navel chakra and the large intestine minor chakra with light green prana. Energize them with light green prana and light blue prana. When energizing with light blue prana, simultaneously will the navel chakra then the large intestine minor chakra to become smaller.

BRAIN CANCER

With brain cancer, the ajna chakra and the back head chakra are overactivated and filled with gray-yellowish-red prana. Apply localized sweeping on the entire head, the ajna chakra, and back head chakra with emphasis on the affected part with light electric-violet prana.

Energize the affected part with light blue prana then with medium or light electric-violet. When energizing, simultaneously visualize the cancer shrinking, becoming smaller, and gradually disappearing.

Energize the back head minor chakra with light whitish-blue prana and simultaneously will it to become smaller. Rescan.

EYE CANCER

With eye cancer, the ajna chakra, the back head minor chakra, and the affected eye minor chakra are overactivated and filled with gray-yellowish-red prana. Apply localized sweeping on the ajna chakra, the back head minor chakra and on the affected eye with light electric-violet.

Energize the affected eye through the ajna chakra with light blue prana then with light or medium electric-violet. When energizing, simultaneously visualize the tumor shrinking, becoming smaller, and gradually disappearing.

Energize the ajna chakra with light whitish-blue. Simultaneously will the ajna chakra to become smaller, then visualize the pranic energy going to the affected eye and will the affected eye minor chakra to become smaller.

Energize the back head minor chakra with light whitish-blue prana and simultaneously will it to become smaller. Rescan.

Eye tumors can still be healed by pranic healing. But the prognosis for eye cancer is very poor.

There are many other types of cancer. The procedure for treatment is similar which is to clean the affected part thoroughly, to inhibit the overactivated corresponding chakra, and to gradually disintegrate the cancer cells with green prana and orange prana. For delicate organs, light or medium electric violet is used.

Author's Note: For rapid cell growth, the meng mein chakra has to be overactivated. In pregnant women and cancer patients, the meng mein chakras are overactivated. It would be interesting if studies and experiments can be done on anti-hypertensive drugs and herbs as possible treatments for cancer. Aspirin, bee propolis, B-17, and chlorophyll contain green prana. Garlic oil contains orange prana. Studies and experiments can also be done on these substances as possible treatments for cancer.

PART III:
SUPPLEMENTARY
HEALING

To each generation is given the part of conserving the essential features of the old and beloved form, but also of wisely expanding and enriching it. Each cycle must add the gain of further research and scientific endeavour, and subtract that which is worn out and of no value.

—*Alice Bailey*
Initiation Human and Solar

Instructive Healing

BASIC CONCEPTS

Instructive healing is based on the concept that the body (bioplasmic and physical) has a consciousness; therefore, it is capable of receiving and following instructions. The intelligence or consciousness of the body is called the physical subconscious mind. The term subconscious is used since it is below the level of ordinary consciousness. By repeatedly instructing the physical subconscious mind, the rate of recovery can be hastened.

It is precisely because the body has a consciousness or intelligence that the different systems of the body are able to function automatically and harmoniously without your awareness or instructions. Without the physical subconscious mind, physical action, like running or dancing, which requires very complex coordination of the muscles, would not be possible. Scientists who are involved with robotics are fully aware of the great effort required to make a computer program to produce a robot capable of walking, climbing, and running.

It is precisely because of the physical subconscious mind that a wound or a burn heals by itself. It is because of the physical subconscious mind that hundreds or even thousands of very complex biochemical reactions are taking place harmoniously within your body without your awareness or instructions. The physical and the bioplasmic bodies are indeed marvelous, living, intelligent machines.

The chakras have an intelligence or consciousness which is called chakral subconscious mind. This is why I use the phrase, "_____ chakra controls and energizes." The word *control* implies intelligence. The chakras or the chakral subconscious minds are under the control of the physical subconscious mind.

The organs have a consciousness or intelligence which is called the organic subconscious mind. The organs and the organic subconscious minds are under the control of the corresponding major chakra, or the chakral subconscious mind. The organic subconscious minds correspond to the minor chakras. A cell has a consciousness or intelligence which is called the *cellular subconscious mind*. The cells and the cellular subconscious mind are under the control of the organic subconscious mind.

An analogy will be used to further clarify the concepts in instructive healing. The physical subconscious mind is similar to a business corporation. The chakras or chakral subconscious minds are directors, executives, and vice-presidents of the divisions. The organs or organic subconscious minds are managers of the departments within the division. The cells or cellular subconscious minds are the personnel in the departments.

The instruction can be given directly to the cells, the organs, the chakras or to the physical subconscious mind of the patient.

PSYCHIC DIAGNOSIS

Diagnosis of an ailment or disorder can be done by asking for information from the physical subconscious mind of the patient.

1. Calm your emotion and mind by doing pranic breathing.
2. Visualize the face of your patient.
3. Ask the physical subconscious mind of the patient about the nature of the ailment or disorder—physical, etheric, emotional, mental, or karmic. For example, "John, what is the cause or what are the causes of the skin inflammation on your armpits and on the throat?"
4. Wait for the reply.

To develop accuracy in psychic diagnosis requires a lot of practice and a high degree of sensitivity.

VISUAL INSTRUCTIVE HEALING

The instruction can be given visually or verbally. If the instructions are given in pictures, then it is called visual instructive healing. It is also called healing by visualization or imaging. This can be done by the healer or by the patient or both. The visualization or imaging has to be done repeatedly as in pranic healing. It is important for the healer to be detached in order to be able to release the visual instruction to the physical subconscious mind of the patient. Visualize the picture or image going inside the ajna chakra of the patient.

The instruction should be given gently but firmly. Avoid using too much will, since the physical subconscious mind may tend to resist the instructions. If the healer overwhelms the physical subconscious mind, there is a tendency for it to be partially stunted and it may not be able to quickly follow the instruction.

The picture or image used could either be actual or symbolic. An actual or literal picture requires a more thorough background in anatomy. Medical doctors will find this approach easier. For persons with a limited anatomical background, it is easier to use symbolic pictures or images. The visualization is done for ten to fifteen minutes per session and once or several times a day until healing is completed.

Procedure:

1. Visualize the face of the patient.
2. Smile or project loving-kindness to the patient. This is to establish rapport and to increase receptivity.
3. Visualize the healing process, then the end result.
4. Repeat the visualization for as long as necessary. The frequency of instructive healing depends on the situation.

For example, to accelerate the healing of a ruptured eardrum: visualize a very light blue solution being applied on the ear hole, and the ear hole being sewn. Visualize the eardrum completely healed. The application of light blue solution is a visual instruction to disinfect the affected parts and the sewing of the hole is a visual instruction to close the ruptured eardrum. The eardrum being completely healed is a visual instruction for the expected end result.

Another example to accelerate the healing process for a tumor: visualize the tumor being eaten up by white blood cells and the tumor disappearing.

Pictures, photographs, or posters can also be used as a form of visual instructive healing. The patient has to look at the picture repeatedly for a prolonged period. The rate of recovery for tuberculosis patients can be further hastened by looking at a picture of healthy lungs.

VERBAL INSTRUCTIVE HEALING

The instructions are given in words. The instructions can be given verbally, subliminally, or telepathically. Healing instructions can be given through ordinary tapes or subliminal tapes. The patient can listen to the tapes several times a day for as long as necessary. This type of healing has been called by many names:

1. Hypnotherapy;
2. Suggestive healing;
3. Healing through self-suggestion;
4. Healing through affirmation;
5. Healing by talking to your body or the affected part;
6. Healing by command;
7. Healing by decreeing.

In verbal instructive healing, the healer verbally or telepathically instructs the physical subconscious mind, or the chakra, or the organ what to do and to get well.

For example, in treating pancreatic diabetes, a pranic healer, after giving pranic healing, can instruct the pituitary gland through the ajna chakra to command the pancreas to produce sufficient insulin required by the body. As another example, to heal a wound, telepathically instruct or command the wound to close and heal during pranic treatment.

Procedure:

1. Visualize the face of the patient.
2. Smile or project loving-kindness to the patient. This is to establish rapport and to increase receptivity.
3. Telepathically instruct the physical subconscious mind what to do and to manifest the expected end result. The instructions can also be recorded on tape and the patient can listen to them several times a day for as long as necessary.
4. Repeat the process for as long as necessary. The frequency of instructive healing depends on the situation.

A congested chakra can be cleansed by energizing it with light whitish-green, then by telepathically instructing it to turn predominantly counter-clockwise and to expel the diseased energy. Once the affected chakra is decongested, instruct it to normalize its rotation.

An overactivated chakra can be inhibited just with an act of the will by the healer. An underactivated chakra can be activated also just by willing.

But better results are obtained if the affected chakra is first thoroughly cleansed and energized.

When cleansing or energizing an affected part, you can telepathically instruct the physical subconscious mind to clear the blocked meridians, thereby, facilitating the healing process.

The patient can also do verbal instructive healing on himself or herself through self-suggestion, affirmation or by talking to the affected chakras and the affected organs. The affirmation can be repeated for five to ten minutes per session and once or several times a day depending upon the need. The patient may also gently and lovingly talk to the body, the affected chakra(s), and the affected part(s) and request them to get well soon. This can be repeated every day for as long as necessary.

Self-suggestion or affirmation is very helpful in hastening the healing process. You may use this affirmation:

> My body is becoming healthier. My _____ (name the affected organ) is healing and getting better.

Many ailments are emotionally induced or are caused by resentment and the inability to forgive. Therefore, it is advisable that the affirmation is not only for the physical ailment but also for the emotion. You may use this affirmation:

> I forgive all those who have caused me injury and pain. I release all the hurts. Divine Father, I humbly ask your forgiveness for all my mistakes. I am at peace and filled with love. My body is becoming healthier and healthier.

You may also use a multipurpose affirmation by Emile Coue:

> Every day, in every way, I am getting better and better.*

The healing affirmation has to be repeated several times a day for as long as necessary.

---

*This well-known phrase comes from Emile Coue: *Self-Mastery through Conscious Autosuggestion*, available from Sun Publications.

INCREASING THE RATE OF VIBRATION

The etheric body can be rapidly energized by instructing the etheric body to increase its rate of vibration by 50 to 100 percent. An affected part can also be rapidly energized by instructing it to increase its rate of vibration by 50 to 100 percent. Before this instruction is given, thorough sweeping has to be done. Otherwise, the diseased energy may spread, thereby worsening the condition.

LIMITATIONS OF INSTRUCTIVE HEALING

In many instances, the use of instructive healing alone will produce wonderful healing results. But in more severe cases, just doing instructive healing is not enough. It is necessary to apply cleansing and energizing. In severe cases, to give instructive healing without applying pranic treatment will not be effective. There are some instructive healers who are able to get good healing results without knowing anything about pranic healing, but these healers have strong etheric bodies. So when the healer visualizes or verbally or telepathically heals the patient, the healer is unintentionally projecting pranic energy to the patient. For rapid healing to take place, it is still necessary to disentangle the health rays, to remove the diseased energy from the etheric body, to remove the diseased energy from the affected chakras and affected organs, and to provide sufficient pranic energy.

Instructive healing is a part of pranic healing. In some instances, it is used during or after pranic treatment to further increase the rate of healing.

Divine Healing

Divine healing uses divine energy for healing. The ultimate source of divine healing energy is God who is the source of all life. The divine healing energy passes through higher beings: great angelic beings, great prophets or avatars, holy masters, saints, great spiritual teachers, healing angels, and others, then to the soul of the healer, the etheric body of the healer, then to the patient's etheric and physical bodies. The healing energy may also be passed from the soul of the healer to the soul of the patient then to the patient's etheric and physical bodies. Divine healing is being practiced in different religions: Christianity, Buddhism, Islam, Taoism, Baha'i, Judaism, Hinduism, and others. No single religion has a monopoly on divine healing. Divine healing is a higher form of pranic healing.

Divine healing energy is seen as electric-violet light or brilliant white light. Divine energy has the properties of all the color pranas. In general, divine energy is used for treating severe ailments, not simple ailments. To use divine energy for treating simple ailments is just like using diamonds instead of coal as fuel. Divine healing is usually used when the healer has to treat many patients with simple or severe ailments in a short time.

Electric-violet light has a consciousness of its own. It knows where to go and what to do. For example, if the divine energy is projected to the ajna

Figure 20-1. Divine healing.

chakra, it will go to the affected chakras and the affected parts. Diseased energy will be expelled. Overactivated chakras will be inhibited. Underactivated chakras will be activated. Organs that are weak will be strengthened. Organs that are inflamed will be soothed.

AFFIRMATION FOR RECEPTIVITY

Divine healing energy is very powerful, but also very subtle. For rapid healing to occur, the patient has to be very receptive. If the patient is not so receptive, then healing will be slow. But if the patient is not receptive at all, then he or she will not be healed. The healer may project a lot of brilliant electric-violet light, but this energy will not be assimilated unless the patient is receptive and wants to get well. If the patient is not so receptive, it is better to use ordinary white prana or ordinary color pranas. They are more effective with patients who are not so receptive since these pranas are grosser than electric-violet light.

The receptivity of patients can be enhanced by silently or verbally reciting the affirmation for receptivity:

> Lord, Thou are the source and fountain of all life, I humbly invoke your divine blessing and healing. I fully accept your divine healing energy. With thanks and in full faith.

Repeat three times.

TOUCHING THE HEART CHAKRA

The crown-hand chakras technique is used for projecting divine energy. As a healer becomes more powerful, it is necessary for him or her to lightly touch the heart chakra with one hand to soften the projected divine energy. Otherwise, the patient may weaken or may even faint.

FOREHEAD-HAND CHAKRAS TECHNIQUE

For healers who are quite powerful, and whose antakharana or spiritual root is bigger than the head, it is better to use the forehead chakra as the source chakra for electric-violet pranic energy than the crown chakra. This technique is called the Forehead-Hand Chakras Technique. For very powerful healers, the use of the forehead chakra as the source chakra is milder, safer, and more effective. The use of the crown chakra as the source chakra by very powerful healers is overwhelming to the patient's body and will produce a slower rate of healing. When using the Forehead-Hand Chakras Technique, it is still necessary to touch your own heart chakra with one hand.

INVOCATION

Before healing, it is advisable for the healer to silently pray:

> *Lord, Thou are the source and fountain of all life,*
> *I humbly invoke for*
> *divine guidance,*
> *divine healing,*
> *and divine protection.*
> *With thanks and in full faith.*

Figure 20-2.   Forehead-hand chakras technique.

The healer may also invoke the divine blessing of archangels, great prophets or avatars, saints, holy persons, your spiritual teacher, angels, and healing ministers for help and healing.

> *To my spiritual teacher, to the healing angels,*
> *and to the healing ministers,*
> *I humbly invoke for*
> *divine guidance,*
> *divine healing,*
> *and divine protection.*
> *With thanks and in full faith.*

After healing, the healer should silently give thanks:

> *Lord,*
> *Thank you for Your divine blessing.*
> *To my spiritual teacher, the healing angels, and healing ministers,*
> *Thank you for your help and for the healing.*

The healer may use other prayers or improvise prayers for healing and thanksgiving.

POINT OF ENTRY

Electric-violet light can be used for cleansing and energizing directly the affected chakras and parts. The upper chakras are more responsive to the electric-violet energy than the lower chakras. In general, especially with grosser patients, the lower chakras are usually not responsive at all to the electric-violet light if energized directly.

The heart chakra—through the back heart chakra—can be used as an entry point for the electric-violet light to go to the different parts of the body. The healer energizes the back heart chakra with electric-violet light and visualizes the divine energy spreading to all parts of the body with emphasis on the affected chakra(s) and the affected part(s). A powerful healer may rapidly project a tremendous amount of the electric-violet light by hitting the patient's back heart chakra with the healer's palm.

The crown chakra, forehead chakra, or ajna chakra can also be used as an entry for the electric-violet light. The projection of divine energy can be done slowly or rapidly. If projected rapidly, the patient may become dizzy or may faint. This is why in charismatic healing or in faith healing, some healers may project a tremendous amount of divine energy by lightly touching or hitting with the palm the ajna chakra or forehead chakra of the patients causing them to faint.

DESCENT OF THE DIVINE LIGHT

The divine healing energy is transferred from the soul of the healer to the soul of the patient, then to the patient's etheric and physical bodies. This is seen as a flood of electric-violet light or brilliant white light coming down, thereby rapidly cleansing and energizing the whole body.

1. Silently say a short prayer requesting for divine healing energy and for divine protection.
2. Instruct the patient to silently recite the affirmation for receptivity.
3. Visualize brilliant white light or electric-violet light descending from above, down to the patient's crown chakra and spreading to all parts of the body.

Figure 20-3.   Descent of the divine light.

4. Mentally instruct the divine healing energy to remain with the patient until it has been fully utilized by his or her body.
5. Repeat treatment several times a week for as long as necessary.

MASS HEALING

A powerful healer can heal patients en masse with divine healing energy.

1. Silently ask for divine blessing for healing and protection.
2. Instruct the patients to silently or verbally recite the affirmation for receptivity.
3. Concentrate simultaneously on your crown chakra and the heart chakra. Divine healing energy is drawn from above, down to the crown chakra, and projected out through the front heart chakra, then through the hands.

Figure 20-4.   Mass healing.

4. Simultaneously visualize all the patients bathing in a sea of brilliant white light or electric-violet light. This is done for several minutes.

DISTANT MASS HEALING

1. Inform the patients that distant healing will be done on a certain date and at a certain time. Instruct them to just relax at the specified date and time, to silently or verbally say the affirmation for receptivity several times, and to wait for about five minutes.
2. The healer is expected to have pictures of the patients. At the specified date and time, go through the pictures by touching each one of them. This is to establish stronger etheric links with the patients.
3. Silently pray for divine healing and divine protection.
4. Concentrate on your crown chakra and heart chakra. Draw divine energy from above, down to your crown chakra, to the heart chakra, then to the hands. Project electric-violet light to the pictures. This is done for one or two minutes.

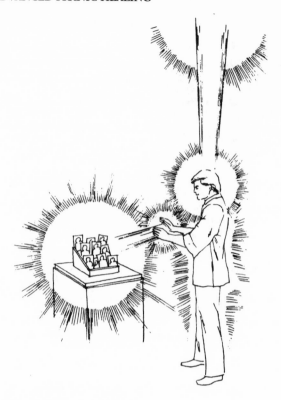

Figure 20-5.   Distant mass healing.

5. Mentally instruct the divine healing energy to remain with the patients until it has been fully utilized by their bodies.
6. Treatment has to be repeated twice or three times a week for as long as necessary.

COMBINATION OF INSTRUCTIVE HEALING AND DIVINE HEALING

This combination healing is done en masse or on an individual basis. The healer says a short prayer asking for divine healing energy and divine protection. The healer says aloud with firm conviction:

> Lord, thank you for healing this patient (or all the patients). You are being healed. You are mentally, emotionally, etherically, and physically being cleansed and healed. Your _____ (specify the af-

fected organs or parts) are being cleansed, energized, and healed. With thanks and in full faith.

This is done once or several times. The patients have to cooperate by silently or verbally reciting the affirmation for receptivity.

Based on clairvoyant observations, the healer is projecting divine healing energy to the patient whether he or she is aware of it or not.

EUCHARISTIC HEALING

The Holy Eucharist is truly sacred. When the wafers or hosts are consecrated, a tremendous amount of divine energy in the form of brilliant electric violet comes down. The hosts are transformed from ordinary bread into "small blazing suns." This is assuming that the priest is sufficiently spiritually developed.

Divine healing of the mind, emotion, and body occurs when the sacred host is taken with proper understanding, devotion, and gratitude. It is advisable to silently say a prayer of acceptance and thanksgiving:

Lord, I fully accept the divine blessing and the divine healing. I mentally, emotionally, and physically accept Thy divine healing energy. With thanks and in full faith.

Repeat the prayer three times, then remain internally still. Be aware of what is happening internally. In some instances, the participant may see his or her body filled with divine light and may experience bliss, divine ecstasy, and divine illumination. For severe cases, it is advisable for the patient to take the sacred host three times a week or more for as long as necessary. Eucharistic healing can be used to heal physical ailments, psychological ailments, and emotional hurts or pain.

Eucharistic healing can also be done by the priest on the patient. The receiving hand of the priest is pointed at the sacred host in order to draw in divine healing energy and the other hand is used for cleansing and energizing the patient. For severe cases, treatment has to be repeated.

My intention is to explain scientifically the mechanism behind Eucharistic Healing. For more information on the inner aspect of the sacraments, please consult the book, *The Science of the Sacraments* by the Rt. Rev. C. W. Leadbeater, published by Theosophical Publishing House, Wheaton, IL.

PART IV:
THE FUTURE OF
PRANIC HEALING

Seed Ideas

The ideas contained here are in seed form; therefore, they will require considerable nurturing to fully develop them. They are given as guides and hints to new research areas.

NUTRITION AND PRANA

Science has studied nutrition from the chemical viewpoint: proteins, carbohydrates, sugars, minerals, fats, and vitamins. So far, science is not aware of the existence of prana, and has not studied nutrition from the pranic viewpoint: the quantity and types of color prana contained in foods, and how prana affects the human body.

Preserved food contains more or less the same amount of proteins, carbohydrates, and other chemicals as fresh food, but fresh food is definitely more nutritious than preserved food because it contains more prana than preserved food. The same principle also applies to synthetic and natural vitamins. Natural vitamins are more effective or potent than synthetic vitamins because the natural ones contain more prana than the synthetic ones. Overcooking food not only destroys some of its chemical nutrients but also releases a lot of its prana due to prolonged heating. In other words, over-cooked food contains considerably less prana than food that is not over-cooked.

To be healthy, it is necessary to have a balanced diet. The idea of a balanced diet should include not only the proper chemical or nutritive mix requirements for the body, but also the proper mix of color pranas required to keep the body healthy. To achieve a balanced pranic diet, it is advisable to prepare dishes having many colors. By noting the color of the food, it is possible to deduce the predominating color prana. For example, green vegetables obviously contain a lot of green prana, while carrots contain a lot of orange prana. But this approach is not always applicable; for instance, red tomatoes contain a lot of yellowish-green prana and very little red prana, and watermelons which have smooth green skin and red pulp contain a lot of green prana and hardly any red prana.

The approach of Western medicine is very different from Chinese medicine or Ayurvedic (Indian) medicine. In Western medicine, the approach is material or chemical. In Chinese or Ayurvedic medicine, the approach is more subtle. What is emphasized in Chinese and Ayurvedic medicine is pranic energy and maintaining pranic harmony within the body. Chinese medicine has developed this approach to a very sophisticated degree by using herbal medicine and acupuncture.

It is commonly known that hemorrhoids tend to worsen by eating hot spicy foods. Why is this so? The answer is quite simple. Since hemorrhoids manifest as pranic congestion of red prana on the anus area, eating hot spicy foods which contain a lot of red prana will definitely aggravate the ailment.

Persons who are susceptible to constipation may improve their condition by regularly eating papaya. Papaya contains a lot of orange prana which stimulates regular bowel movements.

GINSENG

I have done experiments on the effects of Chinese and Korean red ginseng on the etheric body. The dosage ranged from one-half gram to five grams per intake. The subjects' ages ranged from 14 to 55 years old.

It was clairvoyantly observed that the effects of ginseng powder start to manifest almost immediately. Flashes of light were seen coming from the inner and health auras. The inner aura increased from five to about ten inches in thickness. The health aura became brighter and expanded from about two to three feet. The outer aura also expanded. Light grayish matter was being expelled. The chakras became brighter, bigger, and more active. The major chakras increased from about three-and-a-half inches to about five inches. The "synthetic ki" located at the secondary navel chakras increased from about one inch to about three inches in diameter. The "synthetic ki" became denser. Although the pranic energy level of the subjects was very high, they were relaxed and not restless. This is similar to a person meditating. Though a lot of energy is generated when meditating, the meditator is still relaxed and at peace. The subjects are not usually aware of, or do not physically feel, the subtle improvements unless they are either sensitive or weak.

The degree of the effects of the ginseng depends on the dosage, the supplier of the ginseng (different suppliers produce ginseng of different brightness or potency), and the body of the subject. The effects of one-half gram of ginseng will last for about ten to sixteen hours. Within that period of time the effects of the ginseng gradually diminish. Because of this, it is better if one-half gram of ginseng is taken twice a day to maintain one's health. Persons who are ill should preferably take a higher dosage.

Ginseng, when clairvoyantly seen, is very bright compared to other food and medicines. The core (inmost) aura of a fifty gram red ginseng powder is very dense (looks almost like "liquid" gold) and is about six to twelve inches in radius. The outer aura is about three to four yards in radius. Ginseng contains a lot of prana (vital energy) and also a lot of "synthetic ki." The great increase of synthetic ki in the secondary navel chakra is due to the activated major chakras which produce more synthetic ki and also due to the synthetic ki contained in the ginseng itself.

Ginseng has a cleansing effect since grayish matter is being expelled. *It is better to exercise immediately after taking ginseng to facilitate the expelling of used-up prana and to facilitate the assimilation of fresh pranic energy.* Ginseng is also activating and energizing, since the etheric body and its major chakras become brighter, bigger, and denser. *Therefore. the organs controlled and energized by the major chakras are correspondingly cleansed, activated, and energized.*

With these findings, it becomes clear why ginseng is highly regarded by the Chinese and the Koreans. Many Chinese and Koreans take ginseng regularly to improve and maintain their good health. In Chinese medicine, ginseng in combination with herbs having "healing" effects on a specific organ is prescribed for many types of ailments. *Ginseng combined with other herbs is considered as a practically "cure all" medicine.*

To increase the pranic energy level of the healer and to improve his or her healing skill, it is advisable (but not necessary) to take one gram of ginseng before and after healing a large number of patients. It is also advantageous for patients who are very weak to take one to two grams of ginseng before being treated by the healer.

CLASSIFYING DRUGS BY USING
THE PROPERTIES OF COLOR PRANAS

A person who has just embarked on the study and research of the different properties and effects of herbs and drugs is sometimes overwhelmed by the huge body of information available. A different approach to the classification of herbs and drugs is suggested by using the properties of color prana. A chart can be made to give an overall view. The vertical side of the chart will contain a list of color pranas and mixed color pranas, and their corresponding properties. The horizontal side of the chart will list first the body followed by the different organs. Herbs or drugs are then catalogued in the chart. A diuretic drug (promotes secretion of urine) is catalogued under orange prana or yellow-orange prana—expelling property, and the kidneys. An analgesic or pain killer is catalogued under blue prana—soothing effect, and the body. An herb or group of herbs with dissolving effects on blood clots or clogs is catalogued under green prana—breaking down or dissolving effects. To fill the chart would require a considerable amount of time and energy, and the concerted efforts of many experienced herbalists and pharmacists.

ETHERIC BEINGS, CURRENTS, PLANETS

Most scientists assume that life can only exist in a physical form. They send spaceships to other planets looking for signs of physical life, not considering that life may exist in an energy form or in an etheric form. Based on clairvoyant investigation, life also exists in an etheric (energy) form, and there are etheric beings of different degrees of awareness and development. Investigation should be done on the "possible" existence of etheric beings inside or interpenetrating the earth, water, air and fire. This is exactly the basis behind stories about fairies and gnomes.

Investigations should be done on how these etheric beings affect the growth and development of plants, animals, and humans. Investigations should also be directed on the possible existence of humans in etheric form with no corresponding physical body on Earth or on other planets, and also on etheric plants and minerals.

Just as there are water and air currents, there is also such a thing as etheric current. Research should be directed on how to utilize these etheric currents to produce power. Scientists should also investigate the possibility of etheric planets with no corresponding physical form.

Science should also seriously consider the possibility that when the Earth was very young and not hospitable to physical life, "humans" may have already existed in etheric form.

MORE RESEARCH NEEDED
IN THE FIELD OF PRANIC HEALING

Research should be directed toward developing sophisticated equipment that can detect and quantify prana or vital energy. A measuring unit has to be established for prana. Sophisticated equipment will also be needed for measuring the rate of pranic projection and the rate of pranic consumption.

One of the major shortcomings in Kirlian photography is that it can take pictures only of small objects, and the object has to be in contact with the plate or equipment. There is a need for the development of a more practical and advanced type of camera that can take pictures of the energy bodies of objects at a distance or pictures of etheric beings.

How does pranic energy affect the cells? When the skin comes in contact with hot oil, the cells are damaged. However, if pranic healing is applied immediately, the skin will not be damaged or the damage is substantially reduced. How does pranic energy affect the cell and its parts? How was the damage prevented or reduced on the cellular level?

When orange-red pranic energy is directed to a fresh wound, it causes the wound to heal rapidly. Does orange-red prana stimulate the production of a certain chemical or chemicals that accelerate the repair of the wound? If this is so, it might be possible to synthetically produce it. Similar research can be undertaken on other color pranas.

PRANIC PSYCHOTHERAPY

Pranic healing can also be applied in treating psychological ailments. Psychological ailments manifest as malfunctioning (overactivated, underactivated, congestion or depletion) of some major chakras and as traumatic or inhibiting energies lodged in certain major chakras. These traumatic or inhibiting energies are clairvoyantly seen as gray or dark energies.

Diseased energy of psychological ailments can be transmitted. When a patient talks about his or her psychological problem, pent-up negative emotions in the form of diseased energy are released by the patient and are usually absorbed by the psychotherapist, especially if the psychotherapist is quite open, understanding, and compassionate. The release of negative emotional energy is clairvoyantly seen as a brightening of the patient's aura due to the release of grayish energy of different colors.

The unconscious absorption of this negative energy by the psychotherapist produces immediate and long run problems. The immediate problem may manifest as a family problem, since the psychotherapist may try to unconsciously release the negative energy or "take it out" on the immediate members of the family. Under normal circumstances, the body's defense system can expel the negative energy and recover just through a good night's sleep. But since this is done regularly, the negative emotional energy accumulates and inevitably manifests as chakral imbalances. These chakral imbalances may manifest as psychological problems or symptoms similar to the patient's. It may manifest physically as a low energy level or "burnt-out effect," a heart problem or chest pain, rapid aging, and other physical ailments.

GEOMETRIC PRANIC GENERATOR

A four-sided pyramid, a three-sided pyramid, and a cone generate or focus pranic energy or vitality globules within themselves. More air vitality globules are contained within these geometric figures than in the air, hence, they are called pranic generators. The pranic energy or air vitality globules in these geometric figures is as dense, if not denser, than the ground prana or vitality globules. Recuperating inside a geometric pranic generator is similar to resting and recuperating on the ground in order to absorb ground pranic energy. Better results can be obtained by cleansing the body with the application of general and localized sweeping.

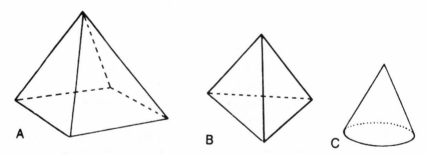

Figure 21-1. Three dimensional pranic generators: (A) four-sided pyramid; (B) three-sided pyramid; and (C) cone.

Experiments can be done by wearing a cone headgear on top of the crown to increase one's learning capacity, to think faster and more clearly, and to make better decisions. This is probably why ancient "magicians" or wise men are sometimes depicted with cone-shaped headgear.

Healing or treating patients inside a geometric pranic generator is a lot easier. Since the healing space or area is filled with dense pranic energy, drawing in pranic energy and projecting pranic energy can be done faster and with greater ease. Very often using a three-dimensional geometric pranic generator is not possible. A two-dimensional geometric pranic generator can then be used. Concentric squares, triangles, and circles are two-dimensional geometric pranic generators. These two-dimensional geometric pranic generators are less potent than the three-dimensional ones but are still considerably potent and useful. The wall or floor where pranic treatment will be given can be designed with a two-dimensional geometric pranic generator. It is better to use only one design, not several combined designs because it may cause confusion in the etheric bodies of persons within the geometric pranic generator. It is better to use the square or the triangle designs than the circle design since some patients may not be able to withstand the type of pranic energy generated by the cone or the concentric circle design.

PRANIC LASER THERAPY

In healing with the use of color lights or chromotherapy, some healers have the wrong concept that it is color alone that heals. Unless this concept is corrected, progress in this field will remain slow. It is not color light that heals, but the vitality globules or pranic energy that has been transformed by the color light to a specific color prana that heals. Obviously, the density or the quantity of pranic energy (vitality globules) in the healing room is a very critical factor. If the healing room contains more pranic energy, then the pranic treatment will be more effective and vice versa. This is why it is advisable to use a geometric pranic generator to increase the quantity of air prana in the healing room.

Another important factor is the degree of permanency or stability of the transformed color pranic energy. This is dependent upon the distance between the treated part and the source of color light. If the distance is too short, the transformed color prana will revert back to white prana. Although the treatment will still be effective, it will not be as effective as when the transformed color pranic energy remains as is. As discussed in an earlier chapter, color prana is faster and more effective than white prana when used correctly.

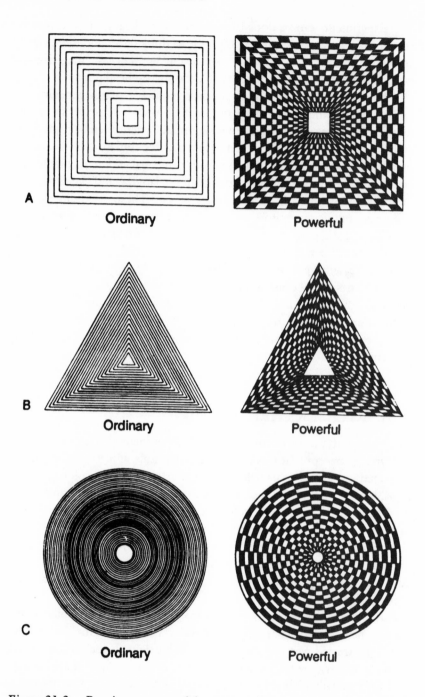

Figure 21-2.   Pranic generators of three types: (A) concentric square; (B) concentric triangle; and (C) concentric circle.

The potency of pranic energy is affected by its velocity and rate of vibration. The velocity of the pranic energy is affected by distance—the further the distance between the treated part and the source of color light, the faster is the velocity of the vitality globules. If the distance is too short, the velocity is not fast enough; therefore, the potency of pranic energy is not strong enough. If the distance is too far, the velocity of the vitality globules will also be very fast. This may result in some damaging effects.

The use of soft laser light in laser pranic therapy is a more advanced form of pranic chromotherapy. The effect of pranic laser therapy is very fast and comparable to pranic treatment done by an advanced pranic healer. It is prophesied by Respected Teacher Mei Ling that a few decades from now, pranic laser therapy will be widely used.

The following are suggested guidelines given by Teacher Mei Ling:

A) The substance used in generating laser light should have carbon content ranging from 50 to 80 percent. Within this range, the pranic laser treatment is quite effective. Below this range, it is not so effective And beyond this range the treatment will have destructive effects. It may be necessary to synthetically produce this substance.

B) The distance between the part to be treated and the source of laser light should range from one to five feet. The distance affects the degree of permanency of the transformed prana and the potency of the projected pranic energy (velocity of the projected prana). If it is too far, the velocity of the projected vitality globules will be too fast and will have a damaging effect.

C) The power or wattage should preferably be low. If the wattage is too low, it will not be very effective. If it is too high, it will be destructive.

D) In general, exposure time should be for a short period. If the exposure time is too long, there will be an overdose. If the exposure time is too short, the projected pranic energy will not be sufficient.

The healing room should preferably have a geometric pranic generator. This is to increase the density or the amount of air vitality globules in the healing room. The patient should be scanned before and after treatment. General and localized sweeping should be applied before energizing. Further localized sweeping may be required after energizing. While energizing, the projected pranic energy is directed to the affected organ and is stabilized.

The given guidelines should not be accepted blindly but should be studied thoroughly, and their validity tested through thorough experiments.

Index